# Foundational Readings in Environmental Policy

FIRST EDITION

# Foundational Readings in Environmental Policy

EDITED BY Younsung Kim

*George Mason University*

SAN DIEGO

Bassim Hamadeh, CEO and Publisher
Peaches diPierro, Associate Acquisitions Editor
Carrie Baarns, Manager, Revisions and Author Care
Danielle Gradisher, Project Editor
Susana Christie, Senior Developmental Editor
Ava Serra, Editorial Assistant
Celeste Paed, Associate Production Editor
Asfa Arshi, Graphic Design Assistant
Greg Isales, Licensing Coordinator
Stephanie Adams, Senior Marketing Program Manager
Natalie Piccotti, Director of Marketing
Kassie Graves, Senior Vice President, Editorial
Jamie Giganti, Director of Academic Publishing



Printed in the United States of America.

# CONTENTS

# PREFACE

Sustainability has emerged as a driving force for changing our modern society. It leads our society to shift to a different pathway that has never been before, pushing us to consider ecosystem value in our daily lives. Climate risk, food insecurity, rampant population growth, mostly in developing countries, document the inevitability of sustainable thinking and environmental policy considerations. It is not difficult to find the current system's perilous state and the optimistic signals for a sustainable future.

There is a glimpse of hope we face in 2021, however. Some eventful changes include the rejoining of the Paris Agreement under the Biden administration in the United States, Green New Deal proposals across the world, strong voices for correcting environmental injustice, climate capital and carbon pricing discussion in the European Union (EU), Environmental, Social, and Governance (ESG) Index-guided green investment opportunities, green funds created by the influential thinkers and leaders like Bill Gates and Jeff Bezos to fund clean breakthrough technologies, to name a few. Those trends and encouragement combined send us a strong signal to explore and educate ourselves concerning sustainability: environmental policy.

As to environmental policy educational resources, one can easily find green information from more than 300,000 websites regarding climate change, blogs, and media. In terms of textbooks for students in higher education, we are fortunate to see many resourceful textbooks in the marketplace. Despite a wealth of information, I found a gap among many selections in that environmental policy textbooks are skewed to U.S. politics and polycentric systems of governance systems. The politics and conflicts are elaborated on, while solutions were less obviously discussed. Also, alternative policy tools such as private–public partnerships, clean innovation, empowerment of citizen science have not been adequately probed. As such, traditional environmental policy learning seems not fully aligned with the ways to cope with today's complicated, intertwined global environmental issues and create tomorrow's sustainable future.

This anthology recognizes the chasm and carries on a more enriched understanding of currently available solutions to address and manage commons problems in partnerships with diverse social actors. In doing so, this book may deepen and broaden the knowledge of the root causes of environmental policy and the direction to mitigate environmental impacts. There are the three key points to be highlighted:

1. ***Environmental issues are discussed with an interdisciplinary approach***: The articles in this anthology provide a multidisciplinary understanding of much complicated global environmental issues, introducing theoretical frameworks in environmental science, management science, and public policy as they relate to environmental policy issues.
2. ***New policy instruments***: Articles in Unit III introduce the new trends in environmental policy and the emerging approaches to environmental policy (e.g., public–private partnerships, collaborative governance, etc.). A solution-based approach is also underscored. The approaches would be useful in bringing out unanswered but important questions to be heard to advance environmental policy.
3. ***Discussion questions that foster deep learning***: At the end of each chapter, you will find probing questions for discussion. They will be used to facilitate in-class discussions and promote self-learning.

In reading articles, I wish you find wisdom, creativity, and hope for a sustainable future by better understanding the complicated nature of wicked environmental issues and learning about today's environmental treaties and tomorrow's technologies and approaches to our planet.

Lastly, I am indebted to my students in and outside of classrooms, from high school interns in my lab to undergraduates, graduate students, and adult learners across the world. They are all passionate about protecting their future from greedy capitalism and are prepared to undertake meaningful engagement in the policymaking process and implement substantive actions. They helped me become a better educator.

This book is dedicated to innovative thinkers and inspiring leaders for our own planet.

McLean, Virginia
Younsung Kim

# INTRODUCTION

This anthology is composed of the three units. The main themes of three units are as follows.

Unit I covers the fundamental principles of environmental policy and politics. The guiding questions are:

- What are the main features of environmental policy?
- How is environmental policy different from public policy?
- How is policy formed?
- Who are the key actors in making and implementing (environmental) policies?
- What was the distinct approach taken at the early stage of the U.S. modern environmental policy?
- How have we (Americans) arrived at adopting environmental laws to address industrial pollution and manage natural resources more wisely?

Unit II outlines environmental issues beyond geographic boundaries and are not limited to the natural/ecological realm. These three issues are the focus: climate change, energy, and biodiversity loss. They are considered not only environmental but political, economic, and technical challenges. The solutions for each transboundary challenge are investigated. The guiding questions are:

- What are the climate change policy approaches that have been considered?
- Which carbon control policies are better?
- Why is the 2015 Paris Agreement Considered to Lead the Monumental Changes in International Climate Politics?
- What are the major challenges for renewable-based electricity?
- What are the governmental actions to promote renewable-based electricity?
- How have the international policy regimes cooperated to address biodiversity loss, particularly loss of endangered species?
- Are the overlaps of international treaties helpful for protecting the endangered species? If yes, how?

Unit III discusses the emerging environmental issues and policy approaches. Indeed, the issue of environmental justice (EJ) has long been reported, but systematic inequality in environmental decision-making has not yet been adequately addressed. Other chapters investigate the key practices that are assumed to promote sustainability in the context of waste management, sustainable business, and urban resilience. The guiding questions are:

- How has environmental inequality been laid out in the United States based on people's socio-economic status and races?
- What are the major challenges for managing wastes these days? How could we promote waste management more radically?
- How has the U.S. federal government attempted to address the issue? Did it work?
- How can we make a business sustainable? Are the firms claiming they are sustainable trustworthy?
- What is the concept of a sustainable city? What would be policy approaches to make cities sustainable?
- How can we increase energy access in developing countries, particularly in rural areas of countries?
- What is a successful example of improving solar-based energy access, not harming the environment?
- What is the concept of sustainability? What are the key challenges of sustainability down the road at the end of the 21st century? Which policy approaches should be more emphasized? Which actors need to be (more) empowered?

UNIT I

# Pollution Control and Politics

READING 1.1

# Tragedy of the Commons and the U.S. Environmental Policy Approaches Since 1970s

By Younsung Kim

Since the 1970s, environmental policy in the United States has noticeably evolved to address deteriorating environmental quality and public health concerns. Major laws to regulate air pollution, water pollution, and waste issues were passed mostly in the 1970s, and the Environmental Protection Agency (EPA) was created to implement environmental laws in partnership with state and local governments. Policies for the conservation of nature also changed profoundly during the modern environmental policy era. As a flagship legislative change, the Endangered Species Act was greatly strengthened in 1973 to identify and list endangered or threatened species of plants and animals. The U.S. environmental quality has shown substantial progress owing to environmental policy drives and public support (Kraft and Vig, 2022).

Despite its overall success, we still face a wide array of challenges surrounding our ecosystems, existing and new. For instance, the U.S. water quality shows relatively modest improvement compared to the air quality (US EPA, 2017). Also, continuously strengthening evidence on climate change and biodiversity crisis indicates the more accelerated speed and scale of governmental intervention, but passing environmental laws is getting more difficult due to a partisan divide and issue polarization (Kraft and Vig, 2022). Understanding the nature of environmental problems and the policymaking process can present an insight into why policies have not been passed successfully. It will also hint at better policy approaches to complicated, transboundary environmental issues, including climate change. This chapter aims to outline the unique characteristics of environmental problems, the policymaking process, and major policy approaches taken over the past five decades. It also presents the merge of environmental and climate issues nowadays, chronicling the pushes and pulls of climate policies since the Obama administration.

## Tragedy of the Commons: Two Types

The Tragedy of the Commons is a foundational concept to make it easier to understand a class of environmental problems. The concept originated from an article by ecological biologist Garret

Hardin published in *Science* (Hardin, 1968). In his article, Hardin indicated that environmental problems belong to a class of no technical solutions, underscoring the insolubility without reducing inputs of pollution to the environment as well as adopting adequate governmental interventions relying on coercive policy mechanisms. The premise of the concept is that humans are rational and are prescient of how to maximize their welfare. Many environmental problems arise due to humans' self-interest maximizing motives that result in excessive use of natural resources and environmental goods when there is a lack of an institutional system to curb human desires. Natural resources have been overexploited, and industrial pollution has been prevalent accordingly.

Under the Tragedy of the Commons analogy, the environmental problem is largely classified into two types. The first type of tragic status in commons is seen when humans have taken something good out of commons. Suppose a herdsman raises cattle in an open pasture. Each herdsman is incentivized to put as many cattle as possible in the commons if there are no limits to adding cattle and the benefits of more cattle are greater than the costs. Putting more cattle is then a rational choice since everyone in the commons would share the costs of additional cows raised. As such, nearby streams of cattle-ranching areas would be polluted, and the soil would get infertile. Deforestation, desertification, and overfishing exemplify this kind of the Tragedy of the Commons, which is the overuse and mismanagement of natural resources.

In another case, the Tragedy of the Commons occurs when something bad is put into the commons. On this occasion, people are driven to emit toxic and noxious gases into the air, discharge harmful water pollutants into freshwater, and dump hazardous chemicals and wastes on land where no regulatory guidelines have been adopted. As such, the benefits of pollution surpass the costs of treating pollutants. Industrial pollution without regulations brings ruin to all, creating a tragic status in the commons. It incentivizes people not to pay for their pollution and induces costs borne by society. As the second type of Tragedy of the Commons, industrial pollution illustrates the high costs of negative externality, which is the spillover effect of transactions when someone's action negatively affects others' welfare.

Those two types of the Tragedy of the Commons cannot be addressed without proper governmental intervention and justify the need for establishing a set of environmental policies with the polluters-pay-principle (PPP). The "polluters pays" principle is the commonly accepted practice that those who produce pollution should bear the costs of managing it to prevent damage to human health or the environment, and it is guided by the 1992 Rio Declaration as part of a set of broader principles to promote sustainable development worldwide. Well-designed environmental policies would be capable of correcting the pricing systems of undervalued natural resources and environmental goods and services (Olmstead, 2022).

## Policymaking Process

Making environmental policy to establish coercive regulatory mechanisms in which people find it cheaper to control the overuse of natural resources and pollution is not straightforward. This is in part due to environmental policymaking requiring the coordination of multiple actors whose stakes vary across the policymaking process under high-level scientific and political uncertainties (Young and Stokke, 2020).

Policy formulation requires an understanding of the policy process. Rosenbaum (2020) defines policymaking as a process that involves a number of related decisions originating from different institutions and actors ranging across the whole domain of the federal government and private institutions. This process involves the five different steps from agenda-setting, option formulation, decision-making, and policy implementation to evaluation. At the stage of policy formulation, a policy agenda is set, and alternative options to solve the policy issues are actively discussed. This is the stage where environmental science, economics, and policy analysis all contribute to the development of a policy agenda. U.S. presidents and the executive branches of the government have played a critical role in agenda-setting, as seen in the latest case of President Obama with his climate-related achievements, including the Clean Power Plan (Vig, 2022).

Policy legitimation is a stage of selecting and endorsing policies through political actions by Congress, the president, and courts. Political support for formal enactment needs to be mobilized during the decision-making status, and many policy proposals tend to fail due to polarized public and partisan divides. Indeed, President Biden's Build Back Better legislative agenda, which includes ambitious climate actions costing about $555 billion over 10 years, couldn't successfully pass the Congress for such reasons (Leonhardt, 2022).

Policy evaluation can create an agenda, reflecting on the performance of certain policies and programs adopted. At the stage of policy evaluation, government agencies, citizen groups, environmental think thank groups having research arms, or Congressional Research Services (CRS) play a vital role in analyzing governmental programs with one or multiple criteria, such as health and ecological considerations, cost efficiency, and moral imperatives (Greenberg, 2007).

Figure 1.1.1 presents the five steps of policymaking, from agenda-setting to policy evaluation. Once a policy is evaluated, the analysis outcomes can be fed into the agenda-setting stage, creating a cyclic model of policymaking.

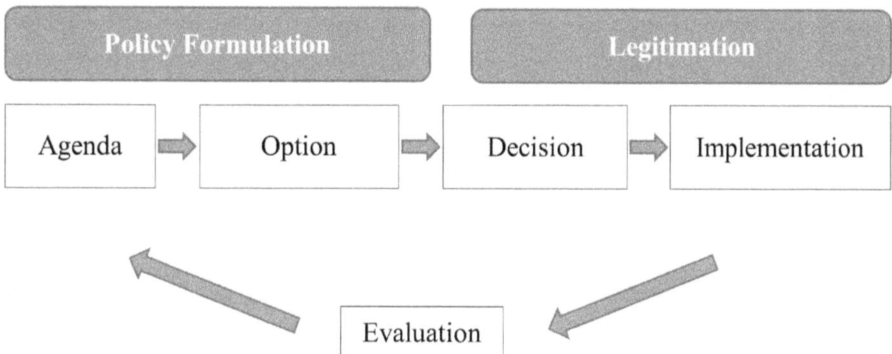


**Figure 1.1.1** Five-Stage Policymaking Process from Agenda-Setting, Option Formulation, Decision, Policy Implementation, and Policy Evaluation.

## Uniqueness of Environmental Issues Creating Conflicts

Environmental politics occur when stakeholders' interests and values for the environment are varied and clash during decision-making. There are two critical features of U.S. environmental policymaking. First, environmental policy conflicts almost concern fundamental differences in values. In most cases, people's values are divided into two groups, environmentalists and cornucopians. Environmentalists acknowledge the pristine value of nature and promote preservation in one spectrum. They also value conservation for recreation and advocate the prudent use of natural resources (Layzer, 2012). Cornucopians believe in humans' ingenuity to invent and engineer solutions to solve natural resource scarcity and pollution as technologies advance. As technology optimists, they tend to place immense value on individual liberty and criticize environmental regulatory policies that would cause unnecessary burdens to society and industry alike. Those two groups converse and are in conflict in every decision regarding public land management, adoption of new environmental policies, and strengthening of environmental regulations.

Also, environmental conflict occurs due to the way problems are defined and the solutions depicted can shape how those values get translated into policies. Environmental issue framing is reliant on the uses of environmental science and environmental economics concepts. Many government agencies, including U.S. EPA, rely on sound science in the belief that the use of scientific information in policy-making can lead to *better* natural resource management decisions and more *effective* environmental policy. However, scientific uncertainty impedes the use of scientific evidence for environmental decision-making. Driven by restricted data, inconclusive outcomes, and measurement error, scientific uncertainty can be reduced but cannot be eliminated. Climate science illustrates how climate deniers use scientific uncertainty to advocate their argument against climate policies. The Intergovernmental Panel on Climate Change (IPCC) has thus updated its assessment reports and sought to reduce scientific uncertainty despite its doubt over what difference more reports will make.

Environmental economics is another competing tool to frame environmental issues and policies in the context of benefits and costs. As environmental policies try to address the issues of mispriced environmental goods and services, environmental protection always comes at a cost. The framing based on projected benefits and costs raises several questions that are hard to be answered. Some questions would be the following: who will bear the costs, who will get benefited from environmental protection, whether the benefits of environmental protection are greater than its costs, how to minimize regulatory costs, how to measure the benefits of environmental regulations, and whether not to adopt regulations with negative social costs is morally acceptable.

Indeed, climate-related policy conflicts demonstrate a prime example of why federal policies with broader impacts often fail to be adopted and implanted. Mounting evidence of climate science (IPCC, 2022; Plumer and Zhong, 2022) and climate risks to humans and ecosystems, particularly coastal communities (Crimmins et al., 2016) only reassure urgent, immediate, impactful actions to reduce greenhouse gases (GHGs).

## U.S. Environmental Policy Approaches

The early stage of the U.S. environmental policy was deterrence-based, as policy responses were led by increasing environmental crises and public outcry over the right to live in an amenable environment. The nation thus relied on business and industry-prescribed environmental protection methods of emissions reduction and technologies like catalytic converters or scrubbers to filter sulfur dioxides. In this approach, the government relied on strict timelines for compliance, and expensive enforcement mechanisms, including audits and penalties, were accompanied. This traditional approach is called command-and-control, top-down, or direct regulation, and the Clean Air Act of 1970 and the Clean Water Act of 1972 set examples. This approach, in part, worked well as most environmental problems back then were local, and not much information was known about pollution abatement costs (Ellerman, 2007; Stavins, 2007).

However, the industry under the command and control approach was less cooperative and didn't comply with the regulations, and legal suits were used as a tactic to avoid or reduce penalties or delay payment. Pollution abatement costs were immense in both industry and society, creating a strong demand for smart regulations in the 1980s and 1990s. With the pre-industrial mantra, the Reagan administration pursued the balancing out of costs and benefits associated with environmental protection. The second generation of environmental policy approach underscoring market-based economic incentives has emerged. Under this approach, the flexibility of how to meet the regulatory standards has become the greatest concern, and policies adopted need to be cost-effective to ensure pollution control with the cheapest options. The approach considers pollution-reducing entities' different capacities for pollution control, allowance-trading programs, pollution taxes, and subsidies for environmentally friendly products or behaviors were highly encouraged. As such, this flexible approach allows businesses to select their own cost-effective strategies for reducing emissions (Press and Mazmanian, 2018).

On top of this approach, the United States has relied on business volunteerism, wherein businesses commit to environmental and sustainability goals that exceed those required. They oftentimes get exemptions from governments' enforcement actions or any mandatory regulatory approaches. Under the Bush administration, tackling climate change has been hinged upon firms' voluntary commitments (Kim and Darnall, 2016) and actions for carbon reductions, and some states' progressive environmental activism (Rabe, 2022). The environmental policy shift from a command-to-control approach to volunteerism illustrates the nature of environmental issues not limited to an environmental medium or species but trancing across ecosystems and the planet.

Table 1.1.1 presents the changes in regulatory approaches from a traditional, command-and-control regulatory approach to volunteerism and policy examples under each approach.

**Table 1.1.1** The Emergence of the U.S. Environmental Regulatory Approaches Since 1970s

| Time Period | Environmental Policy Approach | Examples | Features |
|---|---|---|---|
| **1970s~1980s** | **Command-and-control** | • Clean Air Act of 1970<br>• Clean Water Act of 1972<br>• Resource Conservation and Recovery Act of 1976 | • Strict timeline<br>• Permit-based approach relying on the polluter-pays principle<br>• Heavy penalties<br>• Enforcement mechanisms |
| **1980s~2000s** | **Market-based economic incentives** | • Sulfur dioxide ($SO_2$) allowance-trading program under the Clean Air Act Amendments of 1990 | • Flexibility of how to meet policy goals<br>• Priced-based or quantity-based policy goal<br>• Uncertain of prices or quantities of pollution reduced |
| **2000s~** | **Volunteerism** | • US EPA Performance Track Program<br>• US DOE and EPA's Energy Star | • Promoting eco-labels<br>• Relying on firms' self-regulatory approaches<br>• Process or product-based approaches to distinguishing environmental quality from conventional products or production practices |

## Embracing Carbon Neutrality and Next Steps

The latest IPCC six assessment report witnesses the climate impacts are already more widespread and severe than expected. Droughts, extreme heat, and record floods already threaten food security and livelihoods for millions of people. Since 2008, floods and storms have forced more than 20 million people from their homes each year. The report underscores the irreversible impacts of climate change. (IPCC, 2022; Plumer and Zhong, 2022). The United States has also recognized climate change as a serious threat to human health and well-being. For instance, coastal communities face greater vulnerability to health impacts from flooding (Crimmins et al., 2016).

Nowadays, environmental policy has been integrated into climate policies, and under the Obama administration, the United States has resumed its commitment to the international climate treaty and seemed to regain its leadership for the 2015 Paris Climate Deal. As a national policy goal, the United States during the Obama administration pledged to curb emissions between 26% and 28% below 2005 levels by 2025, with a longer-term goal of an 80% reduction by 2050. Under this goal, the Clean Power Plan was adopted to reduce GHG emissions from power utilities, and its goal was to reduce carbon pollution from the power sector by 32% of emissions in 2005. Fossil fuel–fired power plants are by far the largest source of U.S. carbon emissions, making up 31% of total GHG emissions (U.S. EPA, 2015). Also, Corporate Average Fuel Economy (CAFÉ) standards were strengthened to reduce GHG emissions from the transportation sector, and the most ambitious CAFÉ standard was to increase fuel economy to the equivalent of 54.5 mpg for cars and light-duty trucks by Model Year 2025 (U.S. EPA, 2012). However, these rules were overturned by the Trump administration, demonstrating the instability and reversibility of federal climate policies if laws were not enacted.

Due to the Biden administration's resuscitating push for climate agendas, the United States has rejoined the Paris climate treaty and attempted to restore credibility. President Biden has mapped out a $2.2 trillion clean energy and green jobs plan to cut emissions from electricity to zero by 2035. The plan is assumed to help the United States achieve net-zero emissions by 2050. However, the inclusion of social policies with climate change programs made the Build Better Back Act fail to pass the Senate. Conceived is a critical insight into a political strategy that would focus on key programs once, rather than clumping all issues together in a proposed legislative bill (Dayen, 2021).

However, the EU has successfully passed the Green New Deal in 2019 and placed carbon neutrality as the center of green economy policies. Its momentum has not dwindled even under the global pandemic crisis. The corporate sector, multilateral banking agencies, central banks, and local governments worldwide and in the United States have aligned with such 2050 carbon-neutral initiatives. The worldwide trend and agenda for zero-carbon society questions how the U.S. federal policies could sustainably push forward net-zero carbon emissions, which policy directives need to be pursued, and how the federal government could solidify its collaboration with the private sector, civil society, states, and local governments. And finally, the country's leadership in the international climate regimes needs to be continually conceived in alliance with the national security concern and future economic opportunities.

## References


Crimmins, A., Balbus, J., Gamble, L., Beard, C. B., Bell, J. E., Dodgen, D., Eisen, R. J., Fann, N., Hawkins, M., Herring, S. C., Jantarasami, L., Mills, D. M. Saha, S., Sarofim, M. C., Trtanj, J., & Ziska, L. (2016). Executive summary. The impacts of climate change on human health in the United States: A scientific assessment. U.S. Global Change Research Program, Washington, DC, 24 pp. http://dx.doi.org/10.7930/J00P0WXS

Dayen, D. (2021, October 26). How to fix the democrats' build back better plan. *The New York Times.* https://www.nytimes.com/article/build-back-better-explained.html

Ellerman, A. D. (2007). Are cap-and-trade programs more environmentally effective than conventional regulation? In J. Freeman & C. D. Kolstad (Eds.), *Moving to markets in environmental regulation* (pp. 48–59). Oxford University Press.

Greenberg, M. R. (2007). Introduction: A quick walk through a framework of six environmental policy criteria. In *Environmental Policy Analysis and Practice* (pp. 1–13). Rutgers University Press.

Hardin, G. (1968). The tragedy of the commons. *Science, 162*, 1243–1248.

IPCC (2022). *Climate change 2022: Mitigation of climate change. Contribution of Working Group III to the Sixth Assessment Report of the Intergovernmental Panel on Climate Change.* In P. R. Shukla, J. Skea, R. Slade, A. Al Khourdajie, R. van Diemen, D. McCollum, M. Pathak, S. Some, P. Vyas, R. Fradera, M. Belkacemi, A. Hasija, G. Lisboa, S. Luz, & J. Malley (Eds.). Cambridge University Press. doi 10.1017/9781009157926.001

Kim, Y., & Darnall, N. (2016). Business as collaborative partner: Understanding firms' sociopolitical support for policy formation. *Public Administration Review*, *76*(2), 326–337.

Kraft, M. E., & Vig, N. J. (2022). US environmental policy: A half-century assessment. In N. J. Vig, M. E. Kraft, & B. G. Rabe (Eds.), *Environmental policy: New directions for the twenty-first century* (pp. 3–33). CQ Press.

Layzer, J. (2012). A policymaking framework: Defining problems and portraying solutions in U.S. environmental politics. In *The environmental case: Translating values into policy* (pp. 1–21) (3rd ed.). CQ Press.

Leonhardt, D. (2022). Will climate action happen now: More democrats are focusing on it? https://www.nytimes.com/2022/01/21/briefing/climate-change-bill-democrats.html

Olmstead, S. (2022). Applying market principles to environmental policy. In N. J. Vig, M. E. Kraft, & B. G. Rabe (Eds.), *Environmental policy: New directions for the twenty-first century* (pp. 227–248). CQ Press.

Plumer, B., & Zhong, R. (2022). Stopping climate change is doable, but time is short, U. N. panel warns. *The New York Times.* https://www.nytimes.com/2022/04/04/climate/climate-change-ipcc-un.html

Press, D., & Mazmanian, D. A. (2018). Toward sustainable production: Finding workable strategies for government and industry. In N. J. Vig, M. E. Kraft, B. G. Rabe (Eds.), *Environmental policy: New directions for the twenty-first century* (pp. 269–274). CQ Press.

Rabe, B. (2022). Racing to the top, the bottom, or the middle of the pack? The evolving state government role in environmental protection. In N. J. Vig, M. E. Kraft, B. G. Rabe (Eds.), *Environmental policy: New directions for the twenty-first century* (pp. 35–62). CQ Press.

Rosenbaum, W. A. (2020). Making policy: The process. In W. A. Rosenbaum, *Environmental politics and policy* (pp 30–61). CQ Press.

Stavins, R. (2007). Market-based environmental policies: What can we learn from U.S. experience (and related research)? In J. Freeman & C. D. Kolstad (Eds.), *Moving to markets in environmental regulation* (pp. 19–47). Oxford University Press.

U.S. EPA (2012, August). EPA and NHTSA set standards to reduce greenhouse gases and improve fuel economy for model years 2017–2025 cars and light trucks. EPA-420-F-12-051.

U.S. EPA. (2015). Overview of the clean power plan: Cutting carbon pollution from power plants. https://archive.epa.gov/epa/sites/production/files/2015-08/documents/fs-cpp-overview.pdf

U.S. EPA. (2017). National water quality inventory: Report to Congress. EPA 841-R-16-011. https://www.epa.gov/sites/default/files/2017-12/documents/305brtc_finalowow_08302017.pdf

Vig, N. J. (2022). Presidential powers and environmental policy, In N. J. Vig, M. E. Kraft, & B. G. Rabe (Eds.), *Environmental policy: New directions for the twenty-first century* (pp. 87–110). CQ Press.

Young, O. R., & Stokke, O. S. (2020). Why is it hard to solve environmental problems? The perils of institutional reductionism and institutional overload. *International Environmental Agreements, 20*, 5–19. https://doi.org/10.1007/s10784-020-09468-6

Zhong, R. (2022). These climate scientists are fed up and ready to go on strike. *The New York Times.* https://www.nytimes.com/2022/03/01/climate/ipcc-climate-scientists-strike.html

## DISCUSSION QUESTIONS

1. How does the Tragedy of the Commons analogy relate to climate change?
2. There are policy actors involved in the policymaking process inside and outside the government. In which stage of policymaking would courts be actively engaging in and shaping environmental policy?
3. Policymaking is viewed as a cyclic model, and what are the implications of the cyclic nature of policymaking in the US political system?
4. What are the strengths and limitations of volunteerism-based environmental policy approaches? Would the approach be recommendable for environmental issues with higher health risks?
5. What are the greatest hurdles to achieving the US's carbon-neutral goals by 2050? Which practical and concrete programs have been adopted and proven successful, if any?

READING 1.2

# Wetlands Protection vs. Commercial Development

## The Battle of Sweedens Swamp

By Esther Scott

In 1984, the Pyramid Companies, a prominent developer, unveiled plans to build a regional shopping mall in the southeastern Massachusetts city of Attleboro. The site of the proposed mall appeared ideal in many respects. It was located at the convergence of three major highways, in an area that had no sizable shopping outlets to meet strong consumer demand. It promised to bring jobs and needed tax revenues to the city, and was warmly welcomed by its leaders and residents. The property on which the mall would be built included Sweedens Swamp, which was viewed by many local inhabitants as an unsightly, trash-strewn piece of land that contributed little to the aesthetic or recreational values of the area.

But, littered or not, Sweedens Swamp was also a wetland and, as such, protected under state and federal wetlands regulations. In order to construct its mall, Pyramid would have to obtain permits from Massachusetts and from the US Army Corps of Engineers to fill in 32 acres of the swamp and alter another thirteen. As part of its development package, the company proposed to "mitigate," or compensate for the loss of wetlands by enhancing most of the remaining swamp land on the site and creating a new artificial wetland on a separate parcel of land in the area. The result, the company maintained, would be better functioning and more attractive wetlands than Sweedens Swamp could ever hope to be. Officials both in the state and in the headquarters of the Army Corps seemed favorably disposed to Pyramid's arguments.

But there were those who saw Sweedens Swamp in a completely different light. To environmentalists, this modest wetland performed some of the most valuable functions in nature and was, in particular, an important habitat for local and migratory wildlife. Environmentalists feared, moreover, that allowing Pyramid to build on a wetland, in exchange for "mitigation," would set a precedent that would open the door to unrestrained development of a rapidly diminishing resource. These concerns came to the attention of the Region I office of the Environmental Protection Agency and its administrator, Michael Deland. While responsibility for granting permits lay with the Army Corps,

EPA could bring construction of the mall to a halt by exercising its power to veto a Corps decision to issue a permit. That would be a step Deland would have to consider if the project went forward.

Despite some rumblings of opposition, however, Pyramid was optimistic about its chances of winning the governmental approval it needed. In January 1984, it set about applying for permits to fill in Sweedens Swamp.

## Background: The Protection of Wetlands

In the debate over Sweedens Swamp, few took issue by 1984 with the basic tenet that wetlands in the US needed protection. They had been disappearing from the landscape at a rapid clip. According to one recent Interior Department study, less than 100 million acres of wetlands remained in the contiguous 48 states, out of an estimated 250 million in existence at the time of the first European emigrations.[1] The trend showed no signs of letting up: in the early 1980s, wetlands were being destroyed—either dredged, filled in, or drained—at a rate of anywhere from 300,000 to 500,000 acres per year. The loss of wetlands was viewed with dismay because of the unique environmental services they afforded: they provided wildlife habitat and flood storage capacity; replenished and absorbed underground water supplies; and, through setting and through their vegetation, removed pollutants from water, a process known as "pollution attenuation." For these reasons, some states had adopted regulations which restricted the filling in of wetlands; and the federal government as well, primarily through provisions of the Clean Water Act of 1972 and 1977, had put in place a permit process aimed at limiting development in wetland areas. But while there was little argument about the value of wetlands in general, there was considerable disagreement about the value of Sweedens Swamp in particular.

The object of the controversy was a 49.5 acre wetland located in southeastern Massachusetts, just north of the Rhode Island border, in the city of Attleboro. Water from Sweedens Swamp, which got its name from a farmer who had owned the land in colonial times, drained into the Seven Mile River, and ultimately into Narragansett Bay. The swamp had once covered a considerably larger area, but the construction of Interstate 95 in the early 1960s had sliced through the wetland, leaving a roughly triangular remnant that was bounded on three sides by major roads and highways: I-95, US Route 1 and Route 1A. (See Figure 1.2.1 for map.) The great bulk of its surviving acreage was characterized as a "forested swamp," dominated by red maples and populated by small mammals, amphibians, reptiles, and an array of migratory and year-round birds. (See Figure 1.2.2 for lists of wildlife and plant species.) It was "seasonally flooded," particularly after periods of heavy rainfall; at other times, large sections of the swamp were dry enough to walk on without boots.

How this patch of wooded swamp was viewed was essentially a matter of who was doing the looking. To its defenders, it was an "ordinary" but "hardworking blue collar wetland"; it was a "high-quality red maple swamp," according to the Massachusetts Division of Fisheries and Wildlife, an "urban oasis," in the words of another report, which provided excellent habitat for a rich variety of plant and animal species. To its detractors, it was at best "nondescript," at worst, a "dysfunctional" and degraded "dump," barren of "meaningful wildlife."[2] A July 1985 editorial in the Pawtucket, Rhode Island, *Evening Times,* characterized the wetland as "unsightly and littered with old tires, bedsprings and rubbish." But Sweedens Swamp, the editorial asserted, did have "one great asset: It's in a superb location for a shopping mall." It was this feature that drew the Pyramid Companies to the site in 1983.

## Shopping for a Mall

One of the largest developers of shopping centers in the Northeast, the Syracuse, New York-based Pyramid Companies had been eyeing southeastern Massachusetts in general, and the Sweedens Swamp site in particular, as a possible location for a regional mall. The area was considered ripe for commercial development. It was "no secret," says John Bersani, an attorney who joined Pyramid as its development partner in New England in 1983, "that there was a market opportunity here. There's almost, I think, 900,000 people that live within a fifteen mile radius of [Sweedens Swamp] and there was no regional mall within that area at all. ... There was just a terrific pent-up demand and a terrific market need." Despite Sweedens Swamp's attractive location at the crossroads of three major thoroughfares, however, Bersani was not, as he recalls, initially "enthusiastic about buying this particular site. ... It had a very difficult history."

***Earlier Development Efforts.*** The site Bersani referred to was a roughly 82-acre parcel of land, which included most of what was left of Sweedens Swamp. Over the years, a succession of developers had sought to erect a shopping mall on the property, but had come up empty-handed, as a result of zoning battles and regulatory obstacles. In 1979, a local firm, the Mugar Group, acquired the land and succeeded in its efforts to rezone the property for commercial use and obtain authorization from the Attleboro Conservation Commission to fill in all 50 acres of the swamp to construct a shopping mall; but the project stalled when a group of citizens requested a review of the decision by the regional office of the Massachusetts Department of Environmental Quality Engineering (DEQE). Before the state took up the issue, the property changed hands once again. The Edward J. DeBartolo Corporation of Youngstown, Ohio, bought the parcel and shepherded the shopping mall project through the state environmental review process. In April 1982, however, DEQE issued a "superceding order" rejecting the project on the grounds of its adverse effects on the wetland sections of the property. At that point, DeBartolo decided to abandon its efforts and, says Bersani, "began to look for a prospective buyer." Sometime in 1983, Pyramid decided to take a closer look at the property.

***Pyramid's Concerns.*** Depending upon the point of view, Pyramid was either "an outfit that prides itself on siting malls in places where other companies fear to tread because of environmental opposition,"[3] or a company that "has built a reputation for responsible development."[4] The firm had, Bersani acknowledges, a "not undeserved" reputation as a "very aggressive company" that had tangled with environmentalists and state and local governments in the past over regulatory issues. Pyramid was "an easy black hat target," he says, "for a lot of the environmental groups." On the other hand, he points with pride to a shopping mall that Pyramid built, after a long battle, in the "Pine Bush" area outside Albany, New York, which successfully preserved the habitat of the endangered Karner Blue butterfly.[5]

But Pyramid's past record notwithstanding, Bersani did not immediately jump at the Attleboro site. Its past history, including the early zoning battles, gave him pause. "In a place like Massachusetts," he explains, "where you face many, many additional permitting hurdles and where ... project opponents have opportunities to appeal and reappeal and appeal again to administrative bodies as well as courts, you have to look at the level of animosity and ask yourself, what are the odds of being able to gain approval in that type of environment." Along with the historical zoning issue, there was, he adds, the existence of wetlands on the property and the question of "what type of permitting challenge did that pose."

At the same time, there was a positive side to the long history of the Sweedens Swamp parcel—an extensive paper trail that offered clues to what shape a viable project might take. "This was not a virgin property," Bersani points out, "where we were coming in and looking into a crystal ball and saying, 'What's going to happen if we try to fill a large portion of those wetlands?'" Bersani closely examined the DeBartolo Corporation's files on the site. That company's proposal, he noted, would have filled in the entire 50 acres of swamp land. "They just wanted to pave it over and create a couple of pools where storm water could be held so it wouldn't flood adjacent properties. And that was it," says Bersani. There were no provisions to compensate for the loss of other wetland functions, such as habitat and pollution attenuation. "I looked at that," Bersani recalls, "and said, 'Well, no wonder this thing is hung up. That's just plain and simple an unrealistic proposal.' ... So the first thing that I said to myself was, 'We can come up with a reasonable plan, a good plan.'" He was further encouraged by a letter in the files from DEQE denying DeBartolo's request for a permit. "The letter," Bersani recalls, "said, 'We're turning you down. But if you do x, y, and z, ... if you would consider scaling back your building footprint and preserving some wetlands and creating some others, this may be a permittable project.'"

In addition to examining the files, Bersani paid a visit to Sweedens Swamp to assess the site firsthand. He had, he remembers, expected to see a picturesque marsh. "Instead," he says, "what I saw was something that was almost totally dry and was filled with debris, junk, garbage, roofing shingles, washing machines, old tires, oil drums, barrels. No meaningful wildlife. Certainly no waterfowl. ... You'd see field mice, squirrels, chipmunks, rabbits, certainly nothing extraordinary." The swamp, Bersani concluded, "appeared ... to be of insignificant value, particularly in terms of wildlife habitat." It had value, he notes, for flood storage and pollution attenuation, "but those are values that could readily be replicated with an appropriate project development plan." Increasingly, Bersani says, "looking at the old plan, thinking about what we could do, ... I was beginning to gain a comfort level that this was something that could reasonably be done."

***Alternatives.*** By contrast, the other sites in the area that Bersani looked at as candidates for shopping malls posed what he considered potentially insurmountable obstacles and a greater degree of uncertainty. "I looked at a host of sites," he says. "They all had problems of one type of another." The most notable site, which was to figure prominently in the ensuing controversy, was a 57-acre parcel of land three miles north of Sweedens Swamp, at the intersection of US Route 1 and I-295, in the town of North Attleborough.[6] This site, too, says Bersani, was well known to developers. While it included very little wetland acreage—less than one acre, according to government studies—it had other drawbacks, at least in the eyes of Pyramid. According to a brochure later put out by Pyramid, five prior attempts (including one by DeBartolo) to build a shopping mall on the property had failed. On at least two occasions, Bersani notes, the town meeting had voted down a proposal to rezone the land for commercial use. Moreover, Pyramid considered the location less than ideal—it was not visible from I-95 nor directly accessible to it; and, the company maintained, other developers had been unable to attract major department store tenants to the site. In view of this track record, Pyramid concluded that the North Attleborough site was too problematic for further consideration as a location for a shopping mall.

In December 1983, Pyramid made its move. It purchased the 82-acre Sweedens Swamp parcel in Attleboro from the DeBartolo Corporation, paying "top dollar" for that time, says Bersani, "in excess of $2 million cash, with no option." The company, he continues, did not purposely seek out wetlands because, as some claimed, it was cheap. "We spent millions upfront to acquire this piece of property," he maintains, "at certainly what at that time was probably a record-breaker in terms of land values in that particular area. This was not something where we got some bargain basement deal because it was a swamp."

***Pyramid's Plan.*** Soon thereafter, Pyramid made public its plans for the site. The centerpiece of the plan was the "Newport Avenue Galleria"—a 700,000 square foot, two-level mall, with three major department stores, 150 specialty shops, and a multi-screen cinema complex. (See Figures 1.2.3 and 1.2.4.) To build it, the company would seek to fill in 32.3 of the 49.5 acres of wetlands on the site, which would make it, Michael Deland later wrote, "the largest wetland fill project in Massachusetts in over five years." To compensate for this loss of wetlands, Pyramid formulated both onsite and offsite "mitigation" measures.[7] Onsite, it proposed to alter 13.3 acres of Sweedens Swamp, transforming them from forested wetland to emergent marsh and shrub swamp which, it argued, would provide new wildlife habitat—e.g., for fish, which were then absent from the swamp, and waterfowl—and improved water quality.[8] In addition, Pyramid would add more wetlands on the site by excavating nine acres of upland adjacent to the swamp. Offsite, Pyramid planned to create 35 acres of open water, marsh, and shrub swamp on the site of an abandoned gravel pit in North Attleborough; later, the company moved the site of its proposed wetland to a former sand and gravel pit in the city of Attleboro itself. Pyramid estimated the mitigation cost would be in the millions, but did not specify what that cost represented as a percentage of its overall costs or its return on investment.

These plans, Bersani argues, both complied with the state's wishes, by scaling back the size of the mall and parking lot, and created new wetlands of greater value than those that would be filled in. Most of the existing swamp, he contends, "was pretty low value, because it wasn't very diverse. It was all treed, so it made it inaccessible to waterfowl and more varied wildlife species." Under Pyramid's proposal, "we would plant new species in here, so that instead of just one monolithic red maple swamp, you'd have a diversity of cover types. You'd have some shrub swamp; you'd have some marsh; you'd have some red maple swamp. And that would encourage a better wildlife habitat as well." The company, he adds, had "sought advice and counsel from a wide variety of experts that had done this successfully before," and its proposal had generated considerable enthusiasm. "I heard a lot of people excited about it. They were saying, this is the way development projects should move forward. ... You can clean up what is today a junkyard and make it into something better, and at the same time create new jobs. ... This was a situation where you genuinely could have what we hear our politicians mouthing off about: We can have it all. We can protect the environment and have economic growth."

## The View from Attleboro

The proposed home of the Pyramid mall, the city of Attleboro, was frequently described, rather like the swamp in its midst, as a hard-working blue collar community. It was historically a factory town, says Brenda Reed, who served as mayor from 1984–86, and many of its roughly 35,000 residents continued to work in factories that manufactured such commodities as jewelry, electronic components, and hardware. When Pyramid's plan first surfaced in early 1984, the city had, Reed notes, "suffered through some hard times." The city government was still reeling from the effects of a national economic recession, as well as from federal cutbacks and property tax rollbacks that left it with a deficit of over half a million dollars—a hefty sum for a small city.

Under the circumstances, it was hardly surprising that the city should take a favorable view of Pyramid's proposal. The company projected that the mall would create 1,500 construction jobs and 2,250 permanent full and part-time jobs; $500,000 in local tax revenues; and a $25 million annual increase in the area's economy. In addition to jobs and revenues, residents welcomed the mall as a consumer convenience. The nearest large malls were across the Rhode Island line in Providence and Pawtucket, and residents were eager to have shopping outlets closer to home. The state also stood to gain, since shoppers would pay a five percent Massachusetts sales tax on their purchases, instead of a six percent Rhode Island tax.[9] Such figures gave rise to strong support from Attleboro residents for the project. Reed recalls a survey that indicated that about "95 percent of the community wanted this thing."[10]

Best of all, in Reed's eyes, the projected gains from the mall would not be offset by the loss of a precious local resource. Sweedens Swamp, she maintains, was "a dumping ground and a breeding ground for mosquitoes," an eyesore that citizens clearly did not value. "I physically walked that property," she recalls. "... It's where people dumped their old bathtubs and their old tires and their old everything." Residents did not have, she points out, emotional ties to the wetland. There was "not one person ... who could say to you, 'I go there and picnic once in a while. I take my children there, and we commune with nature.' People didn't go there." In fact, Reed maintains, residents would be much more likely to enjoy the pleasures of nature in the offsite wetlands Pyramid proposed to create.

"There would [be]," she says, "bicycle paths and nature trails and something very special in a place that was at five time a gravel pit; [it would be] a recreational area that residents of Attleboro and other places could enjoy." "Quite frankly," Reed asserts, "... this would have been an improvement on that site even before you get to the jobs."

Not everyone responded positively to the proposed mall, however. A small group of environmentalists, led by the Massachusetts Association of Conservation Commissions and the Massachusetts Audubon Society, voiced their opposition to filling in the swamp and prepared to do battle with Pyramid as the company sought governmental sanction for its plans. The Attleboro Conservation Commission had already approved the much larger project submitted by DeBartolo, without any mitigation provisions, and did not choose to revisit the matter when Pyramid completed its proposal. The first stop, then, for the Newport Avenue Galleria was the state, where the last action on the project had taken place two years earlier—the permit denial issued to DeBartolo. Reed had talked to Governor Michael Dukakis, who was in the midst of a second tour of duty at the helm of the state, and received assurances that the project would get a fair look. Subsequently, in early 1984, Pyramid submitted its application to the Department of Environmental Quality Engineering for a permit to fill 32 acres, and alter another 13, of wetland.

## First Stop: The State

In Massachusetts, the process of applying for a wetlands permit normally began with the local conservation commission. Parties wishing to appeal a local decision could take their case to the appropriate regional office of DEQE, and from there to the central office in Boston. At that point, DEQE would arrange an adjudicatory hearing on the matter, to be presided over by a hearing officer from outside the agency; once the hearing officer published a "tentative decision," the final disposition of the case was in the hands of the DEQE commissioner. The DeBartolo Corporation had taken the process to the point of requesting an adjudicatory hearing in 1982, before finally abandoning its quest to build the mall on the Sweedens Swamp parcel. When Pyramid bought the property, it sought to substitute its name for DeBartolo's on the application for a permit and continue proceedings, without having to file a new "Notice of Intent" to fill wetlands. This was a crucial point for the company: in April 1983, the state had adopted stringent new regulations prohibiting the altering of more than 5,000 square feet of wetlands. Under these rules, the Newport Avenue Galleria could not be permitted; for the project to survive, Pyramid would need to be grandfathered under the old, less strict regulations which had been in effect when DeBartolo had initiated its application. To the chagrin of opponents of the mall, the DEQE approved Pyramid's request that its plans be considered a revised version of DeBartolo's, instead of a wholly new proposal. Even more galling, in June 1984, the department's regional office issued an order tentatively okaying Pyramid's plans for the shopping mall. They contested both decisions in the adjudicatory hearing, which began in August 1984.

At the hearing, opponents of the project (the "intervenors") argued that, under Pyramid, the mall project had been significantly altered, and therefore the application process should be started from scratch—a move that would have effectively killed the mall. Beyond that, they raised questions about the design of the project and the value of the replacement wetlands in comparison with the existing swamp, in terms of such matters as pollution control and prevention, flood storage, and fisheries protection. In each case, the independent hearing officer ruled in Pyramid's favor. In his tentative decision, released on January 28, 1985, the adjudicator first concluded that Pyramid's "modifications to the project" constituted a "positive response to criticisms of the original plan by both the intervenors and the Department [DEQE] and that the general intent of the project remains the same," thereby allowing it to proceed under the original Notice of Intent. In other areas, the hearing officer ruled the project would, if anything, improve the habitat for fish, and that the pollution control functions of the artificial wetlands would be superior to those of the existing swamp. Overall, he concluded that the project was consistent with the intent of the state's wetlands law. "The applicant," he wrote, "has thus far used the most current scientific knowledge and the best and most reliable technology to make sure that the planned development will enhance rather than harm the interests protected by the Wetlands Protection Act." With this finding, the matter moved on to the final state administrative court of appeal: the DEQE commissioner.

***The Commissioner's Decision.*** The commissioner of DEQE at the time, S. Russell Sylva, had assumed his post in November 1984, just a few months before the hearing officer published his decision. Despite a strong interest in wetlands preservation, the new commissioner found himself hemmed in by considerations that, to an extent, had little to do with the particular matter at hand, but much to do with the credibility of his agency and his office. DEQE had "for years used this process of a third-party hearing officer" as a way to "depoliticize" controversial decisions, and no hearing officer, Sylva points out, had ever been "overturned by a commissioner." To start now, he feared, would remove a valuable buffer between the DEQE and the competing interests in cases that came before the department for resolution. It would, Sylva says, "put myself and every other commissioner into the political fire for every decision down the road."[11] Similarly, Sylva felt uneasy about reversing the hearing officer's decision to allow the Pyramid project to be grandfathered under the old wetlands rules. The business community was watching closely, he recalls, to see if the state would honor its commitment to grandfather projects already in the pipeline when it tightened its regulations. "I believed very strongly," says Sylva, "that if we ever raised a question for this agency [about whether] we'd stand behind grandfathering, we'd never be able to increase a regulation."

A further consideration for Sylva, as a relative newcomer to DEQE, was the staff's attitude towards Pyramid's mitigation proposals. The "technical people," he recalls, were "really thinking this was a good solution. ... People were sort of saying, 'Hey, if this works, this wetland is going to be better off than it is currently.'" Some of them also felt, he continues, "that this was a terrific place to test this technology." As a new manager with no background in engineering, Sylva worried what the effect on his staff would be if he were to dismiss their judgment. "Here comes a non-engineer," he imagines, "saying to his staff, 'I'm going to overrule your engineering decisions.' That's a toughie."

In the end, Sylva decided to follow the established practice of his agency and accept the recommendations of the hearing officer. On March 13, 1985, he issued an order authorizing the Pyramid project to proceed. The order, Sylva notes, was "heavily, heavily condition[ed]," so that "if we see problems on this project, we can go back and require [Pyramid] to redo things." Moreover, Sylva believed he was not setting a dangerous precedent in the state that would pave the way for other developers to destroy existing wetlands. "This [project] was kind of a dinosaur," he explains. "It couldn't become a precedent because you couldn't do what they [Pyramid] were doing under the new rules and regulations. ... The new regs are in place, and this isn't going to happen again."

But to opponents of the mall, such assurances were unpersuasive. They promptly appealed Sylva's decision in the state superior court. They also began organizing in earnest, pulling together a consortium of 17 environmental groups—which they dubbed the Coalition to Save Sweedens Swamp—to prepare for the next round of permit reviews, which would be conducted by federal agencies. For environmentalists, the battle would be fought not just to save Sweedens Swamp, but to preserve the integrity of the nation's wetlands protection laws.

## The Environmentalists' Perspective

To environmental organizations and their allies, Sweedens Swamp was, while not pristine, a wetland that had earned its right to protection under the law. It provided, to one degree or another, most of the valuable functions of a wetland: flood storage, pollution attenuation, discharge of groundwater, and wildlife habitat. It was in this latter category that many saw the chief virtue of the swamp. Though the wildlife it hosted was for the most part unremarkable, it was, supporters argued, diverse; moreover, the swamp provided increasingly hard-to-find habitat for migratory and nesting birds. According to a report by the US Fish and Wildlife Service, two visits to the swamp in 1984 yielded sightings of some 31 plant species; 14 bird species, including a mallard duck (which it characterized as a "National Species of Special Emphasis"); as well as green frogs, snakes, and "signs of small mammals such as rabbits." On the basis of such findings, the Fish and Wildlife Service had classified Sweedens Swamp as "Resource Category 2," the second highest rating in its habitat classification scheme.

In addition, defenders of the swamp took issue with those who characterized it as a dump. While they acknowledged that trash had been dumped in the swamp, they maintained that the trash was concentrated in a few areas, largely along the perimeter of the wetland. "A large part of the swamp," says Priscilla Chapman, executive director of the Sierra Club of New England, "had not been degraded with dumping." The image of Sweedens Swamp as a junkyard was exaggerated, she asserts, in part to bolster the argument of mall proponents that the wetland was of little value. Photographs of trash or of old appliances rusting in the grass made an especially vivid impression in the public mind.

"There was a refrigerator [that had been dumped in the swamp]," Chapman recalls. "... Every single time Pyramid wanted to make a point, they would take the press out there and take them right to the refrigerator. Then you'd open up the paper, and there would be [a photograph of] that refrigerator again. ... I told John Bersani that I hoped when it was all over, I would get the refrigerator ... and make [it into] a planter in my backyard or something."

Environmentalists further argued that, unexceptional as Sweedens Swamp was, it was nonetheless irreplaceable—at least by the artificial or, in Chapman's words, "phony" wetlands Pyramid was proposing to build. Critics viewed with particular skepticism the company's plans to create new wetlands on the site of an abandoned gravel pit, which, they contended, because it was an "upland" site, did not have the correct hydrology to allow wetland vegetation to establish itself. Perhaps, Chapman speculates, "by constant manipulation, by pumping water in and continually replanting things, you might be able to keep a wetland going temporarily, but it's unlikely that that would function as a wetland over time." While some artificial wetlands had been built, environmentalists argued, the results, such as were available, were equivocal. "The proposed mitigation plan," maintained Christy Foote-Smith, the executive director of the Massachusetts Association of Conservation Commissions, in testimony in 1984, "that is, the 'build a better wetland' plan, is for the most part uncharted ground. Wetlands replication is a new science, and there is no guarantee of success. Many scientists take the position that it is doubtful that man can precisely create in three years what it has taken nature 10,000 years to develop."

It was, in a sense, the ordinary and unprepossessing appearance of Sweedens Swamp that roused environmentalists to its defense, as the issue moved into the federal arena. "The Clean Water Act," Chapman notes, "does not offer protection to some kinds of swamps or some quality of swamps and deny protection to other kinds of swamps. ... We were very concerned about these arguments that this was a low value swamp," she continues, "because we thought that this kind of argument really undermined the Clean Water Act." If the assertion that Sweedens Swamp was not worth preserving were to prevail, environmentalists "feared," Chapman says, "that that would really bring down the house of cards. Such a decision would open the door for developers all over the United States to find a wetland and go throw a few tires or a few trash bags into [it], and argue that it was no longer an area worth saving." The upcoming federal permit battles, environmentalists believed, would be to some extent a test of the nation's commitment to wetlands preservation. "I think a lot of wetlands that had gotten national attention [in the past] were like the Everglades or some really outstanding area that maybe had endangered species or habitat, or something like that," Chapman observes. "... I think we wanted to see whether the Clean Water Act could protect an ordinary, everyday wetland."

## Federal Wetlands Law

The federal laws governing wetlands protection in the US were to be found chiefly in the Clean Water Act, first passed in 1972 and amended in 1977. Under section 404 of that measure, responsibility for safeguarding the integrity of wetlands was divided between the US Army Corps of Engineers and the Environmental Protection Agency. The former was given authority, under section 404(a), to issue permits allowing the discharge of dredged or fill material into the nation's waters. The regulations that the Corps applied in considering permit requests were written by EPA under section 404(b)(1); that agency also had statutory authority to veto a Corps decision to grant a permit if it concluded that the discharge would have an "unacceptable adverse effect" on the aquatic environment.

In its statement of "purpose and policy" introducing the regulations (often referred to as the section 404(b)(1) "guidelines"), EPA asserted that "[f]rom a national perspective, the degradation or destruction of special aquatic sites, such as filling operations in wetlands, is considered to be among the most severe environmental impacts covered by the Guidelines." The discharge of dredged or fill material would not be permitted, the agency declared, "unless it can be demonstrated that such a discharge will not have an unacceptable adverse impact" on an "aquatic ecosystem." In support of this policy, the guidelines laid down a series of restrictions, some of which would be the source of considerable controversy in the Sweedens Swamp case. Most crucial, perhaps, was the stricture that no discharge would be permitted "if there is a practicable alternative ... which would have less adverse impact on the aquatic ecosystem, so long as the alternative does not have other significant adverse environmental consequences."[12] As a corollary to that, the guidelines stipulated that, in the case of activities that did not "require access or proximity to or siting within the special aquatic site in question to fulfill its basic purpose," practicable alternatives would be "presumed to be available, unless clearly demonstrated otherwise"; moreover, all practicable alternatives which would not involve a discharge would be "presumed to have less adverse impact" than one that did, again unless proven to the contrary. Taken together, these two "rebuttable presumptions" formed the core of the "water dependency" or "alternatives" test that Michael Deland later characterized as the "linchpin of the section 404 regulatory program."

Over time, the "congressionally arranged marriage," in the words of Doug Thompson, chief of the wetlands protection section of EPA's Region I office (which comprises New England), between the Army Corps and EPA had begun to show signs of strain. The Corps, whose purview included the nation's rivers, harbors, and navigable waters, was more development-minded than EPA, and had chafed under the constraints of the 404(b)(1) regulations. In the early 1980s, during a deregulation push initiated by the Reagan administration in environmental and other areas, the Corps had sought to make the guidelines advisory rather than mandatory, and to eliminate EPA's veto powers altogether.[13] While nothing ultimately came of that effort, the two agencies maintained, says Thompson, an "uneasy balance" of interests in their administration of the section 404 program. Still, despite differences in approach, EPA had rarely exercised its right to veto an Army Corps decision: since the inception of the program, the Corps had processed an estimated 11,000 permit applications per year; as of the end of 1983, EPA had initiated veto proceedings on only three. But the Sweedens Swamp case would test that shaky equilibrium. After Pyramid submitted its application to fill 32 acres of wetland and alter an additional 13, the two agencies ultimately found themselves embroiled in what one observer called a "long-simmering turf battle" over control of the wetlands program.[14]

## Next Stop: The Army Corps of Engineers, New England Division

Following established procedure, Pyramid formally submitted its permit request to the New England Division of the Army Corps of Engineers in July 1984, while the state permit process was still in midstream. There, staff engineers would review the application, according to the section 404 guidelines, to determine the impact of the proposed project and its compliance with the conditions set down in the 404 regulations. They would also, as provided in the guidelines, seek the comments of EPA officials in Region I, as well as those of the US Fish and Wildlife Service. At the end of this process, a division engineer would issue a recommendation to deny or approve a permit request. On May 2, 1985, having completed all these steps, Colonel Carl Sciple of the New England Division drafted his "statement of findings and environmental assessment" on the Newport Avenue Galleria project. In it, he recommended that the permit be denied.

Sciple's conclusions rested most prominently on two points in the guidelines which, he noted in his statement, "are regulatory in nature and not simply 'guidelines.'" In those regulations, Sciple observed, "there is an intent expressed that, if you don't need to fill a wetland, don't." Even if, he argued, the offsite mitigation plans Pyramid was proposing were to succeed—an outcome he viewed with some skepticism—"it is contrary to the Guidelines to allow the destruction of a viable wetland, Sweeden's [sic] Swamp, when the project's public need and resulting benefits can be satisfied elsewhere." That "elsewhere," he continued, had been identified: it was the 57-acre parcel of land in North Attleborough which Pyramid had earlier rejected. The North Attleborough site, Sciple wrote, constituted "a practicable alternative to the proposed discharge which would have less adverse impact on the aquatic ecosystem. ..." Unfortunately for Pyramid, the practicable alternative was by this time in the hands of a competitor.

***The Alternative.*** A lot had happened to the North Attleborough site in recent years. On July 1, 1983, a local developer, State Properties of New England—which soon thereafter renamed itself New England Development—optioned a portion of the site (site acquisition was ultimately completed in February 1984), and announced its intention to build a 660,000 square foot mall on the property. Like its predecessors, the company ran into an early roadblock when its effort to have the property rezoned was rebuffed in an October 1984 town meeting. A few months later, however, the needed zoning changes were approved in a town referendum, clearing the way legally for construction of the mall. The North Attleborough site had other problems—it was near an elementary school and close by the water supply of the city of Attleboro, which was threatening to take the land by eminent domain, and there were access problems as well—but these, Sciple maintained, could be "resolved." One problem the site did *not* pose was the need to fill in much wetlands area. Both Army Corps and DEQE engineers agreed that, even under the state's stringent new wetlands regulations, the North

Attleborough property would qualify for a permit. In view of these findings, Sciple concluded that a less damaging alternative to the Pyramid proposal was "available," even though it was not necessarily "available to the applicant"—an interpretation of the term that would be the subject of fierce debate in the coming months.

In making his determination, Sciple was in accord with the views of Michael Deland and the Region I office of EPA. On at least two occasions, in October 1984 and February 1985, Deland had written to Lt. Col. Edward Hammond, deputy division engineer of the New England Division of the Army Corps, strongly expressing his agency's position that the permit should be denied, principally on the grounds that a practicable alternative existed. Deland also argued that the Corps should not accept "the principle of mitigating otherwise avoidable impacts." While the mitigation proposed by Pyramid was "conceptually sound," he wrote, in terms of attempting to improve the hydrologic function of Sweedens Swamp and compensating for wildlife loss, "we do not believe that it can be used to justify noncompliance with the more fundamental precepts of the 404 program. Most importantly, we do not believe that mitigation of impacts can substitute for avoiding them in the first place."

As it turned out, Sciple's permit denial was never made official. In a move that Doug Thompson calls "unprecedented," the headquarters of the Army Corps in Washington, DC asked the regional office to forward Sciple's draft recommendation to Major General John Wall, director of civil works for the Corps, for review. Wall wanted, he later wrote, "to resolve the policy issue of practicable alternatives as applied to non-water dependent activities ... and the use of mitigation to satisfy [the guidelines]." His views on these matters would prove to differ sharply from Deland's.

## Detour: Army Corps Headquarters

The decision of the Washington office of the Army Corps to review Sciple's recommendation came at least in part at the prompting of Pyramid. John Bersani had not anticipated a permit denial from the Corps, once the state had formally approved the mall project in March 1985. He had consulted widely, he says, and "across the board, people's attitudes about the federal program were that if you could secure an approval from Massachusetts—which together with the state of Oregon at that time was viewed as having the most stringent wetland regulations in the country—that if you could satisfy the [DEQE], [then] the feds, as a practical matter, were going to go along." But the state approval, Bersani observes, had galvanized environmental groups, and "then the letters started coming in, and the phone calls" to the New England Division of the Corps and to its deputy division engineer, Lt. Col. Hammond, who was, according to Bersani, "brand new" to his job and inexperienced. "The Corps in [New England]," he says, "came under terrific pressure from the environmental lobby, from [its] sister agencies; the Fish and Wildlife Service and the EPA were very sympathetic to the environmental lobby." When it appeared that the Corps decision would likely go against Pyramid, Bersani continues, "we took our case to people above [Lt. Col.] Hammond in Washington."

The Corps headquarters had reasons of its own for wanting to review the Sweedens Swamp case. It was an unusual step, Bernard Goode, chief of the regulatory branch at headquarters, told a reporter, but "because of policy issues in Attleboro, we felt it was important to help interpret the case."[15] More particularly, the *New York Times* reported in August 1985, "Mr. Goode said the corps' headquarters in Washington decided to take over the decision from the New England office as a good case for giving a showcase to the 'mitigation' policy." At issue was the belief of some headquarters officials that, as General Wall put it, "[i]n certain circumstances ... the provision of mitigation can satisfy the requirements" of the section 404 guidelines.

In his "analysis" of the Pyramid permit application, which was sent back to the New England Division on May 31, 1985, Wall argued that "a plain reading" of the language of the guidelines on practicable alternatives led him to infer that "if mitigation measures can fully compensate for all adverse impacts of a proposed discharge on the aquatic environment, then the adverse effects of the proposed discharge on the aquatic environment is zero."[16] This would mean that "100% mitigation would allow the satisfaction of that 404(b)(1) guidelines requirement even if a practicable alternative site might be available." In the specific case of Sweedens Swamp, Wall contended that the proposed mitigation would in fact result in "a net benefit to the aquatic environment." The swamp, he wrote, "is a wetland of relatively low value," providing few benefits in terms of water quality, flood storage, fisheries habitat, or groundwater recharge. Its greatest utility—as wildlife habitat—extended largely to species of "local importance"; and while it provided good habitat for migratory songbirds, red maple habitat was "commonplace in that part of Massachusetts and thus is not a limiting factor for such species." Between the improved "wetlands functional capability" the onsite mitigation would provide and the compensation for "other losses" that the offsite mitigation would offer, Wall concluded, "the overall rate of mitigation will approximate 1 1/2 to 1."

That was not the only conclusion in Wall's analysis that was to prove controversial. He also addressed the question of whether a practicable alternative had to be available to a particular applicant in order to be considered truly practicable, or whether it sufficed that an alternative would fulfill a project's purpose, regardless of whom it was available to. Under the Corps' own regulations, Wall wrote, he was required to "examine alternatives from both the particular applicant's viewpoint and from the public interest perspective." (EPA's 404 guidelines, Wall observed, were "somewhat ambiguous whether they intend one approach or the other, or both, to be used.") Accordingly, he concluded that, from the applicant's point of view, "it appears that the North Attleboro [sic] site is not available," because it was owned by a competitor. Moreover, the applicant had made "a convincing argument that [the alternative] would not successfully fulfill the purposes of his proposed project, from his particular point of view." From a public interest viewpoint, Wall, noting the popular support for the Attleboro site, wrote that "it is my policy that the Regulatory Program not be used to 'second guess' decisions made by state and local government on a zoning or land use [issue] unless there are significant issues of overriding national importance"—which, in the case of Sweedens Swamp, he concluded, there were not. Consequently, Wall found that the Pyramid project did comply with the 404 guidelines and was "not contrary to the public interest." He directed the New England Division to "reconcile your documentation" with his findings and prepare a notice of intent to issue a permit.

## Reaction

General Wall's findings sent shock waves through the environmental community, and beyond. Environmentalists decried the reversal of the New England Division's recommendation, and labeled Wall's decision a dangerous precedent that would, in the words of a *Boston Globe* report, "give the green light for development on wetlands across the nation."[17] The issue concerned "not just 30 acres of wetlands in Attleboro," a staff member of the Senate Subcommittee on Environmental Pollution told the *Globe*. "It's the national precedent everyone is concerned about here. If this sets the policy, it guts what's left of the [federal wetlands protection] program." Critics perceived the Army Corps headquarters' action as further evidence of a larger intent to weaken EPA's regulatory hold on wetlands development. An official with the National Wildlife Federation contended that under the Reagan administration, the Corps was "determined to frustrate the regulation of wetlands to the maximum extent they can."[18]

***Inside EPA.*** At the Region I offices of EPA, officials shared the consternation of environmental organizations. Pyramid, says Doug Thompson, had launched "a frontal challenge on some important tenets of the wetlands program, such as the need to avoid [adverse impacts] before you compensate and [the issue of] what is a practicable alternative," and the feeling in the agency was that "there were some important legal and regulatory principles at stake." At the time of the Sweedens Swamp case, those principles had not been tested in litigation, and the language of the regulations on which they were based, notes Ann Williams, a lawyer with the Region I office, was "certainly open to more than one interpretation." The meaning of such terms as "practicability, availability, and feasibility," she continues, were "ambiguous," and the issues involved in construing their intent "had not been wrestled with as concretely as what we were faced with in the Attleboro case." As a result of these still-unsettled terms, Thompson adds, "there was tension between [EPA and the Corps] and some jousting as to whose interpretation should have primacy."

For regional EPA officials, the most disturbing matter of interpretation at issue was General Wall's assertion that mitigation could be included in an "alternatives analysis"—i.e., that, in determining whether or not to issue a permit, the Corps could compare the "preferred site with mitigation," Thompson explains, "against the alternative sites without mitigation. ..." Wall's "pronouncement," says Williams, represented "an important policy direction that he was going to be taking the program in if someone didn't say no." If adopted, she continues, "it would pretty much have erased the notion that if you can avoid filling in wetlands, you should." The mitigation issue eventually became "the driving force behind our pursuing this case. ... We felt that General Wall's approach would be extremely damaging to the program, and we were willing to go to the mat on that."

"Going to the mat" would mean deciding to launch the rarely used veto proceeding under section 404(c) of the Clean Water Act. Those regulations authorized EPA to veto a Corps decision if it were determined that the proposed discharge would have an "unacceptable adverse effect" on municipal water supplies, shellfish beds and fishery areas, wildlife or recreational areas."[19] The process of making this determination would formally begin, after an initial consultation period, with the issuance by the regional administrator of a "proposed determination" to prohibit a discharge, followed by a public hearing and a comment period. At the end of those proceedings, the regional administrator would issue a "recommended decision" on the matter; it was then left to the administrator of EPA in Washington to make a "final determination" on the disposition of the permit.

For Michael Deland, a decision to initiate veto proceedings would mean incurring more displeasure, both from state and local officials, who supported the mall, and from the Reagan administration, which had made deregulation a priority in its first term. Deland had already made himself highly unpopular in some parts of Massachusetts by suing the state over pollution in Boston Harbor; as a result of that litigation, the state and many metropolitan Boston communities were spending hundreds of millions of dollars to pay the cost of cleaning up the harbor. Meanwhile, Deland notes, he was also at "loggerheads with ... much of the Reagan administration," which had appointed him to his post in 1983, over his opposition to oil drilling off the coast of New England. Russell Sylva, the DEQE commissioner at the time, recalls speculating on Deland's likely move in the Sweedens Swamp case. "There were a lot of people that were saying, 'Well, Reagan will never let him do it.' ... But I said, 'You know, Mike has gone out on a lot of limbs on Boston Harbor. I think he might [do it]. I can tell you, he's got the [regulatory] tools.'"[20]

As Sylva guessed he might, Deland chose to go out on another limb and proceed with a veto action. "I took a hard look at Sweedens Swamp and what it was contributing from an ecological perspective," he recalls, "and came to the conclusion that while it clearly wasn't a garden of eden, it was ... a wetland that merited protection." As he prepared to make his intention public, Deland was aware that such a step could potentially do further damage to his own standing with the Reagan administration, and provide ammunition to critics who charged that EPA overreached its regulatory purview. "I knew it wasn't going to be popular," he says. But, he adds, "... I felt that I was doing the right thing. The name over the door was the Environmental Protection Agency, and I felt a responsibility to be an activist advocate for the environment." On August 21, 1985, the regional office published a formal notice of a "proposed determination" to prohibit a discharge into Sweedens Swamp. It would mark the first time a veto proceeding had ever been initiated in the Region I office.

## Counterattack

After Deland announced his decision, it was the mall proponents' turn to express outrage. Conservative columnist David B. Wilson, writing in the *Boston Globe,* railed against "environmentalist fundamentalists" for zealously defending a "rubbish-strewn, oil-streaked, 50-acre patch of wetland. ..."[21] Residents of

Attleboro did likewise on September 26, 1985, when some 1,200 of them packed the high school auditorium for a hearing held by EPA on its proposed determination. "People were furious," recalls Priscilla Chapman of the Sierra Club. "… It was a very emotionally charged hearing because it was basically [in residents' eyes], this handful of environmentalists is trying to deprive us blue collar people in Attleboro [of] a job, and what do they care about us? They all go skiing with Robert Redford."

For Attleboro residents, siting the mall in neighboring North Attleborough would mean they would get the worst of both worlds: they would lose the tax revenues the mall would generate, but gain the added traffic it would attract. Brenda Reed, who as mayor spoke out strongly on behalf of the project, recalls the frustration she and others felt at having the city's destiny taken out of their hands. "Local control was taken away from residents of that city," she asserts. "They could not ... make the final decision. … These people were being told in effect by EPA, 'Your decision doesn't matter. We don't care what you think. We care what we think, and we're going to protect you from yourselves.' That is not the way democracy works."

Attleboro residents received strong support from Rep. Barney Frank, whose district at the time included the city. Frank, a liberal Democrat, made numerous appeals on behalf of the Sweedens Swamp project, arguing in one letter to Deland that it was both economically important and "environmentally sound." "I have not seen," Frank later remarked, "from those in opposition to [to the project] specific assertions of harm that will come from the building on Sweeden's Swamp, except for those who believe that in principle we are never to build on any wetland, anywhere, any time, any place."[22]

***Pyramid Reacts.*** But while Attleboro citizens continued to seethe over EPA's intervention, in the months following publication of the notice of a proposed determination, the locus of the controversy over Sweedens Swamp moved beyond a strictly local setting and onto a wider stage, as Pyramid began to press its case in Congress. John Bersani had viewed Deland's action with a mixture of disbelief and outrage. "I remember the day that we got approved by the Corps," Bersani recalls, "feeling this great sense of accomplishment and relief, and about an hour later thinking to myself—because I knew the pressure that had been exerted and all—could the EPA start this veto process? And Pm like, naw." But, he says, when the "environmental lobby" realized the Corps was going to approve Pyramid's proposal, "that's when they pulled out all the stops."

Pyramid was now faced with the possibility of having its permit denied. At this point, the company had plowed many more millions into the project—Bersani estimates it ultimately spent $18 million in purchase price, legal fees, engineering fees, consulting fees. "It all began to mount up," he says. "We had this tremendous investment" in the property. Feeling that environmentalists had gotten the jump on the company (with, Bersani claims, some help from its competitor, New England Development), Pyramid decided to launch a lobbying effort in Washington. In the end, says Bersani, "we mounted quite a campaign."

***Washington Weighs In.*** With the aid of lobbyist Tom Evans, a former Republican congressman, Pyramid enlisted the support of a number of senators and representatives, who wrote letters on behalf of the Attleboro project. Some of the letters went to Deland, but many were addressed to

Lee Thomas, the EPA administrator at the time, who would make the "final determination" on the permit. The letters came from members of Congress serving constituents far removed from Sweedens Swamp—Rep. Arlan Stangeland (R-Minn.), the ranking Republican on the Subcommittee on Water Resources, for example, as well as Strom Thurmond (R-SC) and Alfonse D'Amato (R-NY).[23] The letters spoke, variously, in support of Pyramid and its track record, of the benefits of mitigation in low quality wetlands, of the process the Army Corps had followed in deciding to issue the permit. Some also mentioned EPA's recourse to 404(c) veto proceedings, which had begun to increase in 1984 and 1985. "[W]e are concerned," wrote ten members of the Subcommittee on Water Resources, "that unwarranted use of the Section 404(c) process to overturn well reasoned and amply supported decisions of the Army Corps could undermine the integrity of the Corps' role under Section 404."

Members of Congress were not the only ones to raise their voices in opposition to a veto. The influential Heritage Foundation, a conservative Washington think-tank, published an article in its winter 1986 edition of *Policy Review* excoriating Deland—who was depicted as being part of a "powerful coalition" of environmental groups and other interested parties (including New England Development)—for "trying to thwart the Reagan Administration's environmental policy while developing a 'back-door' regional approach in order to change national standards." In a December 1985 letter to Deland, Louis Cordia of the Heritage Foundation wrote, "The bitter irony is that one would expect the Reagan Administration, especially its EPA, to be in favor of a project that is both *pro-jobs and pro-environment* [emphasis in original]. ... A second irony is that the Reagan Administration has sought to devolve federal government authority back to the state—believing the government closest to the people is more responsive."

Not all the criticism came from Republicans, says Deland. "There was intense pressure," he recalls, "but no more pressure from the Republican side of the street than from the Democratic." Few members of the Massachusetts or New England congressional delegation, from either party, spoke out in support of the step Deland had taken. His strongest backer in Congress proved to be Sen. John Chafee (R-RI), chairman of the Subcommittee on Environmental Pollution and a strong critic of the Army Corps. Some members of Congress from elsewhere in the country also chimed in with letters of support for Deland, urging Thomas to back his position. Still, the tide of congressional opinion at that point largely in Pyramid's favor. "It ended up being a fairly lonely fight," Deland reflects. "But that was not something that bothered me, because I felt I was right. ... I felt that this was an issue that if I were to lose my job over it, so be it. It was one of those [issues] worth taking a stand on."

## Deland's Recommendation

On March 4, 1986, Deland issued his formal recommendation. In it, he expanded on arguments he had made in his letters to the New England Division of the Army Corps and detailed his objections to General Wall's analysis. The document, 70 pages in all, addressed the key issues that had been at the heart of the controversy over Sweedens Swamp.

***Value.*** To begin with, Deland dismissed assertions that Sweedens was a "dysfunctional or low value wetland." He found it provided "to varying degrees" such wetland values as flood storage, groundwater discharge, pollution control, and most particularly, wildlife habitat, which he characterized as "excellent." The trash and debris that had been the focus of detractors' attention affected, according to EPA estimates, less than ten percent of the site. "Although unsightly and visible to the casual observer," Deland remarked, "the refuse has little direct bearing on the wetland values provided by Sweedens Swamp. Wildlife are unlikely to avoid the area because they find it aesthetically displeasing."

***Adverse Effects.*** Deland concluded that the Newport Avenue Galleria mall would have "an immediate and severe impact on wildlife habitat" due to the loss of 32 acres of forested wetland. Even with mitigation, Deland asserted, the project "would still result in a *net loss* of wildlife habitat" [emphasis in original]. The onsite and offsite artificial wetlands, if successful, he pointed out, would be different in type from Sweedens Swamp and "would not provide habitat for the same numbers and type of species displaced or eliminated."

***Practicable Alternatives.*** On the thorny issue of alternatives, Deland addressed two matters of ongoing controversy. First, on the general issue of availability, he came out squarely on the side of those that held that "an alternative need not be available to the applicant" Deland noted the language in the 404 regulations, which stated that a practicable alternative "not presently owned by the applicant which could be reasonably obtained, utilized, expanded or managed ... may be considered." The language, he argued, "does not say explicitly that *the applicant* must be able to obtain, utilize, expand, or manage the alternative area." While acknowledging ambiguity in the regulations, Deland concluded: "Strong policy considerations favor interpreting the guidelines to mean that the availability and feasibility of alternatives are to be viewed from the perspective of the basic project purpose rattier than strictly from the applicant's perspective. This interpretation best serves the guidelines' goal of avoiding the unnecessary destruction of wetlands."

Second, Deland took up the matter of the North Attleborough site specifically as a practicable alternative.[24] He disputed Pyramid's objections to the site—e.g., that its location was inferior, highway access was poor, major stores were reluctant to locate there—arguing that the problems were not insurmountable. "Whether the North Attleborough site is the *best* site within the trade area is not the issue," Deland declared. "In Pyramid's view, the Sweedens Swamp site is by far the preferred site (with its 'excellent' location, access, and visibility). The alternatives test, however, requires only that other sites be feasible, not that they be equally desirable." Accordingly, Deland concluded, Pyramid "has not met its burden to show that Sweedens Swamp is the only feasible alternative."

Finally, Deland considered the question of the availability of the North Attleborough site in particular. Even when alternatives "were evaluated from the applicant's point of view," he contended, Pyramid had not "overcome the presumption of available alternatives." For one thing, Deland wrote, the property had apparently been available at the time Pyramid was scouting for a location for its mall. The company had issued "conflicting statements" on the issue, he noted. In a September 1985 affidavit,

Bersani had testified that the site had already been optioned—in July 1983—at the time Pyramid had begun to investigate the trade area, which he said was not until September of that year. Deland, however, pointed to interviews in the press in which Bersani had indicated that he had considered, and rejected, the North Attleborough site. Moreover, Deland argued, since Pyramid had filed for a permit under the DeBartolo Corporation's notice of intent, it should be bound by the alternatives that were available when DeBartolo originally filed the document, in 1982.

***Mitigation.*** Deland considered the question of mitigation both as a general policy issue and as a specific redress for the loss of 32 acres in Sweedens Swamp. At the policy level, he argued that General Wall's approach "contravenes the language and intent of the [404] regulations and the Clean Water Act itself...." It "so severely skews the alternatives analysis," Deland asserted, "that it completely undercuts the water dependency test. On paper, mitigation could reduce the impacts of virtually any wetland fill project to 'zero.' With enough theoretical mitigation, any project will appear to be environmentally preferable to upland alternatives." Wall's approach, moreover, would permit creation of artificial wetlands of a different type from those they were replacing, a practice that has "little scientific support since it merely reflects the decision-maker's bias for one kind of habitat or another." The notion of "trading artificial for existing wetlands," Deland concluded, "rests on several challengeable assumptions (e.g., that a manmade wetland functions as well as a natural one; or that we know which wetland types, and which wetland values, are most 'important'). Even where successful, mitigation projects usually replace selected wetland attributes, ... not the full spectrum of values most wetlands provide."

In the case of Pyramid's mitigation proposal, Deland found a specific application for these general concerns. He was troubled by the uncertainty of the outcome of such a large undertaking and "by the fact that the artificial wetlands, even if fully successful, would not be of the same type as those that would be destroyed. No doubt," he added, "Pyramid proposes to replace a wooded swamp with an emergent marsh in part because of the difficulty of attempting to create an artificial wooded wetlands." Deland did take note of Pyramid's efforts to address concerns about its mitigation plans. It offered, for instance, to "walk away from the mall project" should the mitigation not succeed, and to establish a "blue ribbon panel" chosen by EPA and Pyramid and "chaired by an environmental celebrity.[25] Permitting the "upfront mitigation" to proceed would, Deland acknowledged, "provide an opportunity to test the success or failure of a large mitigation project and thus be of some educational value." Nonetheless, he determined, "[t]o barter away an existing wetland for a created one of uncertain success and duration when there are practicable alternatives is an environmental brinksmanship simply not allowed under the existing regulations."

Having determined that the adverse impacts were "avoidable," Deland went on to conclude, as required under Section 404(c), that they were "unacceptable." The "avoidance principle of the guidelines," he wrote, "should strongly influence" the decision in particular cases. "Here, the wetland is valuable, the loss is avoidable, and the project purpose can be accomplished without violating the guidelines. On these facts I can only conclude that the adverse effects are unacceptable and must accordingly be prohibited."

## Last Stop: EPA and the Courts

Not surprisingly, John Bersani and Pyramid took a dim view of Deland's findings. Bersani was particularly irked by the suggestion that a practicable alternative would be one that was "available to society" and not necessarily to Pyramid itself. "We had some property interests here," he maintains, "that deserved to be respected and preserved." Those who opposed a mall on the Sweedens Swamp site "were arguing, 'Who cares whether it's Pyramid or New England Development—there's an alternative available out there.' Well, wait a minute. Isn't that a decision for the marketplace, not for a regulator, to make, where this mall is going to be developed?" Pyramid had based its decision to buy the Sweedens Swamp parcel, he adds, on the information then at hand. "At that time," 'Bersani says, "I don't believe there was another alternative reasonably available to us that someone acting prudently would have selected." Pyramid could not be expected to have foreseen that efforts to rezone the North Attleborough site would ultimately succeed, he argues. "I don't think that a developer should be charged with having 100 percent extrasensory perception about what will occur in the future. If people could do that, we could all make a living at the racetrack."

Bersani also believed that environmentalists had overreacted to the idea of using mitigation to offset the adverse effects of a development project. "It scared a lot of people in the environment," he observes. But, he argues, approving the Pyramid proposal would not "open the floodgate to similar proposals by other developers." For one thing, "if this was the standard that others were held up to, I'm not sure there would have been a lot of developers willing to do it. It was a pretty high standard." Moreover, he adds, "I never said, nor would I have ever advocated, anyone trying to do this same kind of mitigation proposal in the context of a higher value wetland."

***EPA's Decision.*** Pyramid and the other parties to the case now took their arguments to Jennifer Joy Wilson, assistant administrator for external affairs and national section 404 manager, to whom EPA Administrator Lee Thomas had delegated the task of making the final determination. On May 13, 1986, two months after Deland had released his recommendation, Wilson issued her findings. In her review of the main issues of the case, Wilson's line of reasoning closely followed Deland's. She differed from him principally in the matter of the definition of "availability," agreeing with Pyramid and Army Corps headquarters that "'availability to the applicant' is the correct test to apply to this case." Nonetheless, "based on the record," she concluded, as had Deland, "that the North Attleborough site must be deemed available to Pyramid." While she would not attempt to reconstruct events, Wilson wrote, "the record clearly shows ... that Pyramid and New England Development were exploring the same trade area at approximately the same time and that Pyramid decided against the North Attleborough site solely on the basis of unsuitability." On this evidence, she continued, she could not conclude that Pyramid had met its burden of showing that the site was unavailable. "To make such a finding would be particularly inappropriate in this case," she noted, "since Pyramid bought Sweedens Swamp with full awareness of the environmental concerns posed by destroying the swamp and with a full appreciation of the importance of finding an alternative site."

Elsewhere in her report, on such issues as the value of Sweedens Swamp, adverse impacts, and mitigation, Wilson was in agreement with Deland's analysis. "I am ... anxious," she wrote, "that we do not set a precedent across the nation of substituting artificial wetlands for natural, functioning wetlands without consideration of the need for destroying those natural wetlands; we simply do not have the scientific ability to certify what techniques will assure the success of such man-made creations."

In her conclusions, Wilson pointed to statistics which indicated that in Massachusetts, "upwards of 50% of the wetlands ... have been lost to date." She continued: "Based on the excellent wildlife value of the wetland in question, its size and setting, the avoidability of the loss, and the significance of such areas in Massachusetts, I conclude that filling Sweedens Swamp to build the proposed mall would have unacceptable adverse effects within the meaning of section 404(c)."

After Wilson's final determination was released, jubilant environmentalists applauded her decision which, said one, sent "a clear message to developers that the path of least resistance in developing inexpensive wetlands is no longer available." But a bitterly disappointed John Bersani felt otherwise. Pyramid, he told reporters, had "complied with every rule set by the Government under the Clean Water Act With this decision, the EPA has gone beyond the limit of the law by changing the national wetland policy established by Congress."[26] Pyramid would, the company announced, challenge EPA's decision in court.

***On the Legal Front.*** Pyramid's appeal of EPA's final determination was not the first legal challenge it had mounted against the agency. In August 1985 and again in February 1986, it had filed lawsuits seeking to block the issuance of the proposed determination largely on procedural grounds; in both cases, the company had lost. The suit it filed in US District Court in New York in May 1986, however, was chiefly concerned with substantive matters. Pyramid asked the court to vacate EPA's determination on the grounds that it was "arbitrary, capricious and otherwise not in accordance with the law." Lawyers for the company argued, first, that in its determination of what constituted "unacceptable adverse effects," EPA improperly relied on the "avoidability" of those effects, through consideration of practicable alternatives, which, they said, was not explicitly authorized in the 404(c) regulations. Second, Pyramid challenged EPA's interpretation of availability, contending that the term should have been interpreted to mean "presently available"—i.e., at the time the agency makes its decision on a permit application—not at the point of "market entry"—i.e., when the applicant entered the market. Should the court rule that the agency's market entry approach to availability was "reasonable," however, Pyramid further claimed that EPA could not "reasonably infer" from the record that it had entered the market before New England Development acquired the North Attleborough site. Finally, even if EPA's interpretations of the regulations were to be upheld as reasonable, Pyramid maintained that the conclusion the agency reached was arbitrary and capricious.

On all these and other points, the court ruled in EPA's favor. In an opinion delivered on October 6, 1987, Judge Thomas McAvoy found that, among other things, EPA's consideration of avoidability in its determination of unacceptable adverse effects was "reasonable"; that its definition of availability was likewise reasonable; that the record supported EPA's contention that the North Attleborough site was available to Pyramid at the point of market entry; and, finally, that EPA's final determination of unacceptable adverse effects was not arbitrary because, consideration of practicable alternatives aside, "another independent and rational basis for its decision"—the loss of important wildlife habitat—"existed."

Pyramid promptly appealed McAvoy's ruling, but the district court decision was upheld by the US Court of Appeals on June 8, 1988, by a two-to-one margin.[27] At this point, Pyramid played its last legal card, appealing to the Supreme Court in October 1988. When the court subsequently declined to hear the case, Pyramid's long battle to build a mall on Sweedens Swamp came to an end.[28]

The court rulings brought gloom to Attleboro, which was effectively eliminated from the mall sweepstakes. "I was saddened for the community," says former mayor Brenda Reed, "because they were not going to have those opportunities [from siting the mall in Attleboro], and it was very clear the opportunities were going to go to another town." That town was, of course, North Attleborough and the co-developer, surprisingly, was Pyramid. In 1987, the company announced that it would form a joint venture with its heretofore arch-enemy, New England Development, to construct a mall on the North Attleborough site. Completed in 1989, Emerald Square, as the mall complex was called, was widely considered a commercial success. Looking back on the long campaign to build a mall in southeastern Massachusetts, John Bersani reflects that New England Development "spent an awful lot of money [there]. We spent an awful lot of money [there]. And neither one of us had anything to show for it at the end of a very, very bloody three-year battle. And eventually, we joint-ventured and made something happen up there [in North Attleborough]." Still, Bersani continued to feel that Pyramid had not lost on the merits of its original proposal. "If this project had been judged on its technical merit, as it was at the state level, it would have been approved," he asserts. Nor did the popularity of the Emerald Square mall alter Bersani's view of what might have been. "It [Emerald Square] is a success," he says. "[But] I still don't believe to this day that it is as good a project site as the original site was."

But environmentalists viewed the outcome differently. They hailed the legal decisions on the Sweedens Swamp case as a victory for all wetlands. Had Pyramid won, said Douglas Foy of the Conservation Law Foundation, it "would have created a hole big enough to drive numerous trucks through the wetlands laws of America."[29] Michael Deland, who would move on the following year to chair the Council on Environmental Quality in the Bush White House, told reporters that he expected the rulings "would set a precedent that EPA does have the right ... to protect wetlands. In general terms it upholds EPA statutory authority to protect wetlands throughout the country."[30] It was, he later reflected, "a win-win situation": southeastern Massachusetts got its shopping mall, and a wetland was preserved. The sometimes reviled Sweedens Swamp had, wrote Priscilla Chapman, "turned out to be a pretty rugged survivor. ..." [31]

Exhibit 1.2.1

PLAINVILLE
MANSFIELD
NORTH ATTLEBORO
RHODE ISLAND
ATTLEBORO
PROPOSED RESTORATION AREA
NEWPORT AVENUE GALLERIA
NOT TO SCALE
N
R.I.
SEEKONK
TONER BLVD.
SOUTH AVE.
WEST ST.
WASHINGTON ST.
Newport Avenue Galleria
LOCATION PLAN
ATTLEBORO , MASS.
(BRISTOL COUNTY)
PLANS ACCOMPANYING PETITION OF
PYRAMID NEWPORT GALLERIA GROUP
PREPARED BY BSC ENGINEERING/BOSTON
JULY, 1985

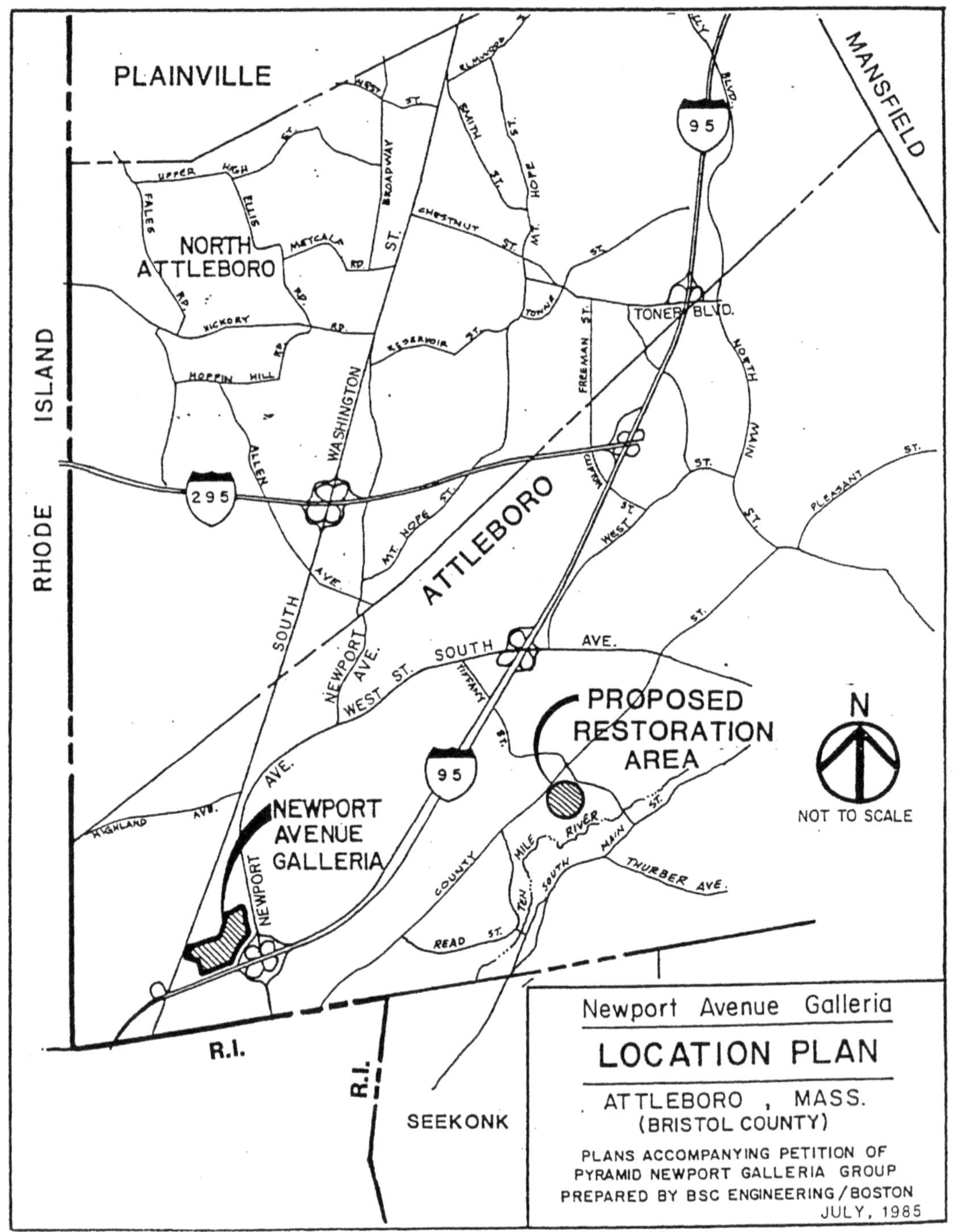

**Exhibit 1.2.2**

**Table 1.2.1** List of Identified Plant Species

| **Sweedens Swamp Attleboro, Massachusetts** | |
|---|---|
| red maple | Acer rubrum (FAC) |
| smooth alder | Alnus serrulata (OBL) |
| Jack-in-the-pulpit | Arisaema atrorubens (FACW) |
| milkweed | Asclepias sp. |
| yellow birch | Betula lutea (FAC) |
| gray birch | Beluta populifolia (FAC) |
| reed bent grass | Calamagrostis canadensis (FACW) |
| fringe sedge | Carex crimita (OBL) |
| sedge | C. lupulina (OBL) |
| sedge | C. lurida (OBL) |
| sedge | C. folliculata (OBL) |
| sedge | Carex sp. |
| sedge | C. vulpinoidea (OBL) |
| catalpa | Catalpa sp. |
| wood reed | Cinna arundinacea (FACW) |
| sweet pepperbush | Clethra alnifolia (FAC) |
| goldthread | Coptis groenlandica (FACW) |
| silky dogwood | Cornus amomum (FACW) |
| red osier | Cornus stolonifera (FACW) |
| dodder | Cuscuta sp. |
| umbrella sedge | Cyperus sp. (prob. OBL) |
| marsh fern | Dryopteris simulata |
| evergreen wood fern | Dryopteris spinulosa (FAC) |
| willow herb | Epilobium sp. (probably OBL) |
| American beech | Fagus grandifolia (FACU) |
| white ash | Fraxinus americana (FACU) |
| bedstraw | Galium sp. |
| manna grass | Glyceria sp. (OBL) |
| witch hazel | Hamamelis virginiana (FAC) |
| winterberry | Ilex verticillata (FACW) |
| jewelweed | Impatiens (probably capensis) (FACW) |

*(Continued)*

**Sweedens Swamp**
**Attleboro, Massachusetts**

| | |
|---|---|
| sedge | Juncus effusus (FACW) |
| red cedar | Juniperus virginiana (FACU) |
| sheep laurel | Kalmia angustifolia (FAC) |
| duckweed | Lemna sp. and Spirodela polyrhiza (OBL) |
| yellow wood lily | Lilius canadense (FAC) |
| spicebush | Lindera benzoin (FACW) |
| Canada mayflower | Maianthemum canadense (FAC) |
| watercress | Nasturtium officinale (OBL) |
| mountain holly | Nemopanthus inncronata |
| black gum | Nyssa sylvatica (FAC) |
| evening-primrose | Oenothera biennis (FACU) |
| sensitive fern | Onoclea sensibilis (FACW) |
| cinnamon fern | Osmunda cinnamomea (FACW) |
| royal fern | Osmunda regalis (OBL) |
| panic-grass | Panicum sp. |
| Virginia creeper | Parthenocissus quinquefolia (FACU) |
| common reed | Phragmites australis (FACW) |
| clearweed | Pilea pumila (FACW) |
| pitch pine | Pinus rigida (FACW) |
| white pine | Pinus strobus (FACU) |
| bluegrass | Poa sp. |
| smartweed | Polygonum sp. |
| cottonwood | Populus deltoides (FAC) |
| quaking aspen | Populus tremuloides (FACU) |
| big-tooth aspen | Populus grandidentata (FACU) |
| cinquefoil | Potentilla sp. |
| black cherry | Prunus serotina (FAC) |
| white oak | Quercus alba (FACU?) |
| scrub oak | Quercus ilicifolia |
| pin oak | Quercus palustris (FACW) |
| red oak | Quercus rubra (FACU) |
| black oak | Quercus velutina |
| European buckthorn | Rhamnus frangula |

**Sweedens Swamp**
**Attleboro, Massachusetts**

| | |
|---|---|
| swamp azalea | Rhododendron viscosum (OBL) |
| blackberry | Rubus sp. |
| trailing blackberry | Rubus sp. |
| poison sumac | Rhus vernix (OBL) |
| willow | Salix sp. |
| pussy willow | Salix discolor (FACW) |
| common elder | Sambucus canadensis (FACW) |
| sassafras | Sassafras albidum (FACU) |
| soft-stemmed bulrush | Scirpus validus (OBL) |
| woolgrass | Scirpus cyperinus (FACW) |
| common greenbriar | Smilax rotundifolia (FAC) |
| peat moss | Sphagnum sp. (OBL) |
| deadly nightshade | Solanum dulcamara (FAC) |
| goldenrod | Solidago sp. |
| steeplebush | Spiraea tomentosa (FACW) |
| skunk cabbage | Symplocarpus foetidus (OBL) |
| tall meadow rue | Thalictrum polygamum (FACW) |
| hemlock | Tsuga canadensis (FACU) |
| broadleaf cattail | Typha latifolia (OBL) |
| highbush blueberry | Vaccinium corymbosum (FACW) |
| early low blueberry | Vaccinium vacillans |
| maple-leaved viburnum | Viburnum acerifolium |
| wild raisin | Viburnum cassinoides |
| arrowwood | Viburnum recognitum (FACW) |
| violet | Viola sp. |

[1]Terminology from National Wetland Plant Database maintained by the U.S. Fish and Wildlife Service. Obligate (OBL) species occur in wetlands exclusively [99–100%]; Facultative wet (FACW) occur in wetlands frequently [67–99%]; Facultative species are present in both wetland and upland habitats [wetland frequency 33–67%]; Facultative upland species occur less frequently in wetlands [1–33%]. If no indication appears it means the plant is either unclassified or is considered an upland species.

OBL = obligate hydrophyte
FACW = facultative hydrophyte
FAC = facultative
FACU = facultative upland

**Exhibit 1.2.2 (cont'd)**

**Table 1.2.2** List of Observed Bird Species

| Sweedens Swamp<br>Attleboro, Massachusetts | |
|---|---|
| Red winged Blackbird | Agelaius phoeniceus |
| Mallard (with brood) | Anas platyrhynchos |
| American Black Duck | Anas rubripes |
| Ruffed Grouse | Bonasa umbellus |
| Red-tailed Hawk | Buteo jamaicensis |
| Northern Flicker (feeding young) | Colaptes auratus |
| American Crow | Corvus brachyrhynchos |
| Blue Jay | Cyanocitta cristata |
| Downy Woodpecker | Dendrocopos pubescens |
| Hairy Woodpecker | Dendrocopos villosus |
| Yellow-rumped Warbler | Dendroica coronata |
| Gray Catbird (feeding young) | Dumetella carolinensis |
| Rusty Blackbird | Euphagus carolinus |
| Common Yellowthroat | Geothlypis triches |
| Dark-eyed Junco | Junco hyemalis |
| Swamp Sparrow | Melospiza georgiana |
| Song Sparrow (feeding young) | Melospiza melodia |
| Northern Mockingbird | Mimus polyglottos |
| Kentucky Warbler | Opornis formosus |
| Blacked-capped Chickadee | Parus atricapillus |
| Tufted Titmouse | Parus bicolor |
| Common Grackle | Quiscalus quiscula |
| Eastern Phoebe | Sayornis phoebe |
| White-breasted Nuthatch (feeding young) | Sitta carolinensis |
| American Goldfinches | Spinus tristis |
| Tree Sparrow | Spizella arborea |

**Sweedens Swamp**
**Attleboro, Massachusetts**

| | |
|---|---|
| Field Sparrow | Spizella pusilla |
| European Starling | Sturnus vulgaris |
| American Robin | Turdus migratorius |
| Eastern Kingbird | Tyrannus tyrannus |
| Red-eyed Vireo | Vireo olivaceus |
| Mourning Dove | Zenaidura macrora |
| White-throated Sparrow | Zonotrichia albicollis |

**Exhibit 1.2.2 (cont'd)**

**Table 1.2.3** List of Observed (*) or Expected Mammals, Reptiles and Amphibians

| Sweedens Swamp<br>Attleboro, Massachusetts | |
|---|---|
| Shorttail Shrew | Blarina brevicauda |
| Opossum | Didelphis marsupialis |
| Woodchuck* | Marmota monax |
| Striped Skunk* | Mephites mephites |
| Meadow Vole | Microtus pennsylvanicus |
| Shorttail Weasel | Mustela erminea |
| Woodland Jumping Mouse | Napaeozapus insignis |
| White-footed Mouse* | Peromyscus leucopus |
| Raccoon | Procyon lotor |
| Norway Rat | Rattus norvegicus |
| Eastern Gray Squirrel* | Sciurus carolinensis |
| Cottontail* | Sylvilagus sp. |
| Eastern Chipmunk* | Tamias striatus |
| | |
| Eastern Painted Turtle | Chrysemys picta |
| Wood Turtle | Clemmys insculpta |
| Eastern Box Turtle* | Terrepene carolina |
| Eastern Garter Snake | Thamnophis sirtalis sirtalis |
| | |
| Spotted Salamander | Ambystoma maculatum |
| American Toad | Bufo americanus |
| Spring Peeper | Hyla crucifer |
| Green Frog* | Rana clamitans |
| Northern Leopard Frog | R. pipiens |
| Wood Frog | R. sylvatica |

Exhibit 1.2.3

N
SOUTH ATTLEBORO
RHODE ISLAND
MASSACHUSETTS
ROBINSON AVE.
ROUTE 1
ROUTE 1A
NEWPORT AVE.
LONG. 71°-21'-41"
BROWN STREET
MENDON ROAD
WASHINGTON STEET
LOCUS
READ
SOUTH
NORTH
STREET
95
95
ROUTE
ROUTE
LAT. 41°-54'-10"
NEW HAVEN RR
NEW YORK
MASSACHUSETTS
RHODE ISLAND
STREET
COTTAGE
City of Pawtucket
VICINITY MAP
SCALE: 1" = 2000'
0
2000
4000
GENERAL NOTES:
1. PURPOSE IS TO CREATE A REGIONAL SHOPPING CENTER AND RELATED PARKING, DRAINAGE AND ROADWAY IMPROVEMENTS.
2. TOPOGRAPHIC INFORMATION FROM PLAN ENTITLED "TOPOGRAPHIC PLAN OF PROPOSED SHOPPING CENTER SITE, ATTLEBORO, MASSACHUSETTS." SCALE 1"= 80'; JUNE, 1977; BY WHITMAN AND HOWARD, INC. REVISED BY BSC ENGINEERING 4/2/84 AND 7/19/84.
3. DATUM: ALL ELEVATIONS BASED ON NGVD OF 1929.
4. CLEAN FILL (INCLUDING PARKING AREA PAVEMENT AND BASE MATERIAL) TO BE PLACED, AND EXCAVATED MATERIAL TO BE REMOVED IN THE LOCATIONS AND AMOUNTS SHOWN ON SHEETS
5. NAME OF WATERBODY: TRIBUTARY OF SEVEN MILE RIVER
Newport Avenue Galleria
VICINITY MAP
ATTLEBORO, MASS.
(BRISTOL COUNTY)
PLANS ACCOMPANYING PETITION OF PYRAMID NEWPORT GALLERIA GROUP
PREPARED BY BSC ENGINEERING/BOSTON
SHEET 1 OF 39
JULY 1984

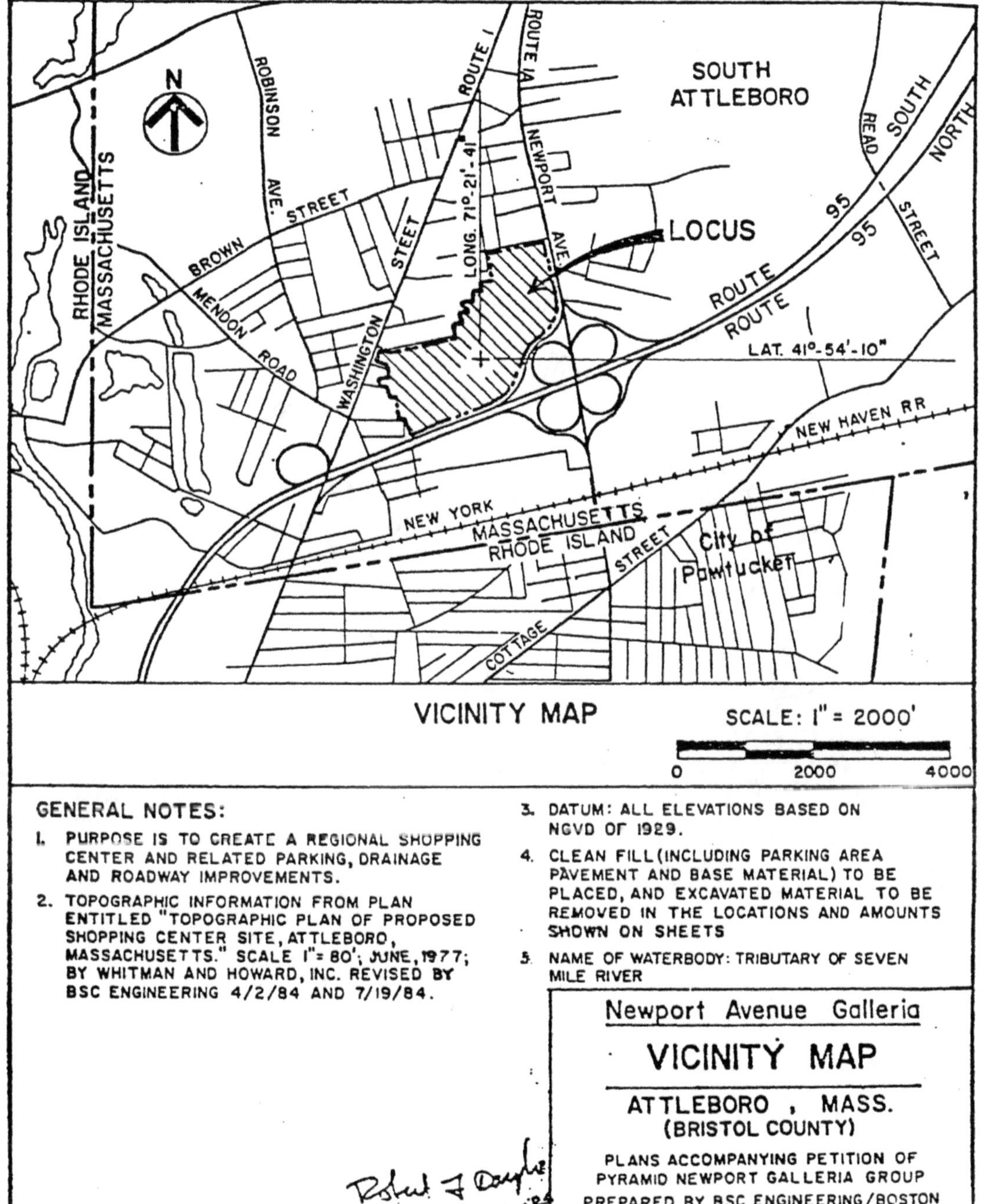

**Exhibit 1.2.4** Mall location within Sweedens Swamp
*Source*: Plan provided by Pyramid

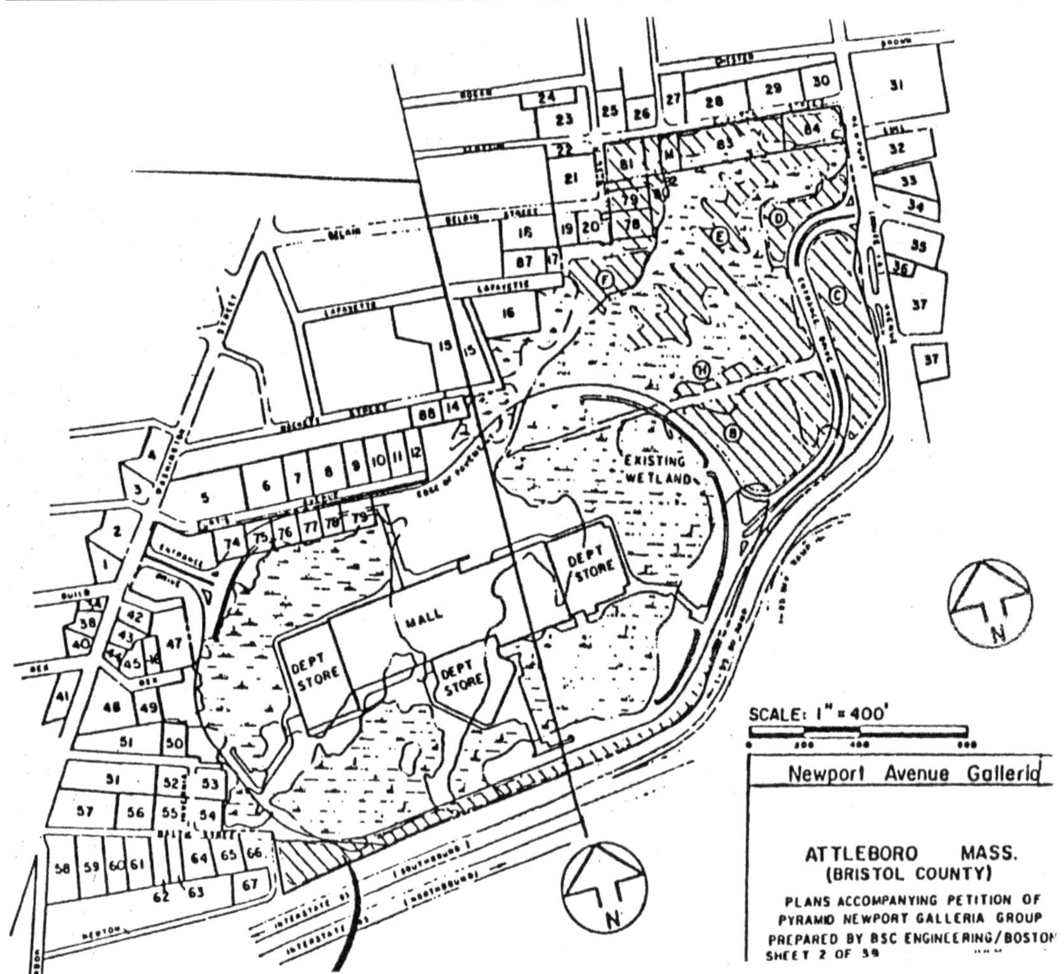

## Endnotes

1. *New York Times,* May 14, 1986.

2. John Gizzi, *Policy Review,* Winter 1986, p. 82.

3. Scot Lehigh, "A Mall at All Costs," *Boston Phoenix,* February 11, 1986.

4. Gizzi, p. 81.

5. Ibid.

6. North Attleborough had once been part of Attleboro. It split off in 1910, establishing its own town charter but retaining the original spelling of the city whose name it shared.

7. The offsite mitigation proposal was not part of the original plan; it was added on in November 1984 in response to concerns about the impact of the project. The term mitigation had a variety of meanings in environmental regulation; in this context, it was used primarily to refer to compensation for wetland losses by creating or enhancing other wetlands.

8. In its existing state, according to Pyramid estimates, about 70 percent of the water in Sweedens Swamp was "channelized"—i.e., contained within stream banks—overflowing its banks only during periods of heavy rain. Pyramid contended that the marshland it would create would enhance the wetland's pollution attenuation function by increasing the contact between water and vegetation.

9. David B. Wilson, "Tax Revenue Lost in the Swamp," *Boston Globe,* March 11, 1986.

10. The chief dissenters appeared to be local merchants who feared losing business to the mall. Their opposition, however, was "very quiet and very subtle," says Reed, and often took the form of covert support for environmentalists opposing the project.

11. The outcome of the Sweedens Swamp case was, however, unusual, according to Sylva. Typically, he says, decisions by a hearing officer "are pro-environment."

12. "Practicable" was defined somewhat ambiguously as being "available and capable of being done after taking into consideration cost, existing technology, and logistics in light of overall project purposes."

13. Lehigh, February 11, 1986.

14. *Inside EPA,* July 11, 1986.

15. *Boston Globe,* July 29, 1985.

16. The language Wall referred to stipulated that "no discharge of dredged or fill material shall be permitted if there is a practicable alternative to the proposed discharge which would have less adverse impact on the aquatic ecosystem, so long as the alternative does not have other significant adverse environmental consequences."

17. *Boston Globe,* July 29, 1985.

18. *New York Times,* August 8, 1985.

19. Adverse effects included "significant loss of or damage to ... wildlife habitat or recreation areas."

20. At that time, Sylva points out, the DEQE commissioner did not have those regulatory tools. State wetlands regulations did not permit him to consider wildlife habitat as a protected wetland value, or to include the existence of practicable alternatives in his own decision on Sweedens Swamp. Later, the state did add a wildlife habitat value to its wetlands regulations.

21. *Boston Globe,* November 7, 1985, March 11, 1986.

22. Gizzi, p. 82. Frank was also reported to have told the *Providence Journal* that some of the apartments he had lived in provided better wildlife habitat than Sweedens Swamp. (*New England Sierran,* May 1986.)

23. South Carolina had been the site of two recent EPA veto proceedings, begun in April 1984; New York was, of course, the home of the Pyramid Companies headquarters.

24. Deland discussed two others sites as well, but the North Attleborough property was by far the best known and most extensively documented alternative.

25. At one point in the proceedings, Pyramid had proposed first building the offsite wetland before beginning construction of the mall. It also offered to post a $1 million performance bond to insure the success of the wetland replication.

26. *New York Times,* May 14, 1986.

27. The dissenting judge strongly disagreed with the EPA's market entry theory of availability.

28. Legal action on the state front had also wound down. In 1986, a state superior court had ruled in favor of mall opponents who had challenged the DEQE's decision to grandfather the Pyramid project. That decision was reversed, however, in a unanimous vote of the state's Supreme Judicial Court.

29. *Boston Globe,* June 10, 1988.

30. *New York Times,* October 8, 1987.

31. *New England Sierran,* November 1987.

## DISCUSSION QUESTIONS

1. What is at the core of the controversy in this case study?
2. The Sweedens Swamp was viewed by many local inhabitants as an unsightly, trash-strewn piece of land that contributed little to the area's aesthetic or recreation values. However, environmentalists believed the wetland still needed to be protected due to some of the most valuable functions in nature. Do you agree with the environmentalists' arguments? If you argue for the wetland protection against commercial development, what would be other reasons you would add more, along with the "pollution attenuation effect"? You may consider the value of wetlands concerning mitigating climate change.
3. Environmentalists considered their fight against commercial development at the Sweedens Swamp is monumentally significant since this case may open the way to impair the integrity of the nation's wetlands protection laws. What are the underlying reasons of the environmentalists' arguments?
4. Requiring alternative actions during the Environmental Impact Assessment can be considered favorable to environmental protection overall? Or is it rather considered to add unnecessary costs that could be avoided as a society?
5. Do you think that the EPA made the right decision for this case, being faithful to its statutory authority to protect wetlands? Why or why not? Note that the EPA decision made by Jennifer Wilson, assistant administrator for external affairs and national section 404 manager, was being accused of the agency exceeding its statutory limit authorized by Congress (p. 22). Please present adequate rationales in either way.

UNIT II

# Environmental Issues beyond Boundary

READING 2.1

# The Paris Agreement

## Analysis, Assessment and Outlook

By Ralph Bodle, Lena Donat and Matthias Duwe

## Introduction

On 12 December 2015, 195 countries and the EU[1] adopted the Paris Agreement. Many consider the agreement a historic milestone in the world's endeavour to tackle climate change. At the same time, it is clear that success of the Paris Agreement will depend on sustained political momentum for actual and progressively more ambitious implementation through domestic policies and actions.

The agreement is the result of almost a decade of negotiations under the UNFCCC. A formal mandate was adopted in Durban in 2011 to "develop a protocol, another legal instrument or an agreed outcome with legal force under the Convention applicable to all Parties".[2] Under the "Ad-hoc Working Group on the Durban Platform for Enhanced Action" (ADP), parties negotiated under two politically linked tracks: Workstream 1 related to the negotiations of the 2015 Agreement, while Workstream 2 was aimed at enhancing ambition until the Paris Agreement is expected to enter into force, i.e. 2020.[3]

Over the last years, governments have also extensively used bilateral and multilateral channels to build agreement on key issues. This included not only traditional fora like the G7, G20 or Major Emitters Forum, but also diplomatic initiatives by the Peruvian and French COP Presidencies or UN Secretary General Ban Ki Moon. These diplomatic efforts had a noticeable impact in moving forward the UNFCCC negotiations. For instance, joint declarations by the United States and China contributed to the emerging consensus on differentiation.

In addition, significant momentum was created when countries after COP20 in Lima started to formulate and submit individual national climate action plans (so-called "Intended Nationally Determined Contributions", or INDCs) during 2015. At the domestic level, for many countries this was the first time they formulated a comprehensive vision for addressing climate change, and it prepared them politically for Paris. At the international level, the INDCs served as an indication of their readiness to contribute to the global effort and to a successful outcome in Paris.

Ralph Bodle, Lena Donat, and Matthias Duwe, "The Paris Agreement: Analysis, Assessment and Outlook," *Carbon and Climate Law Review*, vol. 10, no. 1, pp. 5–22. 

The outcome of the 21st Session of the COP to the UNFCCC is a legally binding treaty ("Paris Agreement", or PA), and an accompanying COP decision ("Paris Decision", or PD). The PA does not replace, but complements the UNFCCC. The PD addresses details and a work programme relating to the PA, as well as issues related to the pre-2020 period. In order to enter into force, the PA has to be ratified by 55 parties to the UNFCCC covering a minimum 55% of global emissions.[4]

This article provides a comprehensive overview of the Paris outcome along the main topics of the negotiations (section II), and an assessment of the cross-cutting political issues (section III). Although Workstream 2 was an important part of the overall political deal achieved in Paris, this article focuses on the Paris Agreement and related parts of the Paris Decision. It concludes with a perspective on overarching achievements of the Paris Agreement (section IV).

## What Has Been Decided on Key Issues?

### *Legal Form of the Paris Agreement*

The "legal form" or "legal nature" of the Paris outcome and its particular obligations was one of the core issues in the negotiations leading up to the Paris Agreement. This includes several issues that should not be conflated: The legal status of the actual Paris Agreement and how it is linked to the other elements that form part of the Paris outcome; the structure of the Paris Agreement's content, i.e. how its individual provisions work together; and the legal nature of individual sections and provisions, for instance in terms of their precision and prescriptiveness.[5]

The legal status of the actual Paris Agreement is straightforward: The Paris Agreement is a treaty under international law. This is clear from several formal indicators, notably that the Paris Agreement provides for its "entry into force" and that it is subject to ratification under the usual procedure for treaties.[6] It does not matter in this respect that the PA is not called a "Protocol".

Besides the actual Paris Agreement text, the overall Paris outcome comprises and anticipates several elements, including UNFCCC COP Decision 1/CP.21 (the Paris Decision) which adopted the Paris Agreement and also specifies further details,[7] some existing elements of the climate regime, future "relevant" decisions by the Conference of the Parties serving as the Meeting of the Parties to the Paris Agreement (CMA),[8] future "Nationally Determined Contributions" (NDCs), and to some extent INDCs.

### *Structure of the Paris Agreement's Content*

In terms of its content, the PA covers the UNFCCC's traditional thematic areas mitigation, adaptation, support and finance, technology, capacity building, and reporting and accounting. Loss and damage is also addressed, albeit separately, in its own article.

The PA is structured around its general purpose (Article 2), which lists three specific, non-exclusive purposes: Staying "well below" 2 degrees or even 1.5 degrees, increasing the ability to adapt, and making financial flows consistent with low emission and climate-resilient development. The purpose is served by a general requirement in Article 3 for all parties to undertake "ambitious efforts", as defined in the specific articles of the PA, towards reaching that purpose. This general obligation notably does not include loss and damage, sinks, forests, cooperation mechanisms and education. The global stocktake (Article 14) regularly assesses the collective efforts of parties towards the purpose. Parties have to submit their intended efforts and update them every five years in light of the stocktake's outcome and the concept of "progression" beyond previous efforts.

The PA is adopted as an annex to a COP decision, which also specifies further details, work programmes etc. of the PA. As a rule of thumb, the PD contains details which are deemed to be unsuitable for a durable and binding treaty, e.g. because they are too technical or subject to change.[9]

### *Mitigation*

For mitigation, key issues in the negotiations were not only the legal nature and content of individual commitments, but also whether and how the agreement should provide a long-term objective and direction.

Temperature limit:[10] One of the most important Paris outcomes is the PA's specific objective of holding temperature "well below" 2°C while also pursuing efforts to stay below 1.5°C. This represents a carefully drafted compromise between the Alliance of Small Island States (AOSIS) and the group of Least Developed Countries (LDCs), who demanded a 1.5°C limit, and some other countries who argued that the temperature goal needed to be credible. While "well below 2°C" is the operational goal, the 1.5°C aspiration is now also established and needs to be ad dressed.[11] Accordingly, the COP invites the IPCC to provide a special report on the impacts of 1.5°C.

Long-term global emission pathway:[12] The PA translates the temperature goal into a long-term emission reduction objective: global emissions should peak "as soon as possible" and then rapidly decline. In the second half of this century, emissions should achieve "a balance between anthropogenic emissions by sources and removals by sinks of GHG". While this "balance" can be interpreted as meaning an equal number on both sides and therefore "net zero GHG emissions", it emphasises "sinks", and it is not entirely clear whether this side of the balance is also limited to "anthropogenic" sinks. To address concerns of developing countries about the global emission objective, some qualifiers were included: peaking can take longer for developing countries, and the entire paragraph is to be seen in the context of equity, sustainable development and poverty eradication. While including a global emission pathway in the PA is an important achievement, it should be noted that it is phrased as an objective ("Parties aim to") and not as an obligation to achieve it.

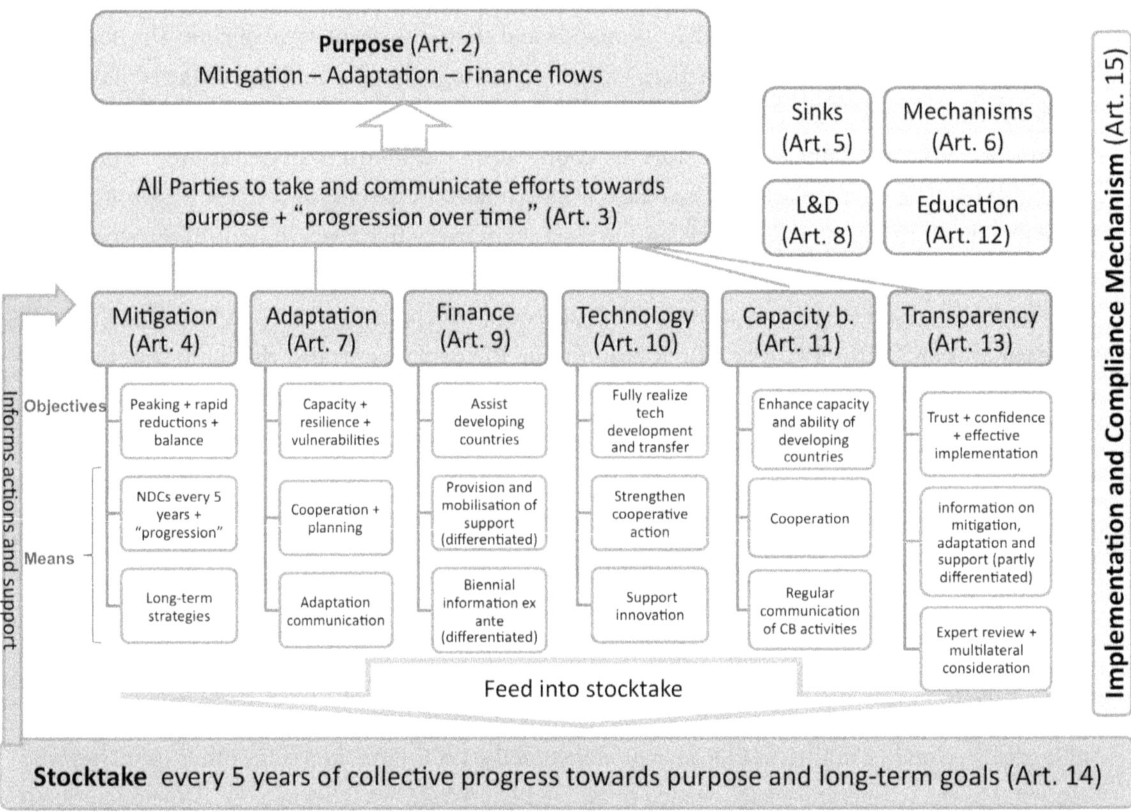


**Figure 2.1.1** Structure of Key Issues in the Paris Agreement
*Source*: Bodle, Donat and Duwe (2016)—modified

Nationally Determined Contributions:[13] One of the few clearly prescriptive obligations under the mitigation Article 4 is the duty of parties to "prepare, communicate and maintain" successive NDCs. These are basically climate action plans setting out what a party intends to do on mitigation over a certain time period. The PD "invites" parties to submit their first NDCs at the latest upon ratification. Per default, the first NDC will be the INDC the party already has submitted, unless the party decides otherwise. The NDCs will be captured in a public registry by the Secretariat and not in the Agreement itself.

Implementing NDCs:[14] The PA does *not* oblige parties to actually fulfil these NDCs, hence their content is not as such legally binding. Parties are only required to pursue measures "with the *aim* of achieving the *objectives* of such contributions".[15] Parties have to account for their contributions, while developing countries receive support for preparing, implementing and accounting for NDCs (see infra).

- Content of NDCs (features):[16] The PA gives only very limited guidance on the content of NDCs: NDCs of developed countries "should" be in the form of economy-wide absolute emission reduction targets, and other countries are encouraged to move towards such targets. There was, however, no agreement on specifying other types of targets or actions. An interim negotiation body, the APA, is mandated to develop further guidance on the features of NDCs.

- Timeframe:[17] Parties were also unable to agree on a common timeframe for NDCs, i.e. whether NDCs should all cover the same period. Most INDCs submitted in the run-up to Paris indicate an implementation timeline up to 2030 and some to 2025; some start in 2020, others in 2021; some indicate a multi-year target period and others a single year target. Harmonising the timeframe would make it easier to compare NDCs, track collective progress towards the global temperature goal and to create momentum at the time of simultaneous submission. The PA now obliges parties to submit an NDC every five years, but does not indicate whether the new NDCs should cover a 5- or 10-year period. This issue is postponed to the first CMA (CMA1).
- Content:[18] To understand the ambition of individual NDCs and track progress of implementation, the quality of information provided is crucial. In this respect, the PA only obliges parties to provide the information "necessary for clarity, transparency and understanding". The PD provides some more detail, but the listed information categories are only optional and not very specific. The APA is mandated to develop further guidance on this issue but this will not apply to the INDCs that have already been submitted.

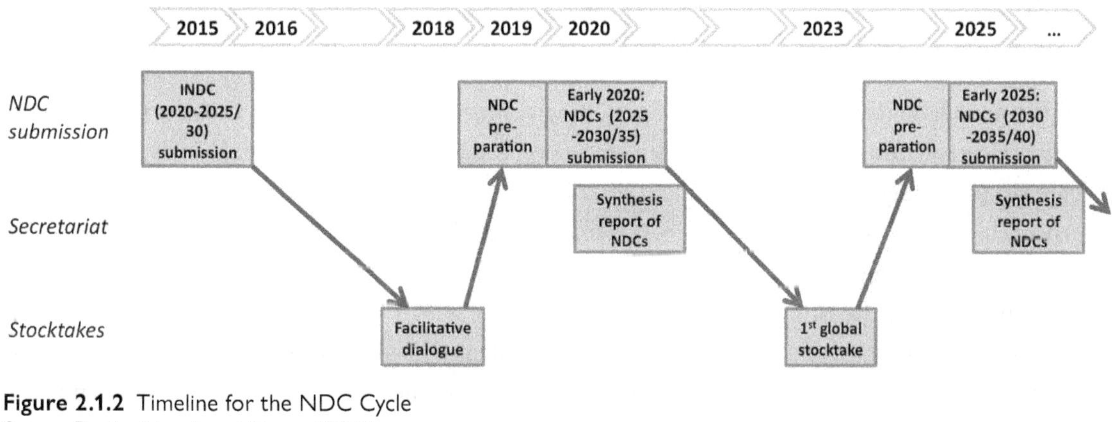


**Figure 2.1.2** Timeline for the NDC Cycle
*Source*: Bodle, Donat and Duwe (2016)

Long-term strategies:[19] Parties are also encouraged to develop and communicate long-term low greenhouse gas emission strategies. The PD further specifies that these should point towards 2050 ("mid-century") and invites parties to communicate the strategies by 2020. The PA is silent on whether and how the strategies are linked to the NDCs.

Increasing ambition over time: The assessments of INDCs handed in before Paris indicate that the combined level of efforts is clearly insufficient to have a high probability of staying below 2°C, let alone 1.5°C. An important yardstick of success of the PA is thus its ability to increase ambition over time. The PA seeks to address this issue via regular updates of NDCs in what has been labelled as "cycles":

- Parties have to submit new NDCs every five years. Each successive update of NDCs is expected to reflect a party's "highest possible ambition" and to be stronger than the previous one (principle of "progression")[20]
- An upward adjustment of NDCs is possible at any time.[21]
- Also every five years, a global stocktake compares collective efforts with the temperature and global emission goal, in light of equity and science.[22]
- The PA provides that each new NDC shall be informed by the outcome of the preceding stocktake. Therefore, the stocktakes were scheduled to give parties time to include the results in the preparation of their next NDC. The first stocktake will take place in 2023 but a "facilitative dialogue" will already take stock of efforts in 2018.[23]
- Parties have to submit their NDC 9–12 months before the relevant CMA and the Secretariat then prepares a synthesis report of NDCs. This gives parties time to understand each others' NDCs before the meeting. However, there is no obligation or process for follow-up, and it remains to be seen whether parties would e.g. revise their NDCs in the light of reactions received.[24]

There is no assessment of the ambition of individual NDCs. The system relies entirely on the national level determining and implementing ambitious efforts and the persuasive impact of publicity, consultations and the so far unspecified global stocktake.

## Adaptation and Loss and Damage

In the negotiations up to Paris, many developing countries were concerned that the political and public focus on mitigation would sideline adaptation to the existing and inevitable effects of climate change. They sought political parity between adaptation and mitigation and wanted to the agreement reflect this, e.g. in the NDCs and the stocktake, a global adaptation goal and finance.

In the Paris Agreement, adaptation and resilience are mentioned as one of the three overarching goals in Article 2. Adaptation may also be a component of NDCs, although parties are not obliged to include it. It is also part of the global stocktake that will take place every five years to assess progress towards the purpose of the PA. How to collectively take stock of the quite different individual adaptation efforts and needs with respect to the long-term goal is likely to require further discussion. The PA also requires that developing countries' adaptation efforts shall be "recognized", probably to give them more political visibility, but what this means and implies is not clear. Finally, the PA aims at achieving "a balance" between financial resources allocated to mitigation and to adaptation. In this respect, adaptation receives the same level of visibility in the PA as mitigation.

However, on substance, the individual obligations regarding adaptation are both less prescriptive and less precise than those on mitigation, and often qualified by adding wording such as "as appropriate". Other provisions are for a large part worded in soft language ("recognize the importance of", "acknowledge"), reflecting the difficulty of prescribing at the international level specific adaptation actions for individual countries.[25]

Global adaptation goal:[26] The PA establishes a global goal on adaptation, namely to enhance adaptive capacity, strengthen resilience and reduce vulnerability to climate change in the context of the temperature goal. The goal is qualitative and does not include a quantitative goal for adaptation finance, despite demands by e.g. the African Group and the Like-Minded Developing Countries in Climate Change (LMDCs, see also infra on climate finance). However, the PA recognizes the link between mitigation ambition and adaptation needs, and that such needs involve costs.

Adaptation communications:[27] There is a soft obligation that parties "should, as appropriate" submit adaptation communications which will be recorded in a public registry. The PA allows for much flexibility: The communications can be submitted in conjunction with or as part of their NDCs, NAPs or NCs, and should not create additional burden for developing countries. Periodical updates are mentioned, but the PA does not specify the timing. Guidance for the content of these communications is vague: they may include adaptation priorities, plans and actions, and support needs.

Adaptation finance:[28] The PA seeks to address the so far relatively small share of climate finance that goes into adaptation: It states the aim of achieving "a balance" between mitigation and adaptation, and developing countries are entitled to "continuous and enhanced" international support for adaptation actions. The PD establishes processes for assessing adaptation needs, for mobilizing adaptation finance and for reviewing the adequacy of support. However, most provisions are descriptive, and the PA does not establish a quantitative finance goal for adaptation. The PA also recognises the link between mitigation ambition and the need for adaptation support. The African Group and other developing countries had also proposed to anchor the Adaptation Fund in the Paris Agreement text, in order to secure its future existence. This was met by concerns mainly because the Adaptation Fund works under the Kyoto Protocol and has a special governance and funding model. The resulting compromise in the Paris decision states that the Adaptation Fund may serve the PA in the future if the CMA and the KP's CMP so decide.

Adaptation institutions:[29] The PA does not explicitly task any institution with adaptation, but sets out that cooperation on adaptation should "take into account the Cancun Adaptation Framework". The Adaptation Committee, established by the UNFCCC's COP, is tasked by the Paris Decision to review the existing UNFCCC institutions on adaptation with a view to improving coherence.

Loss and Damage (L&D):[30] There is no official definition in the UNFCCC context for L&D, but it is often interpreted as damage that cannot be avoided by adaptation. An adequate reflection of this issue in the PA was one of the key demands of Small Island Developing States (SIDS) and also of LDCs. Whether and how L&D should feature in the PA was one of the politically most sensitive questions due to concerns by developed countries that this could entail state responsibility, liability and claims for compensation. L&D now resides in the PA as a distinct issue with its own Article, suggesting that it is not treated as a subcategory to adaptation.[31] The PA recognizes that minimizing and addressing L&D is important, and that limiting global temperature increase to 1.5°C would reduce climate change impacts and thus L&D. However, the PD explicitly excludes liability and compensation claims from the scope of L&D. The question of climate displacement was not addressed in the PA itself, but the PD mandates the Executive Committee of the Warsaw International Mechanism to establish a task force on the subject.[32] A major success for small island states was the establishment of a permanent institution: The Warsaw International Mechanism, established in 2013 by COP19 to discuss questions relating to L&D, but with a limited mandate only, is now anchored in the PA and made a permanent institution.[33]

## Climate Finance

Finance was again a key element of the political package in Paris. It included familiar issues around the obligations of developed countries towards developing countries. The most controversial was whether and how the Paris Agreement would include quantified legal obligations. New issues included addressing more generally the transformational role of financial flows, and whether parties other than those in Annex II should take some form of action in this regard.

Signal for transformation:[34] There was a broad common understanding that climate finance is an enabler for action and that the global mitigation and adaptation efforts require major shifts in financial flows and private investments. The Paris Agreement is a major innovation because it includes this role of financial flows in the purpose of the Agreement, alongside the long-term goal on mitigation and adaptation. The legal link in Article 3 requires all parties to make ambitious efforts towards "making finance flows consistent with a pathway towards low greenhouse gas emissions and climate resilient development."[35] Progress towards this objective is also part of the global stocktake. It has the potential to send a strong signal to all relevant actors, including the private sector, to re-assess and redirect investments. Proposals to capture more specific issues such as fossil fuel subsidies, carbon pricing, mainstreaming and enabling environments are not included in the final text or only play a marginal role.

Quantified finance obligation:[36] There was general agreement that the financial obligations on Annex II parties of the UNFCCC would continue to apply. One of the main political issues in Paris was whether the Agreement should, in addition, anchor and continue the political commitment made in Copenhagen to mobilise USD 100 billion per year by 2020, or even specify higher amounts. The final text of the PA does not contain quantified obligations or a reference to the 100 billion commitment. It restates the continuing existing obligations under the UNFCCC, by referring to developed countries instead of Annex II. However, the PD explicitly refers to the 100 billion goal, stating that developed countries "intend to" continue it until 2025 and that a new collective quantified goal shall be set before that year, with the USD 100 billion as a floor.

Broadening the range of contributors:[37] The flipside of the political discussion over a quantified obligation were demands from developed countries that the Agreement should capture the notion of a broader range of contributors, i.e. that developing countries with the capacity to contribute to climate finance should do so. They argued that this would reflect today's and future economic realities, and that in fact some developing countries were already contributing. Developing countries opposed this notion because they regarded climate finance as a core responsibility of developed countries and because they did not want to formalise their voluntary efforts and raise future expectations. The PA addresses the issue in weak terms by "encouraging" other parties to provide support voluntarily and also to communicate the respective information biennially.

Mobilising climate finance and action for all parties:[38] Apart from *providing* financial support, the PA establishes that developed countries should continue to take the lead in the global effort to *mobilise* climate finance from a wide variety of sources. Developed countries and in particular the EU sought to include that all developing countries should also in some, self-differentiating form take action to help mobilise climate finance. This notion is basically not captured in the Paris outcome—except that it is defined as a global effort and that developing countries are encouraged to provide information on support provided and mobilised by them. Generally, the provisions on finance and transparency of support are quite bifurcated with exclusive or stronger obligations on developed countries.

Transparency ex ante and ex post:[39] Support, including financial support, is included in the PA's transparency framework (see also the following section). The framework defines the purpose of transparency of support as providing clarity not only in terms of support provided, but also received, and also to provide a full overview of aggregate financial support. Broadly similar to the existing system, the information provided under the transparency framework is subject to a technical expert review, but the PA also includes finance in the following multilateral consideration of progress, together with NDC implementation. In addition, there are specific obligations on developed countries to biennially communicate ex ante and ex post information on climate finance provided and mobilised. All this information also feeds into the global stocktake. Developing countries are entitled to support for implementing the transparency provisions. The PA does not address the issue of whether financial resources should be "new and additional", which had long been a bone of contention.

Future role of the Green Climate Fund and the Adaptation Fund:[40] The PA is served by the existing financial mechanism under the UNFCCC, with the Green Climate Fund and the GEF as its operating entities. Demands by developing countries to give the Green Climate Fund a special role were not met. The PA keeps open the possibility that the Adaptation Fund could serve the new Agreement.[41]

## Transparency, MRV and Accounting

Transparency was a key issue for basically all parties, albeit from different perspectives. It is a means to counterbalance the lack of specific and individual mitigation obligations, to improve the credibility of the global effort, and to create mutual trust in a level-playing field. Key issues in the negotiations were how to build on the existing MRV system under the UNFCCC and how to include developing countries.

Transparency framework and obligations:[42] The PA establishes a transparency framework for both action and support under common modalities. It includes regular reports on national greenhouse gas inventories, the implementation of NDCs, support provided and received,[43] and adaptation efforts. The PD specifies that all countries shall report at least every two years, with the exception of LDCs and SIDS. Core requirements are in principle strict obligations on all parties, such as having to report inventories and information on the implementation of NDCs, expert review, and multilateral consideration of progress. For certain MRV elements there are less strict requirements or explicit differentiation between developed and developing countries. The obligation to report on support provided is strict for developed countries and soft for other parties. Reporting on adaptation is also not a strictly prescriptive obligation. The details of the transparency framework need to be decided, and the CMA is mandated with adopting modalities, procedures and guidelines at its 1st session.

Flexibility:[44] The common transparency system applies to all countries but with a long list of caveats. Recognising that not all countries currently have the capacities to comply with regular reporting obligations, parties agreed to allow for flexibility "for those developing countries that need it in the light of their capacities". The system also shall be non-punitive, respectful of national sovereignty, and avoid an undue burden. The PD further specifies that flexibility might be granted on scope, frequency and level of detail of reporting, and that in-country reviews (see below) might be optional. To assist developing countries in meeting their transparency obligations and improve the transparency scheme over time, the PD establishes a specific "Capacity-building Initiative for Transparency".

Transition from the existing UNFCCC system:[45] The PA sets out that the new system shall "build on and enhance" the Convention system, which has to "form part of the experience drawn upon" for the modalities of the new system. The PD further specifies that the transparency rules developed under the PA shall eventually supersede the system of biennial reports and biennial update reports that was established at COP16 in Cancun.

Review:[46] The PA establishes a technical expert review for reported information on mitigation and support, but not on adaptation. The review applies to all parties, but is slightly different for "developing countries that need it": they may receive assistance for identifying capacity-building needs. The following "multilateral consideration of progress" for the first time specifically includes not only efforts on mitigation but also on finance.

Principles:[47] Although the details of the transparency framework are to be determined by the CMA, parties were already able to agree on a set of general principles. These include the "TACCC" principles (transparent, accurate, complete, consistent and comparable), no backsliding from the frequency and quality of UNFCCC reporting, no double counting, environmental integrity, and flexibility in light of capacities.

Accounting:[48] The PA provides basic principles for accounting of emission reductions. Parties have to use the methodologies and common metrics of the IPCC, and ensure "methodological consistency" between the reference levels chosen to define their NDC and the calculations used during their implementation. Parties also "strive to include all categories" of GHG emissions or removals in their NDC but are not obliged to do so. However, they have to explain at least why any category is excluded.

The CMA has the mandate to adopt guidance on accounting modalities. Since the accounting rules will not be adopted before CMA1, they will only apply from the second round of NDCs, but parties may voluntarily already apply them to the first round. The transparency framework also includes developing modalities for accounting for financial support.[49]

## Legal Aspects

It is important to distinguish between the legal form of the Paris Agreement as a whole and the specific content of its individual provisions and elements.[50] The entire text of the Paris Agreement is one treaty. As reservations are not permitted, it has to be ratified as a whole and "as is".[51] Therefore, formally speaking the whole Paris Agreement is binding for its parties once it enters into force. However, not every sentence of the Paris Agreement establishes specific legal rights or obligations or is equally prescriptive or precise. The PA uses a broad range of wordings and qualifiers, which give parties more or less flexibility or discretion regarding *whether* and *how* to implement its provisions. Generally speaking, there are prescriptive and precise obligations mainly relating to procedural aspects such as the NDC cycle and transparency, while there are hardly any on substance.[52]

Legal character of NDCs:[53] The INDCs and NDCs are not formally part of the PA, although it refers to them. Their content is also not binding. Parties have an obligation to have, communicate and regularly update their NDCs, but there is no strict obligation to implement the exact content of the NDCs. Parties are only obliged to "pursue" measures "with *the aim of* achieving the *objectives*" of their NDCs. This means that they do not have to fulfil the NDCs but only to make efforts towards achieving their respective objectives.

Implementation and compliance mechanism:[54] The PA establishes a mechanism "to facilitate implementation of and promote compliance with" the PA. Importantly, the mechanism applies to all parties and covers all provisions of the PA including finance, while highlighting that attention needs to be paid to the national capabilities and circumstances of countries. However, the PA provides only a few basic principles for its operation (transparent, non-adversarial, and non-punitive) and defines the membership of the committee. The decision on the actual modalities and procedures of the mechanism has been postponed to CMA1. Given the strong opposition against a compliance mechanism, especially one that applies to all parties, it remains to be seen whether and how the mechanism will be put into practice. Taking into account that the legal obligations on parties are mainly procedural and relating to making efforts rather than achieving specific results, it will be interesting to see how the compliance mechanism will find its facilitative role.

Entry into force:[55] The PA establishes a double threshold for its entry into force: (1) at least 55 UNFCCC parties have to hand in their ratification instruments, and (2) these parties have to account for at least 55% of global GHG emissions. This double threshold is meant to ensure that the biggest emitters are on board, but not on their own, while making sure at the same time that entry into force can be achieved within a reasonable time. The emissions threshold was a difficult issue because comparable emission data for parties do not exist under the UNFCCC: some parties have last communicated their emission data for 1990, others for 2013. To operationalise the emission threshold, the COP requested the Secretariat to publish a list with the most up-to date emission data from each Party. According to that list on the UNFCCC website,[56] the second threshold would correspond to 20.4 Gigatonnes of $CO_2$eq.

Institutions:[57] The PA is served by the COP, serving as the "Meeting of the Parties to the Paris Agreement" (CMA), the UNFCCC Secretariat, the Subsidiary Body for Scientific and Technological Advice (SBSTA), and the Subsidiary Body for Implementation (SBI). The PA provides that other institutions may serve the Agreement if the CMA decides so. To prepare for the entry into force of the PA, the COP has established a new body, the "Ad-hoc Working Group on the Paris Agreement" (APA). The APA will prepare draft decisions for adoption by CMA1.

Decision-making:[58] Only those parties that have ratified the PA will be able to adopt CMA-decisions with respect to the PA. Following years of political and academic debate about changing the strict consensus requirement, it was discussed until the end whether the PA should establish majority voting rules for the CMA, but this proposal did not gather sufficient support. The PA provides that the rules of procedure of the COP will apply. However, these rules have never been formally adopted and are applied only provisionally without the contested pro visions on voting. In absence of agreed voting rules, the COP has been deciding by consensus. The consensus rule would thus also apply to the CMA—unless parties give it another try to solve the voting question.

## Other Issues

Preamble: The PA's preamble contains some important and sometimes innovative issues, some of which were nevertheless difficult to include in the operative text. Notably, several preambular paragraphs address fundamental issues linked to the transformation that the response to climate change requires, including: development priorities such as eradication of poverty, food security, a just transition of the workforce, human rights, gender equality, the concepts of "climate justice" and "Mother Earth", and sustainable lifestyles and patterns of consumption and production.

Forests:[59] The PA recognizes the role of forests and encourages parties to implement the REDD+ framework already established under the Convention, but does not add to it. The REDD+ framework had been negotiated over many years and adopted in series of decisions at COP19 in Warsaw in 2013. In Paris, COP decisions adopted under the regular Convention agenda complemented the methodological guidelines. The REDD+ framework aims at reducing emissions from deforestation and forest degradation, and enhance conservation, sustainable management of forests, and enhancement of forest carbon stocks in developing countries. One of the concepts behind it is that developing countries may be financially rewarded for such efforts, and the PD highlights the importance of such "results-based payments".

Emissions from aviation and shipping: The PA is silent on emissions from international aviation and shipping, resulting from the combustion of so-called "bunker fuels". This is not a minor omission given that these emissions account for around 3–4% of global GHG emissions—which might become almost 40% by 2050.[60] Text requesting parties to work through the International Maritime Organization (IMO) and International Civil Aviation Organization (ICAO) on measures to reduce these emissions, mainly supported by the EU, EIG and LDCs, disappeared in the final stages of the negotiations—inter alia due to resistance by India and China. The IMO has not been able so far to agree on emission reduction measures, and the ICAO has only established an aspirational goal.[61] However, bunker emissions are anthropogenic emissions and therefore have to be counted in the long-term goal to balance emissions and removals. This might create some momentum in ICAO and IMO.

Markets: The PA does not mention the term "markets" except for "non-market" approaches. But it establishes three different types of international cooperation on mitigation and notably also adaptation, with the aim of increasing ambition. They are available to all parties. "Cooperative approaches"[62] allow parties to engage bilaterally or multilaterally. What kind of cooperation could be meant here has not been further defined, but could potentially cover the linking of emission trading systems. If parties use the resulting mitigation outcomes for meeting their NDCs, parties shall ensure environmental integrity and transparency, apply robust accounting and avoid double counting. Further guidance on this will be developed. The PA also establishes a sustainable development mechanism (SDM)[63] involving both public and private entities, which may in some aspects be similar to the CDM of the Kyoto Protocol. In contrast to the cooperative approaches, the SDM will operate under the authority of the CMA. The SDM is meant to "deliver an overall mitigation in global emissions", i.e. net emission reductions. But it is not clear yet how this is to be achieved. The modalities of the SDM still need to be negotiated. A framework for non-market approaches[64] is also established by the PA, covering not only mitigation, but also adaptation, finance, technology transfer and capacity-building. Further negotiations are required to define how these approaches could work.[65]

Response measures:[66] The PA highlights in several instances the negative impacts that "response measures", i.e. policies to reduce emissions, may have on certain economies. Throughout the negotiations, Saudi Arabia has been a strong demander for such references. The PD specifies that the Forum on the Impact of the Implementation of Response Measures, an arrangement established originally in 2010 by the COP, will serve the Agreement.

Capacity building:[67] Capacity building features strongly in the PA. All parties should cooperate while developed countries should enhance their support for building the capacity of developing countries. A strong push in the negotiations was achieved by agreeing to the establishment of the Paris Committee on Capacity-building that aims to address gaps and needs under the current framework for capacity building. The Committee has a limited mandate, but this may be extended in a review in 2019/20. A specific capacity building initiative for transparency was also established in the PD.

Technology Development and Transfer:[68] The PA underlines the importance of technology development and transfer and makes the Technology Mechanism, established by the UNFCCC COP, a permanent institution of the PA. It establishes a "technology framework" for overarching guidance. The PD specifies that the framework should facilitate technology needs assessments, enhanced support and assess which technologies "are ready for transfer". There is an obligation to strengthen cooperative action and to support innovation, as well as developing countries generally. The COP of the UNFCCC will also undertake a "periodic assessments of the effectiveness and adequacy of support" which informs the global stocktake. Developed countries are required to report on technology transfer, while developing countries are only encouraged to do so. Requests by some developing countries to address intellectual property rights are not reflected in the agreement.

## Assessment of the Paris Agreement

Assessing the Paris Agreement requires a yardstick against which to measure it. Elements of assessment can for instance include what appeared politically feasible on 12 December 2015, what are the changes to the existing regime, or what is scientifically necessary to address climate change. In addition, it also involves expectations regarding how the Paris outcome will be implemented and to what extent it can and will in reality influence the conduct of states or other relevant actors.

The first approach involves the difficulty of supposing what was or could have been "politically feasible". It might put too much emphasis on the mere fact that there is an agreement. Moreover, it seems problematic as it might also be argued that any outcome *per* se reflects what was politically feasible at that time. The second perspective looks at the evolution of the existing climate regime. For the PA this requires a nuanced analysis, because it builds on and in parts restates the existing structures and requirements, while also placing them on a new footing. The third approach would ask to what extent the PA solves the problem of climate change in terms of GHG emissions. This can put the political achievement into perspective. On the other hand, it might not be realistic to expect that the PA prescribes collective or individual actions or emission reductions that are commensurate with a science-based emission pathway. Even if it did, it would be difficult to predict to what extent States would fulfil such obligations for decades to come.

Any assessment will probably mix these and other approaches.

In assessing the PA, it is also essential to distinguish between the PA's political narrative and its text. The provisions of the PA are often drafted in vague wording and leave many legal uncertainties. Few provisions establish clear and prescriptive legal obligation, most leave room for discretion, and there are many caveats. Several provisions are factual statements rather than prescriptive guidance, and many use what would usually be preambular or decision language that has little operational content ("Parties recognize ..."). However, the PA sets out a simple but clear structure and political narrative for the global effort. There is an agreed direction of travel in the form of the long-term goals, all parties are obliged to take action towards that purpose, with efforts that are transparent, assessed against the purpose and regularly enhanced. If parties take this narrative and implementation seriously, the PA's political and real-world impact might go well beyond what is actually written in the text.

Against this background, the following subsections assess the PA along important themes that cut across the particular issues of mitigation, adaptation etc. that have been analysed above.

## Ambition and Long-term Objectives

The science is relatively clear on what the international community needs to do to limit the impacts of climate change: the IPCC's AR5 report has analysed least-cost emission pathways with a likely chance of keeping temperature rise below 2°C. Global GHG emissions would need to equal net zero at the latest by 2100, but this date depends on when emissions peak and how much is emitted in the meantime, i.e. how quickly the respective global carbon budget is used up. UNEP has analysed that if reductions start in 2020, global GHG emissions would have to be zero by 2080. To increase the likelihood of staying below 2°C, or for reducing the temperature limit, reductions would need to be more rapid. From a science point of view, a "good" agreement commits the world as closely as possible to such a pathway, e.g. by establishing a shared objective in line with these scientific underpinnings, and by establishing individual obligations adequate to achieve such objective.

Global ambition:[69] The PA does not establish a clear emission reduction objective. But it does state a temperature limit ("well below 2°C, pursuing efforts towards 1.5°C") and elements of an emission pathway towards 2100: peaking followed by rapid reductions and an eventual balance between emissions and sinks. However, it does not specify specific years for when global emissions should peak or equal net zero. Also, in Article 4.1 the wording "balance" between emissions and removals is ambiguous and is not necessarily synonymous to "net zero".[70]

The purpose of the Agreement in Article 2 is not absolute. The PA explicitly states that its purpose and implementation have to be seen in the context of several other principles and development objectives such as sustainable development, poverty eradication, food security, equity, and common but differentiated responsibilities and respective capabilities, in the light of different national circumstances.

Individual ambition:[71] In respect of how to achieve the necessary reductions and what parties promise to do, the PA is mainly procedural. It obliges each Party to regularly present an NDC and to make it public, and subjects them all to transparency procedures and a regular stocktake. The PA does not prescribe specific mitigation actions or which emission levels should be achieved by when, nor is there an obligation to actually fulfil the NDC. However, Article 3 requires "ambitious" efforts towards the overall purpose, while Article 6 links market and non-market approaches to higher ambition. Article 4.19 suggests that parties should embed their 5-yearly efforts in mid-century long-term low greenhouse gas emission development strategies.[72]

The NDC approach is regarded as a trade-off for having general obligations on *all* parties, including developing countries.[73] The assumption is that not prescribing specific measures or emission reductions will make it easier for countries to join the PA and to develop ambitious NDCs, and that the transparency system and stocktake will create sufficient public pressure on States to do their fair share and implement their NDCs. The fact that almost all parties to the UNFCCC—developed and developing—showed their commitment by submitting an INDC prior to the Paris summit can be regarded as a success in this respect. However, on aggregate the INDCs so far fall short of the ambition required globally. The estimated aggregate level of emissions in 2030 will be at around 55 Gigatonnes of $CO_2$eq in 2030 if the IND-Cs are implemented—but for a least-cost 2°C scenario emissions would need to go down to around 42 Gigatonnes of $CO_2$eq.[74]

Raising ambition over time: To incentivise more ambitious efforts over time, the PA requires parties to update their NDCs every five years. However, the only levers towards increasing ambition are the concepts of "progression" over time and "highest possible ambition", and the idea that NDCs shall be informed by the stocktake. The language on "progression" is factual rather than prescriptive, and there is no guidance on how the concept of progression could be applied to the wide range of very different NDCs—except in that they have to be informed by the global stocktake. Details on how the stocktake could work need to be agreed in the future.[75] The NDCs are complemented by a long-term perspective through long-term low greenhouse gas emission development strategies, which all parties should strive to formulate and communicate. Although the PA specifies no further details, developing these strategies could assist parties in enhancing their individual mitigation efforts in the long run.

The role of transparency is linked to both individual and collective ambition. Understanding what parties say they intend to do in their NDCs is important for other parties in order to compare the fair share of contributions. It is also necessary as a basis for aggregating data and assessing progress towards collective ambition. The lack of standards for the content of the NDCs makes it difficult to understand their potential impact on emissions, and to compare them between parties. The PA establishes the basis of a transparency and accounting scheme for this purpose, but much will depend on the details that have to be negotiated and adopted in the future.

The role of climate finance in raising ambition: One recurrent issue in the negotiations was finance as an enabler of ambitious action. The PA explicitly recognises that more support would allow for higher ambition. Across the PA, developing countries are entitled to receive support for preparing and implementing their NDCs as well as for other actions. The reference to financial flows in the PA's purpose is a key achievement as it recognises that public finance alone will not be sufficient for achieving the mitigation and adaptation purposes. However, the PA does not or only in passing address specific measures that could help mobilise or redirect financial flows, such as subsidies, enabling environments or carbon pricing. There is also only very basic reference to broadening the range of contributors to willing developing countries, but this point might be symbolic as several developing countries are in fact engaged in South-South cooperation. In terms of increasing climate finance in order to raise ambition, the PA envisages a progression and requires that a new quantified goal be set prior 2025 from the 100 billion "floor"

The PA's mainly procedural approach may be explained as an alternative to the Kyoto Protocol, which some perceived as too prescriptive and therefore deterring. It remains to be seen whether the procedures anchored in the PA (cycles, transparency obligations, stocktake) will trigger sufficiently ambitious contributions once the details are agreed, and whether parties will also implement them.

## Differentiation

Since its beginning in 1992, the obligations under the international climate regime have been based on distinguishing countries listed in Annex I to the UNFCCC (considered to be "developed countries") and all other countries ("non-Annex-I countries"). The main obligations are differentiated by reference to these two categories.[76] In recent years, developed countries have argued that this "bifurcation" did not reflect economic, political and emission realities anymore and that an ambitious climate deal also had to involve developing countries, in particular large emitters. The Durban Mandate specified that the Paris Agreement should be "applicable to all Parties". At the same time, all parties recognized that some form and degree of differentiation between countries still needed to be reflected in the Agreement—but parties were divided about how to take into account the national circumstances of countries for each specific issue.

The PA moves beyond the UNFCCC's bifurcated divide with small but decisive steps. The PA explicitly states that *all* parties "are to" take actions towards its purpose, on mitigation, adaptation, means of implementation and transparency. Core prescriptive obligations on mitigation, such as submission of NDCs and transparency, are in principle applicable to all parties, with differentiation and flexibility to be added rather than intrinsic.[77]

At the same time, the provisions of the PA do allow for differentiation between countries in several ways. The PA restates at the beginning the UNFCCC's principle of "common but differentiated responsibilities and respective capabilities", and complements it with the important addition "in the light of different national circumstances". This addition could increase the range of factors that may serve as a basis for determining differentiation.[78] Notably, the PA does not refer to the annexes of the UNFCCC. This could be seen as an "implicit abandonment of the Annexes of the UNFCCC,"[79] and of the division based on 1992 realities. However, it should be noted that many provisions in the PA distinguish between "developing countries" or "developed countries", although without defining these categories. In practice this could mean that the Annexes will for some time provide an important point of reference, with room for (self-) differentiation.

Another indication for the shift beyond bifurcation is that each section of the Agreement takes a slightly different approach to differentiation:

- Preamble: Reiterates the principle of common but differentiated responsibilities and respective capabilities but adds "in the light of different national circumstances." Recognises specific needs and circumstances of developing countries in general, especially the most vulnerable, and LDCs regarding technology transfer and funding.

- Mitigation: Obligations are mostly the same for all parties. As in the preamble, the principle of common but differentiated responsibilities and respective capabilities is supplemented with "in the light of different national circumstances." LDCs and SIDS have more flexibility in formulating NDCs Developed countries "should" take the lead by adopting economy-wide absolute reduction targets, while others are encouraged to move towards such targets. Recognition that that peaking will take longer for developing countries. Overarching obligation to take into account parties with economies most affected by the impacts of response measures.
- Adaptation: Obligations are the same for all parties. Developing countries' efforts have to be recognized (although the meaning of this has to be clarified). Specification that the adaptation communication should not create additional burdens for developing countries. Strong financial entitlement of developing countries and taking account of the needs of developing countries.
- Finance: Most of the finance provisions are almost completely different for the two groups, with obligations for developed countries and soft encouragement for developing countries. Leadership by developed countries in mobilising climate finance as part of a global effort, which implies that developing countries should also make efforts. Across sections, the PA states that support shall be provided to developing countries. Explicit recognition that support "will allow" for higher mitigation ambition.
- Technology: Provisions apply to all parties; support for developing countries.
- Capacity Building: Capacity building is for developing countries. Obligation for all parties to cooperate to enhance developing countries' capacities.
- Transparency: In principle, the same obligations for all parties on reporting on mitigation and adaptation. Reporting on means of implementation is obligatory only for developed countries. Flexibility is mandatory for "those developing countries that need it" in the light of their capacities. Special circumstances of LDCs and SIDS are recognized. Expert review pays "particular attention to the respective national capabilities and circumstances of developing countries".
- Compliance: Compliance mechanism covers all provisions of the PA. It does not refer to developed or developing countries, but is to "pay particular attention to the respective national capabilities and circumstances of Parties".
- Stocktake, loss and damage, and education: No differentiation.

Some country groups also strongly pushed for having their special circumstances recognized. While there was broad agreement that the situation of LDCs required special recognition, it was more difficult, also amongst developing countries, to agree whether other country groups should also be mentioned or singled out, including Africa, SIDS, economies in transition, and small mountainous developing States. The PA recognizes the special circumstances of LDCs and SIDs in the context of NDCs, financial support, capacity building and transparency. Africa is singled out in the preamble of the PD in the context of access to sustainable energy.

The PA is a watershed in differentiating between developing and developed countries. Although the UNFCCC already contains some general obligations that apply to all parties, the PA breaks new ground by supplementing the principle of common but differentiated responsibilities, its core obligations for all parties and range of techniques used to express differentiation. Almost 30 years after the Montreal Protocol established a model structure for including developing countries through differentiation, the PA provides an alternative approach.

## A Signal for Moving Towards Zero Emissions?

The necessary reduction in global GHG emissions requires an unprecedented transformation of economies that will need to bring a multitude of relevant actors on board: different levels of government, from civil society and business. To start this transformation process, one assessment criteria could be whether the agreement sends a credible signal also to non-party stakeholders that the long-term business case for fossil fuels is coming to an end and that States will implement respective policies. This does not suggest that the interests of all actors are the same or that they look for the same signals.

International agreements do not normally oblige non-state actors. There is no obvious or agreed understanding of what would be a desirable "signal" to non-party stakeholders and how an international agreement between states can create such a signal.

The legal form of the PA as a formally binding treaty is a starting point. Although legal form does not say anything about content and does not guarantee implementation, it shows a high degree of political commitment by governments at the international level vis-à-vis other parties, and at the domestic level through the ratification process.

There is also the PA's purpose with its three long-term elements. The explicit and clear temperature limit goes together with the qualitative mitigation goals peaking, rapid reduction and subsequent balance. However, these long-term objectives have short-comings in the fine print: the wording of the "balance" of emissions and removals leaves room for interpretation. Other terms such as "zero" or "decarbonisation" might have been clearer and easier to communicate, but would also entail other difficulties. For instance, there is no agreed definition of the term "decarbonisation".[80] In addition, some caveats and qualifiers spread over the agreement[81] could be regarded as important safeguards by some and as potential loopholes by others. But by and large the purpose and long-term mitigation objectives, together with the obligation to make efforts towards them and the principle of progression, create a simple but robust political narrative that adds weight to the general political commitment.

There are downsides as well: Based on the PA text alone, the procedural structure of the PA and the absence of specific mitigation action obligations may not seem particularly strong signals. Energy in general or renewable energy in particular is not explicitly addressed except for a small reference in the preamble to the PD. Such specific issues are left to individual NDCs. The provisions on "cooperative approaches" are unlikely to send a signal to businesses looking for markets for the time being, because there are no requirements as yet for content and accounting.

With regard to future investments, making finance flows consistent with low-emission pathways is one of the three overarching purposes and an important innovation of the Agreement. This has the potential of being a strong signal to investors. However, as with mitigation, the PA itself does not put much flesh to that bone. Basically none of the proposals addressing means and actions towards this purpose was included in the final Agreement. This includes e.g. reducing fossil fuel subsidies, carbon pricing or improving the conditions for low-carbon investment, i.e. enabling environments.[82] There is one weakly worded reference to the importance of carbon pricing in the PD's chapter on non-party-stakeholders.

The floor of 100 billion USD per year for climate finance as a basis for setting a new goal from 2025 provides some degree of predictability and could push states to mobilise and redirect finance at scale. However, this might not weigh too heavily with investors, given the much larger amounts required for the overall transformation. And for some stakeholders the more important signal might be the intended balance between mitigation and adaptation finance.

The PA has nevertheless triggered widespread reactions around the world from all kinds of actors, including business and investors. Some hold that the PA "has fundamentally shifted calculations about risk and opportunity across many industrial sectors"[83] and provides a "clear pathway to decarbonise the global economy."[84]

While some reactions might be mere rhetoric, the Paris summit has created, at least for the time being, a political momentum that goes beyond the adoption of the PA. In the run-up to Paris and during the conference, many investors and companies were eager to draw up positions themselves, issue statements on climate change, commit to climate targets or change their policies. In this respect, Paris crystallized and triggered many new initiatives by non-party stakeholders.

Investors in particular will have their own way of assessing the PA for their own purposes and potential strategic implications. In this respect the broad political narrative and credibility of the PA is potentially more important than its legal details.

At the same time, the lack of content in the PA means that non-party stakeholders are now waiting for governments to show their commitment to the PA at national level: "The immediate implications for business haven't changed over the weekend and the Agreement is highly unlikely to move markets in the short term. For business, the sharp end of the Agreement is in the national plans or INDCs."[85] It will also be important that the transparency framework is fleshed out in a manner that increases the credibility of governments' promises.

## Conclusions

The PA is a landmark—although it does not require a certain amount or range of emission cuts in a certain amount of time, based on current scientific knowledge. It is a legally binding treaty which does not replace but instead complements the UNFCCC. It needs to be ratified by a sufficient number of parties before it can enter into force. The PA is accompanied by a COP decision that addresses details, further work, and issues related to the pre-2020 period.

One of the most important Paris outcomes is the anchoring of a mitigation objective that is to hold global average temperatures "well below" 2°C while also pursuing efforts to stay below 1.5°C. The PA breaks this temperature limit down into a long-term emission reduction objective. The mitigation objective is part of the overall purpose of the PA, which guides all parties' efforts and also includes adaptation, and finance flows in the PA. All three are significant additions to the UNFCCC's objective.

In respect of how mitigation can be achieved, the PA is mainly procedural. Its core obligations are to have, communicate and regularly update an NDC—and this applies to all parties. However, the PA does not prescribe specific NDC content, mitigation actions or targets. There is no strict obligation to implement the exact content of the NDCs. For raising ambition, the only levers are the concepts of "progression" over time and "highest possible ambition", and the idea that NDCs shall be informed by the global stocktake on progress towards the overall goals.

In order to ensure transparency of efforts, the requirements are in principle strict obligations on all parties, such as having to report inventories and information on the implementation of NDCs, expert review and multilateral consideration of progress. The rules allow for flexibility for developing countries according to their capacities.

The PA's approach is an experiment that relies on the national determination of efforts and the persuasive impact of the transparency framework and the global stocktake towards progression.[86] Details on elements that could safeguard ambition, such as on the content of NDCs, the stocktake, and transparency, are left to be agreed in the coming years. Although it is normal for a complex multilateral treaty such as the PA to leave many technical details to future decisions, the PA is special: its procedural approach means that further details could be crucial for safeguarding ambition.

Adaptation was given a high level of visibility in the PA. A qualitative adaptation goal is established, developing countries' adaptation efforts shall be "recognized", and climate finance aims to achieve a balance between mitigation and adaptation. Apart from that, there is little specific content. L&D now resides in the PA as a distinct issue with its own Article, suggesting that it is not treated only as a subcategory to adaptation. As a trade-off, the PD excludes liability and compensation claims from the scope of L&D.

On finance, the PA establishes the consistency of financial flows with low GHG emissions as one of its overarching purposes. This is a key achievement and might provide a signal to the private sector for adjusting investment strategies. It recognises that public finance alone will not be sufficient for achieving the mitigation and adaptation purposes. However, the PA basically does not address specific measures that could help mobilise or redirect financial flows, such as subsidies, enabling environments or carbon pricing. There are no quantified obligations, and only a hint at a broadened range of contributors or actions for all parties. The PD extends the 100 billion commitment to 2025, when a new, and higher, goal has to be set.

The PA is also a landmark in moving beyond the UNFCCC's bifurcated differentiation with small but decisive steps. It does so by supplementing the principle of common but differentiated responsibilities, by its core obligations for all parties, and by its range of techniques used to express differentiation. The trade-off for including all parties is the procedural approach to determining NDCs and individual action.

Implementation is key to the long-term success of the Paris outcome. It will be crucial to maintain the political momentum that was captured in Paris. The political level has to stay involved beyond the Paris conference in order to connect the Paris system with the real world and keep the relevant political and financial institutions on track to increase efforts. In addition, capacity has to be created for the progressive preparation and technical implementation of NDCs. The "intended" contributions (INDCs) submitted before and in Paris showed an almost universal engagement by all countries, although their content is not ambitious enough for staying below 2°C. This political will needs to be underpinned with the capacity to define and implement actions on the ground.

The Paris Agreement's procedural approach means that further details could be crucial for safeguarding ambition. The forthcoming negotiations have to determine remaining technical details, in particular with regard to the NDC features and the transparency. These details have to provide a counterbalance to the flexibility parties have in defining and implementing their actions. They can ensure public credibility of individual NDCs and actions and thus foster ambitious action by all.

It is essential to distinguish between the PA's political narrative and its text. Despite shortcomings in legal detail, the PA is drafted in a way that presents a clear political narrative of what parties are expected to do towards which aims. The procedural approach is a try, setting out a simple but clear structure for the global effort. The number, and partly also the quality of the INDCs submitted so far are a sign that parties are willing to follow this approach. It remains to be seen whether the procedures anchored in the PA will trigger sufficiently ambitious contributions over time and whether parties will also implement them. In this case the PA's political narrative might have an impact that goes well beyond what is actually written in the text.

## Endnotes

1. For ease of reference, in this article "countries" and "states" should be read as including the EU unless otherwise stated.

2. UNFCCC, Decision 1/CP.17, Establishment of an Ad Hoc Working Group on the Durban Platform for Enhanced Action, UN Doc. FCCC/CP/2011/9/Add.1. 2.

3. For a more detailed account of the UNFCCC negotiation history, see e.g. Daniel Bodansky, "The Paris Climate Change Agreement: A New Hope?", *American Journal of International Law* (forthcoming).

4. For the current status, see on the Internet <http://unfccc.int/paris_agreement/items/9444.php> (last accessed 8 June 2016).

5. See Sebastian Oberthür and Ralph Bodle, "Legal Form and Nature of the Paris Outcome", 6 *Climate Law* (2016), pp. 40 *et sqq*, at pp. 40–46.

6. Arts. 20 and 21 PA.

7. COP decisions are not binding as such, but can be if the treaty so provides or implies. Arts. 4.8, 4.9 and 13.11 PA arguably make the relevant content of decision 1/CP.21 part of the legal obligation contained in these Articles.

8. In particular those that the Paris Agreement makes binding: Arts. 4.8, 4.9, 6.2, 13.11, 13.12, 9.7/13.13 PA.

9. See also Meinhard Doelle, "The Paris Agreement: Historic Breakthrough or High Stakes Experiment?", 6 *Climate Law* (2016), pp. 1 *et sqq*, at p. 5.

10. Art. 2.1(a); para. 21 PD.

11. See also Doelle, "The Paris Agreement", supra, note 9, at p. 8, who even argues that "1.5°C has now become the ultimate standard against which the success of the collective mitigation efforts will be measured."

12. Art. 4.1 PA.

13. Arts. 4.2 and 4.12 PA; paras. 22 and 29 PD.

14. Arts. 4.2 and 4.12 PA; para. 29 PD.

15. Emphasis added. However, Bodansky points out that the difference between the duty of conduct and the duty of result in this case might be minor since "the test of whether a state has implemented its NDC might be seen as whether it has achieved its NDC", Bodansky, "A New Hope?", supra, note 3, at p. 25.

16. Art. 4.4 PA; para. 26 PD.

17. Arts. 4.9 and 4.10; paras. 23–24 PD.

18. Art. 4.8; paras. 26–28 PD.

19. Art. 4.19 PA; para. 36 PD.

20. Art. 4.9 and 4.3 PA.

21. Art. 4.11 PA.

22. Arts. 14, 4.9 PA; paras. 100–102 PD.

23. Art. 14, 4.9 PA.

24. Para. 25 PD.

25. Arts. 2.1(b), 7, 8.4 and 14 PA. See also Bodansky, "A New Hope?", supra, note 3, at p. 30.

26. Arts. 7.1 and 7.4 PA.

27. Arts. 7.10 –7.12 PA.

28. Arts. 9.4 and 7.13 PA; paras. 43, 44 and 46 PD.

29. Paras. 43, 60 PD.

30. Art. 8 PA; para. 52 PD.

31. Cf. the compromise on this issue in Decision 2/CP.19, Warsaw International Mechanism for Loss and Damage associated with Climate Change Impacts, UN Doc. FCCC/CP/2013/10/Add.1, 31 January 2014, 3rd preambular para. and para. 1, which placed the Warsaw international mechanism for loss and damage "under" the Cancun Adaptation Framework, subject to review.

32. Arts. 8.3 and 8.4 PA; para. 50 PD.

33. Art. 8.2 PA; para. 48 PD. For a more detailed assessment of Loss and Damage, see Maxine Burkett, "Reading Between the Red Lines: Loss and Damage and the Paris Outcome", 6 *Climate Law* (2016), pp. 118*et sqq*.

34. Art. 2.1(c) PA; para. 116 and 137 PD.

35. Art. 2.1(c) PA.

36. Art. 9.1 PA; para. 54 PD.

37. Arts. 9.2 and 9.5 PA.

38. Arts. 9.3 and 9.7 PA.

39. Arts. 9.5, 9.6, 9.7, 13.1, 13.6, and 13.14 PA; paras. 55–57, 95–98 PD.

40. Art. 9.10 PA; paras. 59–64 PD.

41. See the section on adaptation, supra.

42. Arts. 13.7–13.10, 13.13, and 13.3 PA; para. 91 PD.

43. Cf. the section on climate finance, supra.

44. Arts. 13.1–13.3 PA; paras. 85–90 PD.

45. Arts. 13.3 PA; paras. 99 PD.

46. Arts. 13.11 and 13.12 PA.

47. Art. 13.3 PA; para. 93 PD.

48. Art. 4.13 PA; para. 31 and 32 PD.

49. Art. 9.7 PA; paras. 57 and 95 PD.

50. For a comprehensive analysis see Oberthür and Bodle, "Paris Outcome", supra, note 5, at p. 40; Daniel Bodansky, "The Legal Character of the Paris Agreement", 25 *Review of European, Comparative, and International Environmental Law* (2016), DOI: 10.1111/reel.12154, forthcoming.

51. Arts. 20, 21, and 27 PA.

52. IISD Reporting Services, "Summary of the Paris Climate Change Conference", 12:663 *Earth Negotiations Bulletin* (2015).

53. Art. 4.2 PA.

54. Art. 15 PA; para. 104 and 105 PD.

55. Art. 21 PA; para. 105 PD.

56. Available on the Internet at <http://unfccc.int/files/ghg_data/application/pdf/table.pdf> (last accessed on 10 June 2016).

57. Arts. 17, 18, and 19 PA; paras. 8–11 PD.

58. Art. 16.2 PA.

59. Art. 5 PA; para. 55 PD.

60. See European Union Directorate General for Internal Policies, "Emission Reduction Targets for International Aviation and Shipping" (2015), available on the Internet at <http://www.europarl.europa.eu/RegData/etudes/STUD/2015/569964/IPOL_STU(2015)569964_EN.pdf> (last accessed on 10 June 2016), at p. 28.

61. But see the new aircraft CO2 emissions standard recommended by the ICAO's environment committee on 8 February 2016, available on the Internet at <http://www.icao.int/Newsroom/Pages/New-ICAO-Aircraft-CO2-Standard-One-Step-Closer-To-Final-Adoption.aspx> (last accessed on 10 June 2016).

62. Arts. 6.2 and 6.3 PA; para. 37 PD.

63. Arts. 6.4-6.7 PA; paras. 38 and 39 PD.

64. Arts. 6.8 and 6.9 PA; paras. 40 and 41 PD.

65. For a more detailed assessment of Art. 6 PA, see Andrei Marcu, *Carbon Market Provisions in the Paris Agreement (Article 6)* (Venice: International Centre for Climate Governance, 2016).

66. Art. 4.15 PA; paras. 33 and 34 PD.

67. Art. 11 PA; paras. 72–89 PD.

68. Arts. 10, 13.9, and 13.10 PA; paras. 66–71 PD.

69. Arts. 2, 4.1, and 14 PA.

70. See supra.

71. Arts. 3, 4.2, 4.3, and 4.19 PA.

72. The reference to mid-century is in para 35 PD.

73. Although it should be noted that the UNFCCC already contains obligations that apply to all parties, e.g. in Arts. 4.1 and 12.1 UNFCCC.

74. UNFCCC Synthesis Report, UN Doc FCCC/CP/2015/7, available on the Internet at <http://unfccc.int/resource/docs/2015/cop21/eng/07.pdf> (last accessed on 10 June 2016).

75. On the review of NDCs and the stocktake, see also Annalisa Savaresi, "The Paris Agreement: A New Beginning?", 34 *Journal of Energy & Natural Resources Law* (2016), pp. 16*et sqq.*

76. For financial obligations, the differentiation is between a list of countries contained in Annex II of the UNFCC, a subset of those listed in Annex I, and everyone else, Non-Annex II countries.

77. See also Christina Voigt and Felipe Ferreira, "Differentiation in the Paris Agreement", 6 *Climate Law* (2016), pp. 58 *et sqq.*

78. See also Doelle, "Paris Agreement", supra, note 9, at p. 18.

79. Ibid., at p. 18.

80. IPCC defines "decarbonisation" as "reducing the carbon *intensity* of energy" (emphasis added), see IPCC AR5 SYR SPM, 5. Others understand "decarbonisation" as the end point of an energy system or economy with no $CO_2$ emissions.

81. Such as national circumstances, food security, just transition of the workforce, sustainable development, poverty eradication, human rights, response measures.

82. See also Doelle, "Paris Agreement", supra, note 9, at p. 16.

83. Investment Week, "Which Sectors Could be Impacted by the Paris Climate Agreement?", 6 January 2016, available on the Internet at <http://www.investmentweek.co.uk/investment-week/analysis/2440883/which-sectors-could-be-impacted-by-the-paris-climate-agreement> (last accessed on 10 June 2016).

84. Unilever "Paul Polman Praises Historic Paris Agreement", 12 December 2015, available on the Internet at <https://www.unilever.com/news/news-and-features/2015/Polman-praises-Paris-Agreement-121215.html> (last accessed on 10 June 2016).

85. PriceWaterhouseCoopers, "PwC COP21 Briefing: Paris Climate Summit", 14 December 2015, available on the Internet at http://pwc.blogs.com/sustainability/2015/12/pwc-cop21-briefing-paris-climate-summit.html (last accessed on 10 June 2016).

86. See for a similar view, Doelle, "Paris Agreement", supra, note 9, at p. 4, and Bodansky, "A New Hope?", supra, note 3, at p. 35.

## DISCUSSION QUESTIONS

1. An important yardstick of the Paris Agreement's success is its ability to increase ambition over time via the cycles of NDCs. What are NDCs? Do you believe that NDC cycles are strongly designed to ensure the Paris Agreement is accomplished? Why? If not, how can NDCs be improved?
2. One of the unique peculiarities of the Paris Agreement is climate finance. Why is climate finance considered to be a key element? What are the appropriate roles for the Green Climate Fund and the Adaptation Fund?
3. The PA recognizes the role of forests in mitigating and adapting to climate change and adopts the REDD framework to reduce emissions from deforestation and forest degradation, enhance conservation and management of forests, and enhance forest carbon stocks in developing countries. What is the current state of REDD+ framework? Do you believe that the results-based payments would promote climate-equitable development in the Global South? If not, what are the mechanisms that could support REDD+ framework function more appropriately?

READING 2.2

# Renewable Electricity

## Falling Costs, Variability, and Scaling Challenges

By Richard Heinberg and David Fridley

The universal availability and use of electricity has come to define modern life, at least for the vast majority of people in the industrialized world. Electricity is accessible in nearly every home and commercial building. We rely on power from wall sockets 24 hr a day, 365 days a year for a myriad of uses that range from toasting a bagel to powering an MRI machine. Electricity is remarkably versatile, and we have built a massive infrastructure to generate, distribute, and consume it.

Electricity constitutes only a portion of the energy the world uses daily. In the United States, 21% of final energy is used as electricity (for the world, the figure is 18%); of the U.S. electricity supply, 38% is generated from coal, 31% from natural gas, 19% from nuclear power, 7% from hydro, and 5% from other renewables (Figure 2.2.1).[1]

Since most solar and wind energy technologies produce electricity (as do hydro, geothermal, and some biomass generators), replacement of fossil fuels by renewable energy sources is happening fastest in the electricity sector. Further, this means that hopes for accelerating the energy transition hinge on the electrification of a greater proportion of our total energy use.

For proponents of renewable energy, there has been plenty of good news in recent years regarding falling prices for solar and wind, and soaring growth rates in these industries. Still, as we will see in this chapter, there are significant challenges to be addressed.

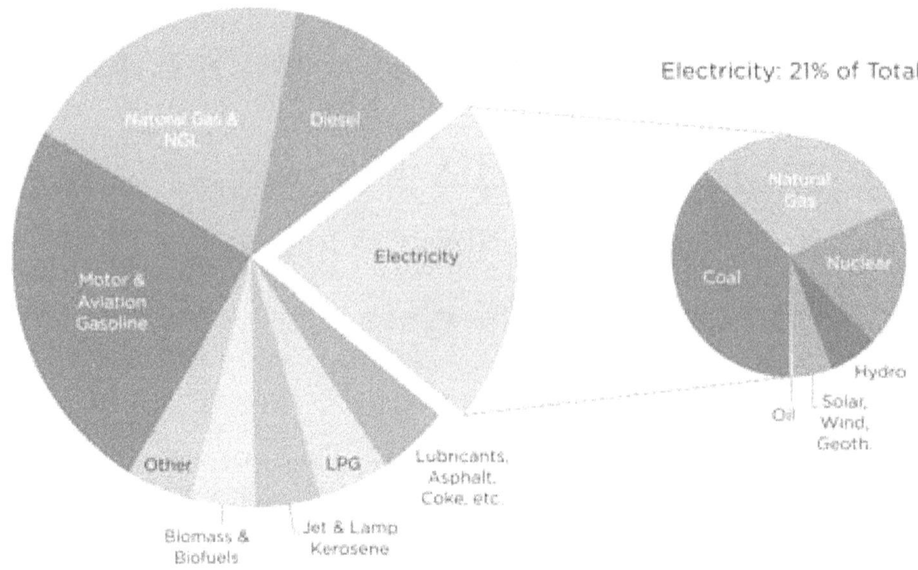


**Figure 2.2.1** U.S. Final Energy Consumption by Fuel Type, 2012. NGL = Natural Gas Liquids; LPG = Liquefied Petroleum Gas.
*Source*: International Energy Agency and U.S. Energy Information Administration.

## Price Is Less of a Barrier

Solar and wind are growing fast. In 2014, global a solar capacity grew 28.7% over the previous year and has more than quadrupled in the past four years.[2] This is an astounding rate of growth: if it were to continue, solar would become the world's dominant source of electricity by 2024. A wind energy capacity is growing at a somewhat slower pace (doubling about every five years), but it has a larger current base: in 2012 (the last full year of U.S. Energy Information Administration [EIA] global data by generation type), solar delivered 94 terawatt-hours (TWh) (billion megawatt-hours [MWh]) per year versus wind's 522 TWh per year, of a global generation of 22,600 TWh.[3]

Remarkably, in the United States, solar and wind power are currently growing faster than coal—not just in percentage terms but in absolute numbers: for 2014, the United States increase in coal consumption amounted to 4.6 TWh, while solar and wind added 23 TWh.[4] Even in China, solar and wind are expanding quickly, while coal consumption is hardly growing at all or even starting to taper off (owing to a substantial slowdown in industrial consumption).

Solar and wind's spectacular growth is occurring for several reasons, but perhaps the most significant driver has been the fall in prices for new solar and wind capacity as compared to costs for coal and natural gas. The price drop is most apparent in the case of solar: the price of photovoltaic (PV) cells has fallen by 99% over the past 25 years and the trend continues. In a 2014 report, Deutsche Bank solar industry analyst Vishal Shah forecast that solar will reach "grid parity" in 36 of 50 U.S.

states by 2016, and in most of the world by 2017 (grid parity is defined as the point where the price for PV electricity is competitive with the retail price for grid power).[5] Shah also estimates that the installed solar capacity will grow as much as sixfold before the end of the decade; see Figure 2.2.2 for a snapshot of just the last few years of solar capacity growth.

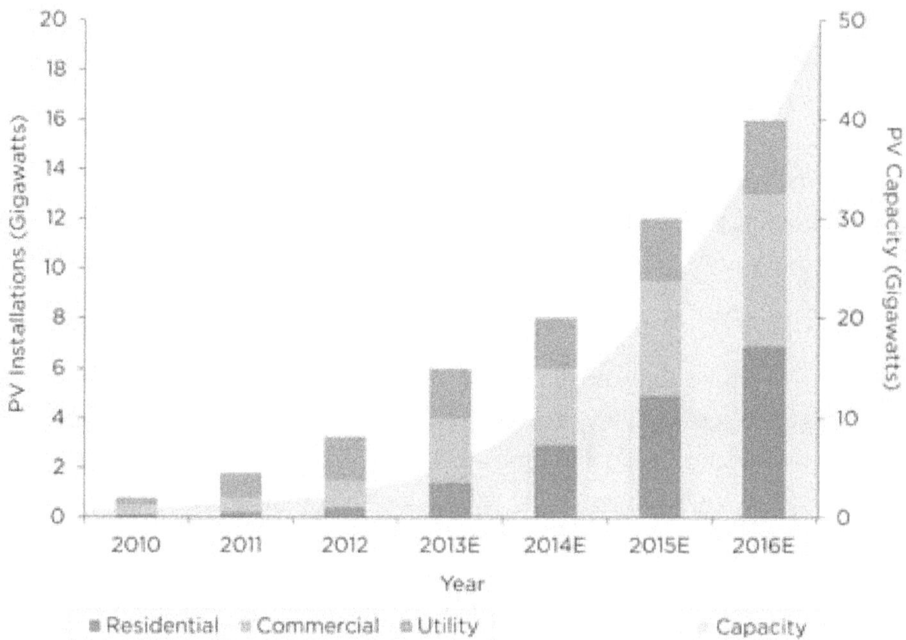


**Figure 2.2.2** U.S. Total Photovoltaic Installations and Capacity.
*Source*: Shah, V., Booream-Phelps, J., & Min, S. (2014). 2014 Outlook: Let the Second Gold Rush Begin. Deutsche Bank, Market Research, North America United States. Retrieved January 6, 2014, from https://www.deutschebank.nl/nl/docs/Solar_-_2014_Outlook_Let_the_Second_Gold_Rush_Begin.pdf

The fall in PV prices is being driven by two factors: improvements in technology (both in manufacturing methods and in PV materials) and increased scale of manufacturing. Manufacturing scale improvements have resulted largely from the Chinese government's decision in 2009 to support widespread deployment of PV, which in turn has led to a spate of price cutting across the industry, as well as a global flood of cheap panels—though some characterize China's actions as product dumping or unfair competition, with many American and European manufacturers having gone bankrupt due to their inability to match Chinese prices.

Power purchase agreement prices for wind energy projects are currently competitive with prices for power from coal and natural gas plants in many markets. Wind prices are falling because of lower cost wind turbines (taller wind towers and longer and lighter blades) that allow for a better capture of the wind resource, and therefore increased economic performance.

In general, technologies tend to become more efficient and more cost-effective over time, as engineers identify improvements and as devices are produced on a larger scale.[6] Fossil fuel technologies (mining, drilling, hydrofracturing, refining) are also becoming more efficient; however, those technologies are being used to harvest depleting resources, so an accelerating decline in resource quality will inevitably outstrip the ability of engineers to improve recovery efficiencies.[7]

Is the current rapid growth in solar and wind capacity sustainable? Can the pace in fact be substantially increased? Will price declines increase or reverse themselves as higher penetration rates are achieved? The answers to these questions will depend on the renewable energy industry's ability to solve a few looming problems.

## Intermittency

As stated earlier, we have designed our energy usage patterns to take advantage of controllable inputs. Need more electricity? If you're relying on coal for energy, that just requires shoveling more fuel into the boiler. Sunlight and wind are different: they are available on nature's terms, not ours. Sometimes the sun is shining or the wind is blowing, sometimes not. Energy geeks have a vocabulary to describe this—they say solar and wind power are *intermittent*, *variable*, *stochastic*, or *chaotic*. In contrast, energy experts refer to coal, gas, oil, hydro, biomass, nuclear, and geothermal sources as *predictable*; sources that can be quickly brought into service or shuttered to meet transient demand (usually natural gas or hydro plants) are called *dispatchable*. It should be noted, though, that these latter sources are also subject to a certain amount of variability: natural gas, coal, and nuclear power plants sometimes need to be shut down for maintenance, or can go offline due to accidents, and hydropower can be distinctly seasonal depending on rainfall patterns. They're just much *less* variable than solar and wind.

The availability of sunlight follows fairly consistent diurnal and seasonal patterns. We can calculate in advance the position of the sun in the sky for any moment in time, for any location. We know that sunlight will be more readily available in summer months than in winter months, and that this seasonal variability will be more extreme the farther we are from the equator. We also know that sunlight is likely to be most intense at noon and is absent at night. Yet within this expected variability, there is also a more chaotic intermittency: sometimes the sun is hidden for moments, hours, days, or even weeks by clouds.

Wind tends to follow different diurnal and seasonal patterns. Some locations have far more consistent winds than others. Also, winds tend to be stronger, and more consistent, at greater heights above the earth's surface (thus taller turbines tend to be more efficient). The wind resource varies greatly by location. In some regions, it is out of phase with energy demands—weak during the day but stronger at night; in other places, winds are stronger during the day. Transient weather patterns can bring hurricane-force gales or days and weeks of calm, when virtually no electricity can be generated.

Therefore when discussing solar panels and wind turbines, it is important to understand the difference between *nameplate capacity* (how much power could be generated with constant sun or wind) and these resources' *average* power output (Figure 2.2.3). The ratio of these numbers is the *capacity factor*. A coal- or gas-fired baseload power plant might have a capacity factor of 90%; wind farms have capacity factors ranging between 22 and 43%.[8] In the United States, PV systems have capacity factors ranging between 12 and 20%, depending on the location.[9]

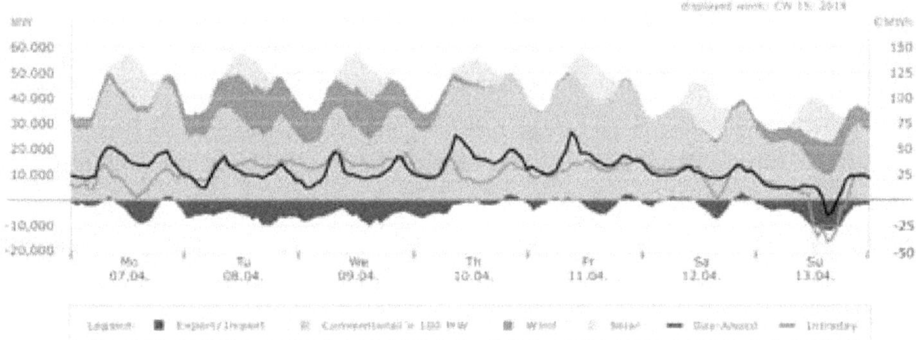


**Figure 2.2.3** Intermittency of Renewable Energy Electricity Generation and Its Effect on Price. This Chart Shows Germany's Electricity Production and Spot Prices for the Week of April 7, 2014. As Renewable Energy Production Fluctuates, Conventional Production, and the Spot Prices Respond.
*Source*: Mayer, J. (2014). Electricity production and spot prices in Germany 2014. Fraunhofer ISE. https://www.ise.fraunhofer.de/en/renewable-energy-data

Uncontrollable resource variability is a problem for grid operators who need to match electricity generation with demand on a minute-by-minute basis. Daily and seasonal demand cycles are fairly easy to predict in general terms: electricity use tends to peak in the afternoons and dip at night; and in most temperate and tropical regions, it increases during the hottest part of the summer when air conditioners are in use. Solar output tends to follow this cycle fairly well up to a point, but often cannot be dispatched to meet a surge of demand or turned off if demand is low (more recently built PV farms have "spinning" reserves where some proportion of the power output must be available for ramping). Wind power's variations often balance out those of solar; but sometimes both reinforce one another, producing an unusable surge of electricity that grid operators must somehow shed. And sometimes both sources are in a lull (the weather is cloudy and still), even though electricity demand is high. (Modern wind farms also have grid benefits, since they can be damped easily, which is useful for reactive power [voltage] control.)

Intermittency has long been recognized as a hindrance to the adoption of solar and wind technologies, and so a lot of thought has gone into finding ways to reduce or buffer that intermittency. Also, many countries now have experience integrating solar and wind into their grid systems. In short, there are strategies for dealing with intermittency—though each has limitations and costs.

## Storage

The most obvious way to make up for the variability of solar and wind energy is by storing energy when it is available in surplus so that it can be used later. There are several ways energy can be stored, but before we survey them it will be helpful to know a little about how to evaluate storage systems.

Let's start with two factors: (1) the amount of *energy* the system can store (as expressed in watt-hours) and (2) the amount of *power* the system can absorb or deliver at any moment (as expressed in watts). A system that stores lots of energy won't be very useful if it can only receive or return that energy a little at a time. And a system with enormous power won't be helpful if it needs recharging after only a few minutes. Storage systems need to do well in both respects.

Energy density is especially relevant for alternative ways to power transportation. For electric vehicle (EV) batteries, it is useful to know the energy density both by weight (megajoules per kilogram, MJ/kg) and by volume (megajoules per liter, MJ/L). EVs are often burdened by heavy batteries (the battery pack of a Tesla Model S, e.g., weighs in at over 1,300 pounds). On the other hand, storing energy in the form of compressed hydrogen takes up a lot of space (see Figure 1.3).

Another metric of energy storage has to do with economic and environmental factors. What's the carbon footprint of a given storage technology? How much energy was used to construct it? And what's the energy cost of maintaining the technology over its projected lifetime? These three questions are closely related. Researchers Barnhart and Benson at Stanford University have proposed using the metric *energy stored on investment* (ESOI) as a way of tackling these issues.[10] It expresses the amount of energy that can be stored over the lifetime of a technology divided by the amount of energy required to build that technology. The higher the ESOI value, the better the storage technology from an energy point of view—and, most likely, from an environmental perspective as well.

A final consideration with regard to energy storage has to do with limiting resources, such as lithium for batteries. For electricity, the three most widely discussed options for energy storage are geologic storage, hydrogen, and batteries.

### Geologic Storage: Water Reservoirs, Compressed Air in Caverns

In the most common instance, this means pumping water uphill into a reservoir when electricity is overabundant, then letting it run back downhill to turn a turbine when more electricity is needed. Pumped storage is the most widely used grid-scale energy storage option; yet, for the United States, a current pumped storage capacity is roughly 2% of the capacity of the electric grid.[11]

**Figure 2.2.4** Pumped Hydro Power Station. (Credit: A. Aleksandravicius, via Shutterstock.)

Pumped storage is the cheapest option for grid-scale energy storage (batteries have much higher embodied energy costs). Barnhart and Benson (2013) determined that a typical pumped hydro facility has an ESOI value of 210,[12] which means it can store and deliver 210 times more energy over its lifetime than the amount of energy required to build it. Storage of compressed air in underground caverns also has a high ESOI value; however, this option is today rarely used.

The limits and downsides to geologic storage include the fact that it works only for stationary systems (not vehicles). It also suffers from low energy density: physicist Tom Murphy points out that "to match the energy contained in a gallon of gasoline, we would have to lift 13 tons of water (3,500 gallons) 1 km high (3,280 feet)."[13] Therefore, we would need a lot of reservoir volume to store really significant amounts of energy. But geologic storage requires appropriate topographic and geological conditions. In the final analysis, it is unclear whether it can be expanded enough to store anywhere near the amounts of energy we might need in an all-renewable future.

## Hydrogen

Using electricity to produce hydrogen, then storing the hydrogen, offers another possible vector for buffering out the intermittency of renewable energy sources. Current hydrogen storage is minuscule. However, some analysts suggest hydrogen storage could be used widely at the household scale to store a large total amount of energy that could be flexibly used.[14]

Pellow et al. (2015) have determined that a hydrogen energy storage system would have an ESOI rating of 59,[15] which is much lower than the figure for pumped storage but higher than that of the best battery technology available today. Nevertheless, Pellow et al. (2015) also found that the low round trip efficiency of a regenerative hydrogen fuel cell (RHFC) energy storage system "results in very high energy costs during operation, and a much lower overall energy efficiency than lithium ion batteries (0.30 for RHFC vs. 0.83 for lithium ion batteries)."[16] Hydrogen storage represents a relatively efficient use of *manufacturing energy* to provide storage. But its *operational efficiency* must improve before it can compete with batteries in that regard.

In sum, hydrogen may be economic in some applications. It is potentially better than batteries for large-scale storage, and it can be adapted for use in vehicles and homes—though operational energy losses remain a problem.

## Batteries

There is much ongoing research into the technology of converting electrical energy for storage as chemical energy in a battery. Just a couple of decades ago, lead–acid batteries (invented in 1859) were the primary available option for large-scale applications; today nickel- and lithium-based batteries are also available. Batteries are getting cheaper and better. In 2015, Tesla Motors Inc. unveiled a new generation of patented lithium-ion batteries designed for home and industrial use to store energy from the sun and wind. This provoked speculation that higher volume production and further technical improvements could yield batteries cheap and powerful enough to solve the intermittency problems of renewable energy.

Since battery costs and efficiencies are a moving target, perhaps it is useful to consider the physical limits to battery improvements. Science writer Alice Friedemann has performed the thought experiment of examining the periodic table of elements to identify the lightest elements with multiple oxidation states that form compounds (oxidation–reduction reactions generate a voltage, which is the basis of electric cells or batteries). Ignoring problems such as materials scarcity, she finds that the theoretical upper energy density limit to the best materials would be around 5 MJ/kg.[17] The best batteries currently commercially available are able to achieve about 0.5 MJ/kg, or 10% of this physical upper bound. Improvements would also be required in materials such as electrolytes, separators, current collectors, and packaging. Given all this, Friedemann concludes that "we're unlikely to improve the energy density by more than about a factor of two within about 20 years." Energy density is primarily a limiting factor in batteries for mobile purposes; still, for stationary purposes, low energy density implies the need for more materials, and therefore typically translates to greater energetic cost in manufacturing.

The ESOI of batteries is quite low compared to that of pumped storage, and lower than that of hydrogen. Lithium-ion batteries perform best with an ESOI value of 10.[18] Lead–acid batteries have an ESOI value of 2,[19] the lowest in the Barnhart and Benson study.

Batteries imply an added energy cost; what happens when this energy cost is added to the energy cost of building and installing renewable energy generation systems? Clearly, it reduces the energy "affordability" of the system; but if you're starting with an energy source that has a high EROEI, this is less of a problem. Using EROEI analysis, Charles Barnhart et al. found that storage is less "affordable" for PV than it is for wind.[20] Also, the manufacturing of batteries adds to carbon emissions. Technology writer Kris De Decker performed a life cycle analysis on existing PV-plus-batteries generating systems and found that they entail lower carbon emissions than conventional grid power, but not that much less.[21]

For small rolling vehicles and off-grid, self-contained electricity systems, batteries may provide the best available energy storage solution. Nevertheless, low energy density and low ESOI appear to be inherent drawbacks for chemical storage of electricity on a large scale; and while improvements are on the way, they are unlikely to change the overall situation.

## Other Storage Options

While geologic storage, hydrogen, and batteries are the options most often discussed, there are others, such as compressed air canisters (for cars) and flywheels (for the grid); however, these are not widely used and are unlikely to offer substantial improvements over our three main candidates.[22]

There has also been talk of storing energy in electric fields (by way of capacitors) or magnetic fields (using superconductors). A company called EEstor claims a new capacitor capable of storage of 1 MJ/kg, which is about twice as good as the best current battery. Electromagnets of high-temperature superconductors can theoretically achieve about 4 MJ/kg. The ultimate physical potentials for such storage technologies would represent improvements over existing batteries but would still lack the energy density of hydrocarbon fuels.

Electrical energy could also be stored in synthetic fuels more chemically complex than hydrogen, including liquid fuels. These would offer greater energy density than battery storage and would therefore be better suited for use in vehicles; however, they would suffer from energy conversion inefficiencies.

In a recent paper, Mark Jacobson et al. (2017) propose the use of yet another storage medium—underground thermal energy storage (UTES).[23] Industrial waste heat, or heat from combined heat and power (CHP) plants or solar thermal collectors, would be channeled to storage tanks of water, pits of water, or fields of boreholes up to 300 m deep. For solar thermal plants, heat would be collected in the summer and released and used in winter. The heat is primarily used for space conditioning, though it can also be used for power generation, depending on the storage temperature. The technology (which is currently in use on the 52 household Drake Landing Solar Community in Alberta, Canada, with 25,000 sq. ft. of solar collectors) has high investment costs (3,400–4,500 euros/kW) but fairly low operation and maintenance costs.

Scaling up this technology is likely to be a big challenge. UTES (or any thermal energy storage design) is best used and optimized when done in conjunction with new construction or renovations;

but given that the average building lifetime in the United States is 75 years, the rate of penetration growth is likely to be inhibited. A joint technical paper on the subject by the International Energy Agency (IEA) and the International Renewable Energy Agency (IRENA) confirms this is the case for Europe, where building stock turnover is only 1.3% per year and the renovation rate is only 1.5% per year.[24] It would be very expensive to try to retrofit existing buildings to take advantage of this process. It is also unclear how it could be fit into an existing dense urban area. UTES design is site specific, and subsurface storage technologies are site specific. This adds to cost and complexity.

UTES is also characterized by low energy density. Water-based systems can achieve up to 50 kWh/m$^3$ (180 MJ/m$^3$ or 0.18 MJ/kg), which is about at the level of a Li+ battery. The consequence of that is low area density (a scheme in Crailsheim, Germany, for 260 houses, one school, and one sports hall uses 79,000 sq. ft. of solar collectors, 3,500 cubic feet of peak load storage, 17,000 cubic feet of buffer storage, and 1.5 million cubic feet of borehole storage with 80 probes), and of course entails a lot of drilling, along with large quantities of probes, pipes, and other equipment. The IEA/IRENA technical paper notes that the barriers include system integration, regulation, high costs, material stability, and complexity, while R&D is needed for insulation and high-temperature materials.

Currently, only 8–10 gigawatts (GW) of sensible thermal energy storage exists in the world, but Jacobson et al. propose capacity sufficient to support 467 terawatts (TW) of charge from solar thermal collectors. To say that this is a highly ambitious proposal may be an understatement.

The bottom line for energy storage: many options exist, and research is likely to expand their number and improve them. But each of the categories of options is subject to limits and costs, even assuming substantial technical improvements. Given different criteria (energy density, carbon emissions, cost), some storage options offer advantages over others. However, current electricity storage is only a tiny percentage of the amount that will likely be required in an all-renewable energy future—we need to build *a lot* of storage. And supplying large amounts of storage will add significantly to the financial, materials, energy, and carbon costs of systems.[25] A real-world example: California's Energy Storage law AB2514 directs utilities to install 1.3 GW of storage capacity by 2020. The total installed generation capacity today is 78 GW, of which 12.26 is renewable (excluding large hydro). The law says storage must be economically feasible, but utilities have so far balked at implementing it.

## Grid Redesign

The electricity grids of the 20th century were designed to distribute power from large, centralized coal, gas, nuclear, and hydro generating plants to far-flung end users. Grid managers learned to track electricity demand patterns (usually based on times of heavy use of domestic heating and air conditioning), which tend to feature daily peaks. These demand spikes are now met by *peaking power generators* (usually fired by natural gas) that are used only for short periods each day. The low utilization of peaking generators, along with the necessary redundancy in the electricity grid, results in high costs to the electricity companies, which are passed on to customers.

The renewable electricity system of the 21st century will be different: it will accommodate numerous smaller and more geographically distributed power inputs, most of which are uncontrollably variable. Meeting demand will require, among other things, significant smart grid upgrades. The term "smart grid" doesn't refer to a specific technology, but rather to a set of related technologies whose goals are to gain a better understanding of what is happening on the grid in order to reduce power consumption during peak hours and incorporate grid energy storage, both of which make it easier to integrate more solar and wind. Disregarding the renewable energy transition, smart grids are expected to deliver increased efficiency and reliability, saving grid operators and consumers money. Add distributed renewable power generation and the grid may evolve beyond a centralized system to become something of a collaborative network of electricity producers and consumers.

The main elements of a smart grid consist of integrated communications, sensing and measurement devices (smart meters and high-speed sensors deployed throughout the transmission network), devices to signal the current state of the grid, and better management and forecasting software; as renewable energy inputs are added, energy storage systems will inevitably become part of the network. Smart grids with a large share of renewables will also need additional transmission capacity to move more power longer distances to balance loads as output from distributed solar and wind generators varies.

A paper from Siemens Corporate Technology in Germany weighs the relative contributions of grid extensions and electricity storage to a hypothetical 100% renewable European grid, and finds that, with storage, renewables could supply up to 60% of power without additional grid capacity or backup, and 80% with an "ideal" grid.[26] These conclusions are similar to those of a National Renewable Energy Laboratory (NREL) study, which relies heavily on dispatchable biomass power generation to achieve the renewable target (about 15% biomass generation in 2050). They note regarding the grid that "electricity supply and demand can be balanced in every hour of the year in each region with nearly 80% of electricity from renewable resources, including nearly 50% from variable renewable generation, according to simulations of 2050 power system operations."[27]

How much will all this cost? A 2011 study by the Electric Power Research Institute (EPRI) found that smart grid upgrades in the United States would require the investment of between $338 and $476 billion over the next 20 years, but would deliver $1.3–2 trillion in benefits during that period.[28] Another study, this one by the U.S. Department of Energy, calculated that a more modest modernization of U.S. grids would save between $46 and $117 billion over the same 20-year time frame.[29]

Assuming that smart grid investments are a good deal over the long run, who pays for these upgrades over the short term? Experts disagree on whether recovery of a utility's smart grid upgrade costs should come from raising rates to customers or from some "nontraditional" source, such as government. There is also concern that utilities and regulators are accustomed to buying power equipment that lasts 40 years or more, whereas some electronic sensors and communications devices now being installed on the grid may last half that time, or as little as a decade.[30]

The electricity grid has been described as the largest machine ever created by human beings; as we make it larger and smarter in order to accommodate more variable and distributed renewable energy inputs, we also make it even more complex. Is there another solution? There is: do away with the centralized grid altogether and have energy generation and storage happen at the scale of communities. This would require every city and possibly every neighborhood to have enough generating and storage capacity, as well as needed control equipment, to sustain itself. The result would likely be a more expensive electricity system overall, and one that would, left entirely to the free market, result in much greater energy inequality (a subject to which we will return in Chapter 8), since some households and communities would be able to afford robust systems, others none at all. The intermittency of wind and sunlight would also likely pose a greater challenge for more localized minigrids, unless they were linked over large geographical areas to take advantage of distant resources to make up for local shortfalls.

Decentralizing the grid would encourage energy use more in line with natural flows of renewable energy; also, households/communities would be more self-sufficient, and the system would entail less complexity and fewer interdependencies, resulting in less vulnerability to breaks in a brittle system. In light of all the factors mentioned, the likely outcome will be some mix of both centralized and decentralized grid systems, combining long-distance transmission infrastructure (high-voltage lines) with local distribution.

## Demand Management

Given electricity sources whose unpredictably variable output doesn't coincide with times when electricity is typically used, one set of solutions (which we have just discussed) aims to make that output more predictable using *storage and control systems*; another set of solutions, generally referred to as *demand response*, is geared to manage *when* consumers use energy and *how much* they use, through voluntary programs or economic incentives. Although the purpose of demand response programs today is to avoid construction of costly generation capacity to meet peak demand, the practices are similarly applicable to managing the increased penetration of variable electricity generation such as solar and wind. Aligning electricity demand with supply entails two main substrategies: dynamic pricing, and smart appliances and equipment. One potentially important example of the latter is the use of electric car batteries for grid storage, discussed later in the chapter.

Dynamic pricing—changing the price of electricity according to its hour-by-hour availability—has led large industrial and commercial users to shift their usage to times when supplies are abundant and prices are low. This requires knowing when those times are, which in turn requires ways to communicate with users. In California, links between the independent system operator (ISO)—which coordinates, controls, and monitors the operation of the electrical power system—and large interruptible users have already been established; further, one of the goals of smart meter programs is to communicate real-time pricing information to residential and commercial customers so they can shift usage times. As this requires sensors, communication links, software, and data management, dynamic pricing is inseparably connected with the project of redesigning the grid, discussed earlier in this chapter. Using dynamic pricing to enlist market forces in demand management will unquestionably help reduce times of over- or undersupply of electricity, thus increasing power affordability.[31]

**Figure 2.2.5** Battery of a Toyota 86 Electric Vehicle. (Credit: Tokumeigakarinoaoshima, via Wikimedia Commons.)

Dynamic pricing can happen with the old grid infrastructure, it just requires feedback of the spot price to consumers who face that price. However, most domestic consumers currently don't have an easily accessible way to track the spot price in real time or are subject to flat rate pricing, and thus have no incentive to change their usage patterns.

When we're at home, we don't check electricity prices hour by hour to see when prices are high or low. How, then, can residential electricity customers be integrated into dynamic pricing programs? By automating the process via the so-called Internet of Things. Once most appliances are computerized and connected by Wi-Fi or hard line, they could in principle be set to respond to data from the utility company so they adjust their energy usage based on the current price of electricity. (Another potential for grid demand management entails allowing the utility to dial down power usage of appliances like refrigerators and air conditioners remotely during peak times.) This doesn't require a smart meter; in fact, most smart meters don't have this capacity. All that is required is a switch that the utility can turn on and off.

There are, of course, limits to these strategies. The Internet of Things implies additional material resources—which require extraction, manufacturing, transport, and operation—and also increased system complexity. It also raises privacy issues: already televisions are tracking (and potentially selling) users' usage data. Finally, some electricity usage is easily amenable to demand shifting; at home, for example, we may be quite willing to load up the washing machine, set its dial, and wait for the machine itself to determine when to wash our clothes based on hourly electricity price fluctuations. But if we're working at a computer, we might be less than pleased to see its screen go black following the momentary display of a message reading, "Sorry, electricity prices have just gone up."

Among smart appliances, electric cars have often been touted as having the greatest potential for helping match grid electricity demand with supply. Since automobiles are parked an average of 95% of the time, if EVs were left plugged in during that time, electricity could flow to power lines and back, with a value to the utilities of up to $4,000 per year per car.[32] The use of EV batteries to provide decentralized storage of electrical energy, either by delivering electricity into the grid or by throttling their charging rate, is known as vehicle-to-grid (V2G). Grid managers could incentivize vehicle owners to participate in V2G programs by offering discounted electricity at night to charge vehicles and by offering fees to offset the cost of battery wear and tear from additional cycling. It is unclear, however, whether such incentives could realistically be greater than the value of the batteries to their owners.

Since proposed V2G programs center on the use of batteries for storage, all of the limits to battery storage technology previously discussed apply here. Currently, only pilot V2G programs exist, and the number of EVs in use worldwide is still too small to provide much real-world data on the likely benefits and drawbacks of a program large enough to impact grid reliability and price stability.

## Capacity Redundancy

Another way to reduce the impact of energy source intermittency is to add redundant generation capacity: when the sun isn't shining and the wind isn't blowing, then simply rely on other electricity sources, which can be throttled down when sun and wind are abundantly available (this is already done with natural gas generators, though using them this way is much less energy efficient than as combined cycle *base load*, in which they operate continuously and are available 24 hr a day). Redundancy obviously adds to total system costs, and therefore proposals for future 100% renewable electricity systems typically attempt to reduce the need for it with strategies already discussed (storage, grid upgrades, and demand management). Nevertheless, capacity redundancy is the primary strategy that currently enables intermittent renewables to be integrated into electricity grid systems.

So far, solar and wind have remained proportionally small contributors to overall electrical energy in most nations, and variability has been buffered primarily by fossil energy resources (especially by natural gas–fired peaking plants, which can be powered up or down quite quickly). In effect, the grid itself becomes the battery for solar and wind generators. Renewable energy resources other than solar and wind could fill more of that role; these would likely include biomass, hydro, and geothermal. But are these resources up to the job? Let's take a look at each in turn.

## Biomass

Burning wood, crop residues, and biogas is a dispatchable electricity source: as with coal or natural gas, if more electricity is needed then, it's just a matter of firing up the boiler and adding fuel. However, this resource is limited, and long-term sustainability is uncertain. Forests cover 7% of the earth's surface, but net deforestation is occurring around the globe, especially in South America, Indonesia, and Africa.[33] The use of ever-larger areas of land and quantities of water for growth of dedicated "energy forests" also raises concerns about competition with food and fiber crops.

World electric power generation from biomass was about 405 TWh in 2013 from an installed capacity of 88 GW, with much of the growth based on a growing international trade in wood pellets (at some distance from the source, transport of wood pellets consumes more energy than the pellets will deliver).[34] Cogeneration or CHP plants can burn fossil fuels or biomass to generate electricity while also using their "waste" heat for space or water heating (biomass CHP is more efficient at producing heat than electricity, but it can be practical if there is a local source of excess biomass and a community or industrial demand nearby for heat and electricity). Most biomass generation plants are located in northern Europe, the United States, and Brazil, with increasing amounts in China, India, and Japan, and the capacity has been growing at over 10% per year over the last decade.[35] However, biomass power plants are only half as efficient as natural gas plants, and they are limited in size by a fuel-shed of around 100 miles. Except in cases of long-distance trade in wood pellets, biomass availability is highly seasonal, and biomass storage is particularly inefficient with high rates of loss due to degradation.

In its favor, biomass is well suited for use in small-scale, region-appropriate applications where using local biomass is sustainable. In Europe there has been steady growth in biomass CHP plants in which scrap materials from wood processing or agriculture are burned, while in developing countries CHPs are often run on coconut or rice husks. Burning biomass and biogas is considered to be carbon neutral, since, unlike fossil fuels, these operate within the biospheric carbon cycle, though the increased reliance on wood as fuel raises concern about the time lag between combustion of the wood and the pace of carbon reuptake in new growth.

While biomass is a renewable resource, it is not a particularly expandable one. Often, available biomass is a waste product of other human activities, such as crop residues from agriculture, wood chips, sawdust, and "black liquor" from wood products industries, and solid waste from municipal trash and sewage. In a less fossil fuel intensive agricultural system, such as may be required globally in the future, crop residues may be needed to replenish soil fertility and won't be available for power generation. There may also be more competition for waste products in the future, as manufacturing from recycled materials increases.

## Hydroelectric Power

Hydro dams have the potential to produce a moderate amount of additional, high-quality electricity in less-industrialized countries, but they are often associated with severe environmental and social costs. Particularly in northern Europe, hydropower already serves to balance the growing proportion of variable renewable electricity production, though hydropower itself can be subject to strong seasonal variations, which may be exacerbated by climate change-induced changes in rainfall. Globally, there are many undeveloped dam sites with hydropower potential, though there are far fewer in the United States, where most of the best sites have already been dammed. With over 1,000 GW of hydropower capacity installed globally,[36] the International Hydropower Association estimates that about one third of the technical potential of world hydropower has already been developed.[37]

## Geothermal

Geothermal energy is derived from the heat within the earth. It can be "mined" by extracting hot water or steam, either to run a turbine for electricity generation or for direct use of the heat itself. High-quality geothermal energy is typically available only in regions where tectonic plates meet, where volcanic and seismic activities are common, and where heat is fairly close to the surface. Currently, the only places being exploited for geothermal electrical power are ones where hydrothermal resources exist in the form of hot water or steam reservoirs. In these locations, hot groundwater is pumped to the surface from wells 2–3 km deep and is used to drive turbines. In a theory, power can also be generated from hot dry rocks by pumping turbine fluid into them through boreholes that are 3–10 km deep. This method, called enhanced geothermal system (EGS) generation, is the subject of ongoing research and the construction of demonstration plants, and the first grid-connected commercial plant with a capacity of 1.7 MW came online in Nevada in 2013 as a part of an existing geothermal field.[38] Because EGSs use fluid injection to open existing rock joints, there is some concern that this technology could generate earthquakes as an unintended side effect.[39] In general, early high hopes for EGS technology appear not to be panning out.

In 2013, the world geothermal power capacity reached 12 GW with output rising to 76 TWh.[40] The annual growth of geothermal power capacity worldwide has slowed from 9% in 1997 to 4% in 2013.[41] Geothermal power plants produce much lower levels of emissions and use less land area than fossil fuel plants. However, technological improvements are necessary for the industry to continue to grow. Water can also be a limiting factor, since both hydrothermal and dry rock systems consume water.

There is no consensus on potential resource base estimates for geothermal power generation. Hydrothermal areas that have both heat and water are rare, so the large-scale expansion of geothermal power depends on whether lower temperature hydrothermal resources can be tapped. A 2006 Massachusetts Institute of Technology (MIT) report estimated U.S. hydrothermal resources at 2,400–9,600 EJ, while dry-heat geothermal resources were estimated to be as much as 13 million EJ (as you'll recall, the world currently uses over 500 EJ per year), but the U.S. Department of Energy estimated in 2014 that technical advances needed to access the latter may still be 10–15 years from commercial maturity,[42] which may reflect inherent problems with EGS.

Biomass, hydro, and geothermal are probably the best three renewable electricity sources available for base load renewable power, though there are others (notably tidal and wave generators, which currently produce only very small total amounts of electrical power). This book focuses on solar and wind as the main candidates for expansion of renewable energy because these are the sources with the most immediate capacity for growth. No doubt some combination of biomass, hydro, and geothermal, used as base load and/or backup capacity, can help buffer the intermittency of solar and wind, but since these sources (with the possible exception of geothermal) have limited prospects for expansion, this could ultimately also limit the total amount of energy production capacity in an all-renewable future energy regime.

How about buffering the intermittency of solar and wind with more solar and wind? After all, even if the weather is cloudy and still in a given location, it might be windy and sunny a few hundred miles away. This kind of capacity redundancy would require more grid interconnections and, of course, more solar panels and wind turbines. Since we couldn't know far in advance which other regions would be likely to provide capacity redundancy for ours, we would need enough redundancy in several places, and enough transmission capability to meet possible supply shortfalls. All of this adds to the system cost.

The actual experience of grid operators integrating solar and wind into the grid has led to an emerging consensus that the cost of integrating renewables will shoot up as solar and wind make up a very high percentage of grid power.[43] In the early stages of solar and wind build-out, it is fairly easy to incorporate new uncontrollable inputs into the grid because redundancy already exists in the form of coal, natural gas, nuclear, and hydro generation plants, which have plenty of capacity to balance out added variable renewable electricity and match it with demand—which is also variable. However, as total solar and wind input surpasses 30% of grid electricity, the costs of integration are likely to gradually increase. Past 60–80%, the need for storage and redundancy will likely explode. The goal of a near 100% renewable, grid-based electricity system is a subject of great controversy and research, but it remains theoretical, because no society has created one yet, except for a couple of small islands in the Canary Islands (El Hierro)[44] and Denmark (Samsø), where wind and pumped hydro have been deployed to serve their small populations; or Uruguay, which generates the great majority of its electricity from hydropower.

## Scaling Challenges

If we're to achieve a 100% renewable electricity system soon enough to significantly mitigate climate change, we'll have to build fast. The good news is that solar and wind are already growing quickly, as we have already seen. The bad news is that there appear to be some financial, energy, and environmental hurdles in the path toward scaling up these sources at the rates needed.

The energy transition will be expensive. While some estimates suggest that a renewable energy regime will be more affordable than a business-as-usual pathway dominated by fossil fuels (especially so once the climate and health impacts of the latter are taken into account),[45] it is doubtful that the business-as-usual pathway is itself affordable. And health and environmental costs avoided do not translate to money in the bank ready to be invested in alternative energy projects. Estimates of the total cost of moving to an all-renewable global electricity system are too preliminary to be exact, but they are nevertheless expressed in the tens of trillions of dollars.[46] Where will the money come from? If the utility industry simply replaces coal, natural gas, and nuclear plants as they reach retirement age with solar, wind, geothermal, hydro, and biomass capacity, then most of the capital cost of the transition would come from the utility industry using its usual financing methods. But, again, to achieve the speed of transition needed, we would also have to retire fossil-fueled plants that are still well within their projected operating lifetime. That would imply higher rates of investment than the utility industry is accustomed to. Also, as the need for storage, capacity redundancy, and grid expansion and redesign increase, these will impose still more added costs.

Until recently, rapid expansion of solar and wind has relied on incentives, including rebates to homeowners installing PV systems and feed-in tariffs (long-term contracts to buy electricity from renewable energy producers, typically based on the cost of generation rather than existing market prices for electrical power). But those incentives are being reduced, eliminated, or thrown in doubt in countries such as Italy, Spain, and the United Kingdom, and in states such as Kansas and Arizona. While the falling costs of wind and solar are making them more directly competitive with incumbent fossil electricity sources, the loss of government financial support would slow the renewables transition.

A recent MIT study of the prospects for solar electricity found that, due to factors related to intermittency, "Even if solar PV generation becomes cost-competitive at low levels of penetration, revenues per kW of installed capacity will decline as solar penetration increases until a breakeven point is reached, beyond which further investment in solar PV would be unprofitable."[47] Therefore, further subsidies for renewables (or penalties for nonrenewables) would probably be required if this energy source is to be scalable to replace the bulk of fossil-fueled generation.

Financing for solar and wind generation is fundamentally different from that for coal and gas plants. In the former case, investment is almost entirely upfront; from then on the "fuel" is free and maintenance is relatively inexpensive. In the latter, the cost of building the generation plant is proportionally less, with ongoing fuel costs being factored into wholesale and retail electricity prices. There is an obvious advantage to solar and wind from an investment standpoint (no worries about fluctuations in fuel prices), but there is also a drawback: front-loading of investment means that the availability of low-interest credit plays a major role in making new wind and solar capacity affordable.

Incumbent coal and gas power plants have the advantage of a lower tax burden, as fuel costs can be deducted from taxable income, while solar and wind cannot benefit from this deduction. Property taxes can also be an issue for large solar and wind installations, which take up much more land per unit of generating capacity than fossil fuel plants.

Aside from these financial problems, there is also an *energy* hurdle to the rapid transition to renewable electricity. Just as the financial investment in solar and wind generators is front-loaded, so is the energy investment in their construction: from an energy perspective, these generators must "pay" for themselves over time. This means that, if lots of generation capacity is built too quickly, it may constitute an energy sink rather than a true net energy source until rates of installation begin to slow (Figure 2.2.4). A 2013 study by Benson and Dale at Stanford University, cited earlier, showed that solar PV generation capacity installed between the years 2000 and 2012 paid for itself in energy terms only toward the end of that period; this was due to the high rates of growth, the energy costs of panel production and installation, and the relatively low EROEI of PV.[48] Wind power, with its higher EROEI, is less subject to this problem; nevertheless, the principle still holds: if the rate of installation of an energy-generating technology whose energy costs occur almost entirely in the manufacturing

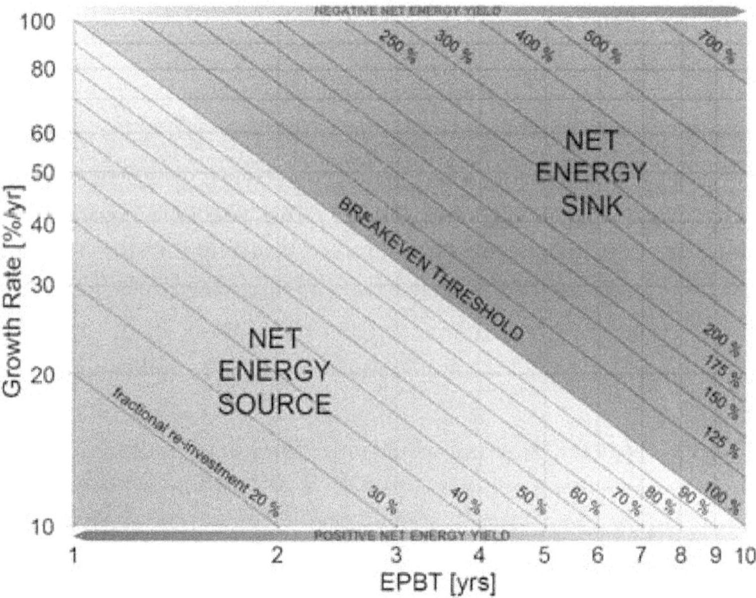


**Figure 2.2.6** Conceptual energy balance. This figure shows growth rate (%/yr) as a function of energy payback time (EPBT) (yrs) for a number of fractional reinvestment rates (%) (diagonal lines).
*Source*: Carbajales-Dale, M. (2015). Fueling the energy transition: The net energy perspective. GCEP Workshop on Net Energy Analysis at Stanford University, April 1, 2015.

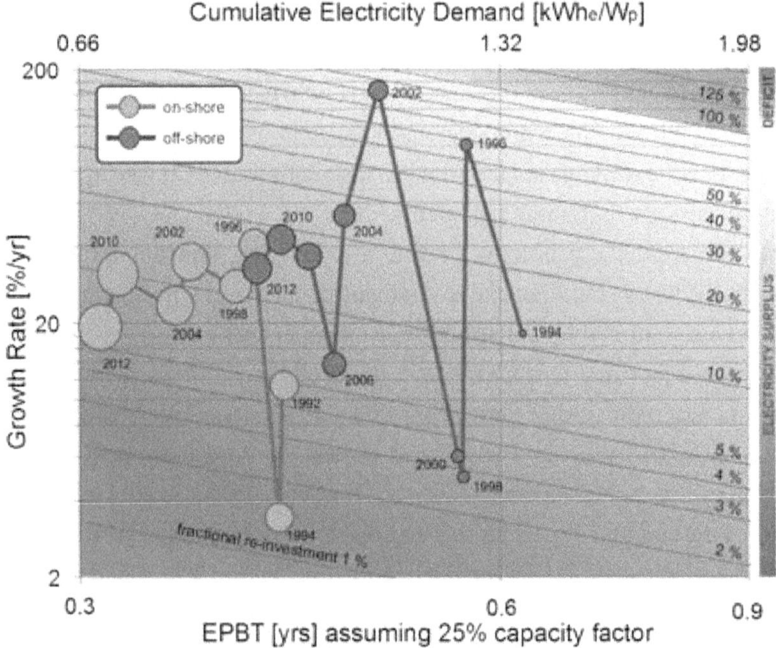


**Figure 2.2.7** Wind energy payback period.
*Source*: Carbajales-Dale, M. (2015). Fueling the energy transition: The net energy perspective. GCEP Workshop on Net Energy Analysis at Stanford University, April 1, 2015.

stage is steep, then the net energy available from that technology during the ramp-up period will be significantly lower than the gross energy produced by the installed generators (Figure 2.2.5).

This also means that, from an energy standpoint, a rapid deployment of solar and wind generators will almost certainly be subsidized mostly by fossil fuels. Which in turn implies that, during at least part of the transition period, society will need *more* energy from fossil fuels than it is currently deriving—unless existing energy demand can be throttled down, while a larger proportion of remaining fossil energy consumption is devoted to all the activities needed to build and deploy wind turbines and solar panels.

Another scaling challenge for solar and wind comes from the need for raw materials, including rare earth minerals for electromagnets in wind turbines and lithium for batteries. At current rates of installation this is not a significant barrier, but world supplies of these elements are limited and could constrain production; for example, at 10% annual growth in annual extraction rates, currently lithium reserves would last a mere 50 years.[49]

Questions about the technical potential of wind power pose yet another scaling challenge for renewable electricity sources. Early estimates of the potential ranged from ten to a hundred times current total world electricity generation capacity from all sources. Research by Adams and Keith notes "[w]ind resource estimates that ignore the effect of wind turbines in slowing large-scale winds may therefore substantially overestimate the wind power resource."[50] However, other researchers dispute this claim.[51]

Then there are location issues. Older design wind turbines near urban areas have been reported to create low-frequency noises that are disturbing to at least some people (this is not a problem with offshore turbines—at least not for humans).[52] Solar panels can often be unobtrusively sited on rooftops, but producing really substantial amounts of energy from PV or concentrating solar will require real estate. Already, large concentrating solar thermal projects in the deserts of the American Southwest are forcing tradeoffs with habitat for species such as the desert tortoise. In addition, large solar arrays in desert areas require periodic washing of dust in order to maintain high levels of efficiency. Concentrating solar thermal plants need water for cooling as well, but this requires amounts of water that can be significant in these environments.[53]

## Lessons From Spain and Germany

The world is still in the early phases of its renewable energy transition, but some clues about that transition's future, and some lessons on how to optimize it, can be gleaned from the experience of countries that have gone the farthest and fastest. Spain (with 27.4% of its electricity derived from solar and wind in 2014)[54] and Germany (with about 30% of electricity from renewable sources, including hydro)[55] are two of the leaders in this regard, but their stories are very different. And their efforts have both supporters, who characterize the transition so far as a great success, and detractors, who paint it as an expensive failure.

The Iberian Peninsula is sunny and has large wind resources; further, in terms of grid connections with other nations, Spain is relatively isolated. These factors together make the Spanish experience with PV and wind an interesting test case. Spain's experience with the rapid introduction of renewables started in 1997, with early strong support for solar and wind. The government instituted a standard offer (feed-in tariff) policy requiring that utilities purchase electricity generated by renewables at premium rates. Power companies, including Acciona, Endesa, and Iberdrola, saw this as an opportunity to start building their own wind farms. Spain's renewables subsidies led to a nearly 40 fold increase in the wind capacity over the next dozen years to 16.7 GW in 2008.[56]

In 2004, the Spanish government also instituted a generous feed-in tariff of 46 euro cents per kWh for solar. Again, investors rushed to cash in on this lucrative promise of long-term profits, and rates of solar installation soared. The government target for 2008 was 400 MW of new solar capacity; 3,500 MW was actually installed. During 2008, Spain installed more than 2.5 GW of PV capacity, nearly half of the global total that year. At the same time, subsidies supported the construction of nearly 2 GW of generation capacity from large solar thermal electric plants.

Out of necessity, Spain pioneered the integration of large amounts of variable renewable electricity into the grid. The nation's grid operator, Red Eléctrica de España (REE), had argued that it would be impossible to integrate wind power at more than 12% of total electricity demand. However, in 2006 REE built a centralized dispatch system and required all wind farms to connect to it. This was the first system of its kind in the world, and it enabled Spain's wind power to grow to 20% of annual demand in 2014, providing over 60% of electricity at times of peak generation.[57]

**Figure 2.2.8** The Solnova Solar Power Station Near Seville, Spain. (Credit: Abengoa Solar, via Wikimedia Commons.)

But this rapid deployment of renewables meant the government was paying out more in subsidies than it had bargained for. An existing law that set limits on retail electricity rate increases required the government to make up for discrepancies between the utility industry's revenues and costs. By 2009, this rate freeze was causing Spain's utility system to run a deficit of 4 billion euros—roughly 20% above utility company revenues.[58] After the global economic crash of 2008, the Spanish government was simply unable to continue funding such deficits. The sitting center-left government reduced the feed-in tariff rates; in 2012 its center-right successors froze renewable energy incentives and introduced a complicated system that rewarded renewable energy producers even less.

Today Spain's renewable energy transition is moving very slowly. In retrospect, failures of the boom years can probably be chalked up to a combination of bad policies that failed to pay fairly for electricity and that lacked an upper limit on subsidies, and bad luck in the form of the global financial crisis.[59]

Germany offers a more encouraging example. Its *Energiewende*, or energy transition, has historical roots reaching back to the 1970s, when popular skepticism of nuclear power and support for renewables were already decisive political issues. Like their Spanish colleagues, German policy makers believed that early subsides for renewables would eventually lead to much lower prices for solar and wind—as they indeed have. But in Germany, subsidies have been more consistently managed. Feed-in tariffs were instituted in 2004 and have been modified many times since. As of July 2014, subsidized rates for PV electricity ranged from 12.88 euro cents per kWh for small rooftop systems to 8.92 euro cents per kWh for large utility-scaled systems.[60]

Today in Germany, wind, solar, and biomass combined account for almost the same portion of net electricity production as brown coal (biomass was 39% of the total).[61] Peak generation from the combined wind and solar achieved 74% of total electricity production in April 2014.[62] In terms of generating capacity, Germany reached its 2010 target for wind power in 2005, its solar target for 2050 in 2012.

**Figure 2.2.9** An Enercon Wind Farm in Lower Saxony, Germany. (Credit: Philip May, via Wikimedia Commons.)

The 2011 Fukushima nuclear disaster in Japan led Germany's government to rethink the nation's reliance on nuclear power. Chancellor Angela Merkel announced the immediate, permanent shutdown of 8 of its 17 reactors and pledged to close the rest by the end of 2022. As a result, the largest four German utility companies—all owners of nuclear power plants—have seen declining electricity output. Meanwhile, the nation doubled down on its determination to develop renewable energy sources.

Germany has not only encouraged large-scale renewable energy systems but has also financed enormous numbers of distributed household- and community-sized generators. Six percent of German households were producing their own energy in 2014, and 20% said they aimed to do so by the end of the decade.[63] Compare this to California, where household solar ownership rates are about 1.2%.[64] Similarly, rather than relying only on grid-scale storage, Germany has created incentives for homeowners to add batteries to their residential PV systems.[65]

> The *Energiewende* does have its detractors. A recent *Wall Street Journal* opinion piece noted, "Average electricity prices for companies have jumped 60% over the past five years because of costs passed along as part of government subsidies of renewable energy producers. Prices are now more than double those in the U.S. Yet nearly 75% of Germany's small- and medium-size industrial businesses say rising energy costs are a major risk, according to a recent survey by PricewaterhouseCoopers and the Federation of German Industry."[66] However, businesses are not fleeing the country as a result. In fact, it could be said that manufacturing is flourishing in Germany to a greater degree than in the United States, where electricity is so much cheaper: in 2012, industrial production made up 30.7% of the German economy, while it comprised only 20.6% of the U.S. economy.[67] Perhaps the biggest difference between critics and boosters of the energy transition is that critics assume that maintenance of the current largely fossil-fueled electricity system is a viable option, while boosters understand that, even with its challenges, the transition to an all-renewable energy economy is both necessary and inevitable.

What lessons can we take away from the examples of Spain and Germany? Subsidies for renewable electricity are still necessary, as are coordinated efforts to integrate and manage variable solar and wind inputs to the grid. These technical and economic issues are important, but perhaps less daunting than potential political roadblocks. As a recent analysis puts it, "The rapid deployment of large volumes of renewables requires both political will and a consistent policy."[68] When new governments overturn strong renewable energy policies instituted by previous governments, potential investors in wind and solar flee and may be shy to return. The nations that have had the most success with the renewable energy transition have implemented some form of feed-in tariff as a subsidy and have stuck with that basic strategy even while adjusting tariffs somewhat as generation costs and other factors changed. Though solar and wind electricity prices have fallen significantly, it is difficult to imagine the renewables transition occurring at greater than old-plant replacement speed without such subsides or incentives.

## Pushback Against Wind and Solar

The recent rapid growth of wind and solar has posed problems for utility companies. As more and more solar and wind electricity generation capacity is installed—and this applies especially to rooftop solar—the utility companies' current business model faces an existential threat. Solar panel owners benefit from electricity free of generation costs, but utility companies have to pay for grid maintenance and are now forced to deal with uncontrollable energy inputs that may have to be offset, shed, or stored—and that costs money. The solar owner benefits, the utility pays.

Utilities are stuck with the bill for grid upgrades and grid-scale energy storage and, absent government subsidies, have no choice but to pass these costs on to customers in the form of higher rates. But then, facing higher grid rates, customers who can afford stand-alone solar systems may see it as being in their long-term advantage to go off grid. This hypothetical self-reinforcing feedback process has been called the utility death spiral.[69]

A 2010 study from the German Renewable Energies Agency concluded that nuclear power is inherently "incompatible with renewable energies."[70] Because solar and wind generators require no fuel, they can be the cheapest sources of electricity at the moment of production (their "levelized cost" includes payment on capital); therefore, renewable electricity is often used as much as possible when it is available (though policies such as renewable portfolio standards [RPSs] play a role in this regard as well). When this happens, fossil-fueled and nuclear plants are throttled back if there is too much power relative to immediate demand—but not all power plants can do this. Older nuclear and coal power plants that can't be throttled back easily are therefore poorly suited for an electricity system with large and growing amounts of intermittent solar and wind power.

In the United States, utility companies—especially ones with large investments in nuclear and coal—have begun a coordinated campaign whose first phase included a push for state laws raising prices for solar customers. This has largely failed in legislatures around the country, as solar energy has proven popular even with political conservatives. More recently, the effort has centered on public utility commissions, where utility industry representatives have pushed for solar fee hikes, including high monthly charges for net metering, which pays solar customers for electricity they feed into the grid.[71]

Costs to utility companies from the introduction of distributed solar PV are somewhat balanced by the fact that the added solar capacity helps reduce the strain on electric grids on summer days when demand soars and utilities must buy additional power at high rates. Nevertheless, as more residential and business customers install their own PV systems, revenues to the utility industry are starting to decline.[72] Industry-sponsored studies warn that the trend could eventually lead to a radical transformation of energy markets, on a scale similar to the restructuring of the telecommunications industry following the advent of the internet and cell phones.

One partial solution is to entirely separate the businesses of power generation and grid operation (a situation that largely already exists in many places). That way, grid operators can concentrate on dealing with the task of optimizing the electricity system for renewable inputs, while nuclear, coal, gas, solar, and wind generators battle among themselves for market share. In any case, there is obviously a need for planning and policy at the governmental level to smooth the transition as much as possible.

* * *

This rather lengthy chapter has explored issues surrounding the renewable energy transition in the electricity sector. It is in this sector where most of the growth in renewable energy has occurred so far. But we must not forget that only about 18% of final energy is consumed in the form of electricity globally (21% in the United States). As we have seen, even in this portion of the overall energy economy, substantial roadblocks to an all-renewable future remain (a very significant one that we will address later is the problem of embedded energy in the electricity sector—energy used in the processes of building and manufacturing solar panels, wind turbines, storage devices, and the rest of the infrastructure that will make up the renewable electricity system of the future). The next two chapters explore nonelectricity uses of energy, which pose their own, often greater, challenges.

## Endnotes

1. International Energy Agency, "World: Balance (2012)." International Energy Agency, "United States: Final Consumption (2012)," accessed October 1, 2015, http://www.iea.org/sankey/#?c=United States&s=Final consumption.
2. BP, "Data Workbook—Statistical Review 2015," accessed October 2, 2015, http://www.bp.com/en/global/corporate/energy-economics/statistical-review-ofworld-energy/downloads.html.
3. BP, "Data Workbook—Statistical Review 2015."
4. Chris Mooney, "Here's How Much Faster Wind and Solar Are Growing Than Fossil Fuels," *Washington Post*, March 9, 2015.
5. Vishal Shah, Jerimiah Booream-Phelps, and Susie Min, "2014 Outlook: Let the Second Gold Rush Begin," Deutsche Bank, January 6, 2014, https://www.deutschebank.nl/nl/docs/Solar_-_2014_Outlook_Let_the_Second_Gold_Rush_Begin.pdf.
6. Deborah Lawrence, "Investment in Solar Stocks Crushed Big Oil," *Energy Policy Forum*, November 4, 2014, http://energypolicyforum.com/2014/11/04/investment-in-solar-stocks-crushed-big-oil/.
7. James. Martinson, "The True Benefits of Wind Power," *Newsweek*, April 21, 2015,http://www.newsweek.com/true-benefits-wind-power-323595.
8. U.S. Energy Information Administration, "Table 6.7.B. Capacity Factors for Utility Scale Generators Not Primarily Using Fossil Fuels, January 2013–July 2015," accessed October 2, 2015, http://www.eia.gov/todayinenergy/detail.cfm?id=11991.

9. Michael Dale and Sally M. Benson, "Energy Balance of the Global Photovoltaic (PV) Industry: Is the PV Industry a Net Electricity Producer?" (see chap. 1, n. 6).

10. Mark Schwartz, "Stanford Scientists Calculate the Carbon Footprint of Grid-Scale Battery Technologies," *Stanford Report*, March 5, 2013, http://news.stanford.edu/news/2013/march/store-electric-grid-030513.html.

11. U.S. Energy Information Administration, "Pumped Storage Provides Grid Reliability Even with Net Generation Loss," *Today In Energy*, July, 8, 2013, http://www.eia.gov/todayinenergy/detail.cfm?id=11991.

12. Charles Barnhart and Sally Benson, "On the Importance of Reducing the Energetic and Material Demands of Electrical Energy Storage," *Energy & Environmental Science* 6, no. 4 (2013): 1083–92, doi:10.1039/C3EE24040A.

13. Tom Murphy, "Pump Up the Storage," *Do the Math*, November 15, 2011, accessed October 2, 2015, http://physics.ucsd.edu/do-the-math/2011/11/pump-up-the-storage/.

14. David Biello, "Inside the Solar-Hydrogen House: No More Power Bills—Ever," *Scientific American*, June 19, 2008, http://www.scientificamerican.com/article/hydrogen-house. See also Shannon Page and Susan Krumdieck, "System-Level Energy Efficiency Is the Greatest Barrier to Development of the Hydrogen Economy," *Energy Policy* 37, no. 9 (2009): 3325–35, doi:10.1016/j.enpol.2008.11.009.

15. Matthew Pellow et al., "Hydrogen or Batteries for Grid Storage? A Net Energy Analysis," *Energy and Environmental Science* 8 (2015): 1938–52, doi:10.1039/C4EE04041D.

16. Matthew Pellow et al., "Hydrogen or Batteries for Grid Storage?"

17. Alice Friedemann, "Making the Most Energy Dense Battery from the Palette of the Periodic Table," *Energy Skeptic*, April 15, 2015, http://energyskeptic.com/2015/making-the-most-energy-dense-battery-from-the-palette-of-the-periodic-table/.

18. Mark Schwartz, "Stanford Scientists Calculate the Carbon Footprint of Grid-Scale Battery Technologies."

19. Mark Schwartz, "Stanford Scientists Calculate the Carbon Footprint of Grid-Scale Battery Technologies."

20. Charles Barnhart, Michael Dale, Adam Brandt, and Sally Benson, "The Energetic Implications of Curtailing versus Storing Solar-and Wind-Generated Electricity," *Energy & Environmental Science* 6, no. 10 (2013): 2804–10.

21. Kris De Decker, "Off-Grid: How Sustainable Is Stored Sunlight," *Low-Tech Magazine*, accessed October 1, 2015, http://www.lowtechmagazine.com/2015/05/sustainability-off-grid-solar-power.html.

22. Shalke Cloete, "The Fundamental Limitations of Renewable Energy," *Energy Collective*, September 6, 2013, http://theenergycollective.com/schalk-cloete/257351/fundamental-limitations-renewable-energy.

23. Mark Jacobson et al. "Low-Cost Solution to the Grid Reliability Problem with 100% Penetration of Intermittent Wind, Water, and Solar for All Purposes," *Proceedings of the National Academy of Sciences USA* 112, no. 49 (December 8, 2015): 15060–65, doi:10.1073/pnas.1510028112.

24. International Energy Agency, Energy Technology Systems Analysis Programme and International Renewable Energy Agency, *Thermal Energy Storage: Technology Brief*, January 2013, https://www.irena.org/DocumentDownloads/Publications/IRENA-ETSAP%20Tech%20Brief%20E17%20Thermal%20Energy%20Storage.pdf.

25. Kurt Zenz House, "The Limits of Energy Storage Technology," *Bulletin of the Atomic Scientists*, January 20, 2009, http://thebulletin.org/limits-energy-storage-technology.

26. Florian Steinke, Philipp Wolfrum, and Clemens Hoffmann, "Grid vs. Storage in a 100% Renewable Europe," *Renewable* Energy 50 (February 2013): 826–32, doi:10.1016/j.renene.2012.07.044.

27. T. Mai, D. Sandor, R. Wiser, and T. Schneider, *Renewable Electricity Futures Study: Executive Summary* (Golden, CO: National Renewable Energy Laboratory, 2012), http://www.nrel.gov/docs/fy13osti/52409-ES.pdf.

28. Electric Power Research Institute, *Estimating the Costs and Benefits of the Smart Grid*, March 29, 2011, http://my.epri.com/portal/server.pt?Abstract_id=000000000001022519.

29. Lannis Kannberg et al., GridWiseTM: *The Benefits of a Transformed Energy System*, Pacific Northwest National Laboratory, (Springfield VA: U.S. Department of Commerce, September 2003), http://arxiv.org/pdf/nlin/0409035v1.pdf.

30. William Atkinson, "Beyond Deployment Smart Meter Maintenance, Repair and Replacement," *Intelligent Utility*, January/February 2009, http://www.intelligentutility.com/magazine/article/107546/beyond-deployment-smart-meter-maintenance-repair-and-replacement. See also K. T. Weaver, "Congressional Testimony: 'Smart' Meters Have a Life of 5 to 7 Years," *Smart Grid Awareness*, October 29, 2015, http://smartgridawareness.org/2015/10/29/smart-meters-have-life-of-5-to-7-years/.

31. Marco Silva, Hugo Morais, and Zita Vale, "An Integrated Approach for Distributed Energy Resource Short-Term Scheduling in Smart Grids Considering Realistic Power System Simulation," *Energy Conversion and Management* 64 (2012): 273–88, accessed October 3, 2015, http://www.sciencedirect.com/science/article/pii/S0196890412002087.

32. Elizabeth Boyle, "V2G Generates Electricity—and Cash," *University of Delaware UDaily*, December 9, 2007, http://www.udel.edu/PR/UDaily/2008/nov/car112807.html.

33. Pekka E. Kauppi et al., "Returning Forests Analyzed with the Forest Identity," *Proceedings of the National Academy of Sciences* 103, no. 46 (2006): 17574–79.

34. REN21, *Renewables 2014 Global Status Report* (Paris: Ren21 Secretariat, 2014), 31–37, http://www.ren21.net/status-of-renewables/global-status-report/.

35. REN21, *Renewables 2014 Global Status Report*, 13.

36. REN21, *Renewables 2014 Global Status Report*, 13.

37. The International Energy Agency estimates that the world can double hydroelectric output by 2050, https://www.iea.org/topics/renewables/subtopics/hydropower/, accessed October 1, 2015.

38. REN21, *Renewables 2014 Global Status Report*, 39.

39. On induced seismicity, see Geoscience Australia, *Induced Seismicity and Geothermal Power Development in Australia*, (undated), http://www.ga.gov.au/corporate_data/66220/66220.pdf.

40. REN21, *Renewables 2014 Global Status Report*, 38

41. Benjamin Matek, *2015 Annual U.S. & Global Geothermal Power Production Report*, Geothermal Energy Association (2015), 15, http://geo-energy.org/reports.aspx.

42. Idaho National Laboratory, *The Future of Geothermal Energy: Impact of Enhanced Geothermal Systems (EGS) on the United States in the 21st Century* (U.S. Department of Energy, November 2006), https://mitei.mit.edu/system/files/geothermal-energy-full.pdf. Adam Goldstein and Ralph Braccio, *2013 Market Trends Report: Geothermal Technologies Office* (U.S. Department of Energy, January 2014), vi, http://www1.eere.energy.gov/geothermal/pdfs/market-report2013.pdf.

43. See for example T. Mai et al., *Renewable Electricity Futures Study Volume 1: Exploration of High-Penetration Renewable Electricity Futures* (Golden, CO: National Renewable Energy Laboratory, 2012), http://www.nrel.gov/docs/fy12osti/52409-1.pdf.

44. Lauren Frayer, "Tiny Spanish Island Nears Its Goal: 100 Percent Renewable Energy," *National Public Radio*, September 28, 2014, http://www.npr.org/sections/parallels/2014/09/17/349223674/tiny-spanish-island-nears-its-goal-100-percent-renewable-energy.

45. See, for example, The Solutions Project, http://thesolutionsproject.org/.

46. "Will Renewables Replace Fossil Fuels?," recorded discussion with Mark Jacobson, David Blittersdorf, and Tom Murphy, *The Energy Xchange*, September 1, 2015, https://energyx.org/will-renewables-replace-fossil-fuels.

47. Massachusetts Institute of Technology Energy Initiative, *The Future of Solar Energy* (2015), xii–xx, http://mitei.mit.edu/futureofsolar.

48. Michael Dale and Sally Benson, "Energy Balance of the Global Photovoltaic (PV) Industry: Is the PV Industry a Net Electricity Producer?"

49. Ugo Bardi, *Extracted: How the Quest for Mineral Wealth Is Plundering the Planet* (White River Jct., VT: Chelsea Green, 2014), 131.

50. Amanda Adams and David Keith. "Are Global Wind Power Resource Estimates Overstated?" *Environmental Research Letters* 8, no. 1 (2013): 015021, http://iopscience.iop.org/article/10.1088/1748-9326/8/1/015021.

51. Kate Marvel, Ben Kravitz, and Ken Caldeira, "Geophysical Limits to Global Wind Power," *Nature Climate Change* 3 (2013), 118–21, http://www.nature.com/nclimate/journal/v3/n2/full/nclimate1683.html.

52. Alice Salt, "Wind Turbines Can Be Hazardous to Human Health," Cochlear Fluids Research Laboratory, Washington University, St. Louis, April 2, 2014, http://oto2.wustl.edu/cochlea/wind.html.

53. Dave Levitan, "Is Anything Stopping a Truly Massive Build-Out of Desert Solar Power?" *Scientific American*, July 1, 2013, http://www.scientificamerican.com/article/challenges-for-desert-solar-power/.

54. Red Eléctrica de España, "The Spanish Electricity System 2014" (REE: Madrid, 2015), 11, http://www.ree.es/sites/default/files/downloadable/the_spanish_electricity_system_2014_0.pdf.

55. Fraunhofer ISE, "Annual Electricity Generation in Germany," accessed October 1, 2015, https://www.energy-charts.de/energy.htm.

56. BP, "Data Workbook—Statistical Review 2015," http://www.bp.com/en/global/corporate/energy-economics/statistical-review-of-world-energy/downloads.html.

57. Red Eléctrica de España, "The Spanish Electricity System 2014."

58. Toby Couture, "Booms, Busts, and Retroactive Cuts: Spain's RE Odyssey," *E3 Analytics*, February 2011, http://www.e3analytics.eu/wp-content/uploads/2012/05/Analytical_Brief_Vol3_Issue1.pdf.

59. Andres Cala, "Renewable Energy in Spain Is Taking a Beating," *New York Times*, October 8, 2013, http://www.nytimes.com/2013/10/09/business/energy-environment/renewable-energy-in-spain-is-taking-a-beating.html?_r=0; Toby Couture, "The Lesson in Renewable Energy Development from Spain," *Renewable Energy World*, July 30, 2013, http://www.renewableenergyworld.com/rea/news/article/2013/07/a-lesson-in-renewable-energy-development-from-spain.

60. Harry Wirth, ed., *Recent Facts about Photovoltaics in Germany* (Freiburg: Fraunhofer ISE, 2015), 10, https://www.ise.fraunhofer.de/en/publications/veroeffentlichungen-pdf-dateien-en/studien-und-konzept-papiere/recent-facts-about-photovoltaics-in-germany.pdf.

61. Bruno Burger, *Electricity Production from Solar and Wind in Germany in 2014* (Freiburg: Fraunhofer ISE, December 29, 2014), https://www.ise.fraunhofer.de/en renewable-energy-data.

62. Kiley Kroh, "Germany Sets New Record, Generating 74% of Power Needs from Renewable Energy," *Climate Progress*, May 13, 2014, http://thinkprogress.org/climate/2014/05/13/3436923/germany-energy-records/Germany/.

63. Craig Morris, "Rebuttal: Renewables Make Millions of Germans Multidozenaires," *Renewables International*, May 16, 2014, http://www.renewablesinternational.net/renewables-make-millions-of-germans-multidozenaires/150/537/78900/.

64. California Energy Commission and California Public Utilities Commission, "California Solar Statistics: Program Totals by Administrator," accessed October 25, 2015, https://www.californiasolarstatistics.ca.gov/reports/agency_stats/.

65. Solar Server, "Energy Transition 2.0: Energy Storage and Solar PV," October 15, 2013, http://www.solarserver.com/solar-magazine/solar-report/solar-report/energy-transition-20-energy-storage-and-solar-pv.html.

66. Matthew Karnitschnig, "Germany's Expensive Gamble on Renewable Energy," *Wall Street Journal*, August 26, 2014, http://www.wsj.com/articles/germanys-expensive-gamble-on-renewable-energy-1409106602.

67. World Bank, World Development Indicators, "Industry, Value Added (% of GDP)," accessed October 1, 2015, http://data.worldbank.org/indicator/NV.IND.TOTL.ZS.

68. Christian Roselund and John Bernhardt, "Lessons Learned along Europe's Road to Renewables," *IEEE Spectrum*, May 4 2015, http://spectrum.ieee.org/energy/renewables/lessons-learned-along-europes-road-to-renewables.

69. Christopher Helman, "Will Solar Cause a Death Spiral for Utilities?," *Forbes*, January 30, 2015, http://www.forbes.com/sites/energysource/2015/01/30/will-solar-cause-a-death-spiral-for-utilities/.

70. Janine Schmidt, "Renewable Energies and Base Load Power Plants: Are They Compatible?," *Renews Special* 35 (June 2010), German Renewable Energies Agency, http://www.unendlich-viel-energie.de/media/file/302.35_Renews_Special_Renewable_Energies_and_Baseload_Power_Plants.pdf. See also Chris Nelder, "Why Base Load Power Is Doomed," *ZDnet*, March 28, 2012, http://www.zdnet.com/article/why-baseload-power-is-doomed/.

71. Joby Warrick, "Utilities Wage Campaign against Rooftop Solar," *Washington Post*, March 7, 2015, http://www.washingtonpost.com/national/health-science/utilities-sensing-threat-put-squeeze-on-booming-solar-roof-industry/2015/03/07/2d916f88-c1c9-11e4-ad5c-3b8ce89f1b89_story.html.

72. Joby Warrick, "Utilities Wage Campaign against Rooftop Solar."

## DISCUSSION QUESTIONS

1. One of the challenges of renewable-based electricity generation is intermittency. A storage system can help make up for the variability of solar and wind energy. What are the currently available storage systems (focus on the systems introduced)? Compare them by the metric energy stored on investment (ESOI) value.
2. Smart grid systems and dynamic pricing can control the limitations of renewable-based electricity supply. What are the two systems? How do they work to reduce power consumption during peak hours and incorporate grid energy storage?
3. Solar and wind-based renewable energies have been grown quickly, and there is increasing hope for a 100% renewable-based electricity system. However, there are still financial, energy, and environmental hurdles in the path toward scaling up these sources at the rates needed. Discuss the financial, energy, and environmental limitations to scaling up the renewable-based electric system.

READING 2.3

# The Convention on International Trade in Endangered Species of Wild Fauna and Flora (CITES)

## Responding to Calls for Action from Other Nature Conservation Regimes

By John Lanchbery

The Convention on International Trade in Endangered Species of Wild Fauna and Flora (CITES) is unusual among international environmental regimes in that its main mode of operation, the regulation of international trade, tends to drive it to interact and cooperate with a number of nonenvironmental institutions, in particular concerning trade. From its entry into force in 1975, it has thus worked not only via its parties and their domestic police and customs organizations but also directly with the World Customs Organization (WCO), the International Criminal Police Organization (Interpol), and the General Agreement on Tariffs and Trade (GATT) that later became part of the World Trade Organization (WTO).

Furthermore, CITES interacts with a number of other international regimes concerning the conservation of wildlife,[1] of which CITES is probably the leading example and has in some ways formed the center. Wildlife conservation regimes often work together as a group of treaties, assisting each other to meet common objectives. This is because they share a common, overall goal (the conservation of wild animals or plants), but differ either in the species they cover or in the way they pursue the goal. Thus, while CITES regulates international trade in endangered species, the Convention on Migratory Species of Wild Animals (CMS) provides for conservation measures "on the ground," the International Convention on the Regulation of Whaling restricts the taking of whales, and so on.

John Lanchbery, "The Convention on International Trade in Endangered Species of Wild Fauna and Flora (Cites): Responding to Calls for Action from Other Nature Conservation Regimes," *Institutional Interaction in Global Environmental Governance: Synergy and Conflict among International and EU Policies,* ed. Sebastian Oberthür and Thomas Gehring, pp. 157–179.

The fact that the conservation agreements are interrelated in this way is no accident. Many of them have common origins, often in the form of calls for their establishment by the World Conservation Union (IUCN), and they were often specifically designed to operate in different but complementary ways. The IUCN was the initial instigator of most of the major wildlife treaties concluded in the second half of the twentieth century, including both CITES and the CMS. Cooperation between the wildlife treaties is actively promoted by the IUCN, both directly and via the secretariats to the treaties, which it commonly provides with the United Nations Environment Program (UNEP).

This chapter focuses mainly on the interactions between CITES and two other nature conservation regimes: the CMS and the Convention for the Conservation and Management of the Vicuña (Convenio para la Conservación y Manejo de la Vicuña, CCMV). These cases of interaction were selected chiefly because they are examples of how the nature conservation treaties often act in concert and of the central role of CITES in this. In particular, they demonstrate how regimes with limited memberships have used CITES, with its larger, global membership, to assist them in meeting common nature conservation goals. CITES responded to a call for action by the CMS to protect the Asiatic subspecies of the houbara bustard, a bird recognized as endangered by both CITES and the CMS. The CCMV asked CITES for assistance in protecting the vicuña, which was again recognized as threatened by both regimes.

The chapter begins with a description of CITES, its origins, and its mode of operation. It then provides an overview of the interactions of CITES with a broad range of other international institutions and EU legislative instruments. Subsequently, the two cases of interaction with the CMS concerning the houbara bustard and the CCMV concerning the vicuña are investigated in greater detail. In each case, the other treaty is described and an account of the concrete case of interaction is provided. The chapter ends with some general conclusions.

## The Convention on International Trade in Endangered Species of Wild Fauna and Flora (CITES)

CITES seeks to protect wild species by regulating trade in both the species themselves and products made from them. Its aim is to conserve endangered species, but it does so by attempting to control trade. In doing so, it implicitly recognizes that it is often hard for international regimes to effectively prescribe what their parties should do at home, whereas it can be comparatively easy to regulate an international activity, such as trade.

CITES' focus on attempting to limit trade appears to be well justified. International trade in wildlife is enormous, and controlling it to sustainable levels would undoubtedly do much to conserve many species. The Directorate General Environment of the European Commission estimates that international wildlife trade, both legal and illegal, is worth at least U.S.$10–20 billion annually. From

1995 to 1999, legal trade in CITES-listed species alone involved 1.5 million live birds, 640,000 live reptiles, about 3 million reptile skins, 150,000 furs, almost 300 tons of caviar, over 1 million pieces of coral, and 21,000 hunting trophies (Mulliken 2002).

The idea of limiting international trade in endangered species is not new. It dates back to the first decade of the twentieth century, when there was a call for a treaty limiting trade in the exotic bird feathers then used in ladies' hats (Lyster 1985). Later, the 1933 London Convention on the preservation of fauna and flora in Africa included provisions for restricting trade and also introduced the concept of having easily changeable annexes or appendixes listing endangered species (Lyster 1985; Sand 1997). Many later regional fauna and flora treaties followed the example of the London Convention, paving the way for the global CITES agreement that limits trade in species listed in exactly the same way (Lanchbery 1995).

Substantive political moves for a global agreement on trade in endangered species began in the 1950s, together with other wildlife agreements, notably the Ramsar Convention on Wetlands (Lyster 1985; Burns 1990). In 1963, the Governing Council of the IUCN called for "an international convention on regulating the export, transit and import of rare or threatened fauna and flora species or their skins or trophies."[2] Subsequent progress on negotiating a treaty was, however, slow until the 1972 Stockholm United Nations Conference on the Human Environment reemphasized the need for such an agreement. By March 1973 CITES had been negotiated and signed by its first twenty-one parties (Sand 1997). By spring 2005 it had 167 parties (http://www.cites.org), the largest membership of all wildlife conservation treaties, of which it is very much the "flagship" (Wijnstekers 2003).[3]

The main features of the mode of operation of CITES are three appendixes that are reviewed and can be changed at its Conference of the Parties (COP), which has met roughly every two years. The first appendix lists species in which trade is banned in all but the most exceptional circumstances. Appendix II includes species not necessarily threatened with extinction, but in which trade must be controlled in order to "avoid utilization incompatible with their survival" (Article II.2.a of CITES). Appendix III contains species that are protected in at least one country, which has asked other CITES parties for assistance in controlling the trade (Article II).

The treaty lays down detailed rules governing the import and export of species or products made from them. It also requires parties to establish national Management Authorities and Scientific Authorities. It further determines that the COP to CITES should meet every two years. Some operational features of the treaty have evolved considerably over time, extending and strengthening the remit of CITES over and above the provisions in the original text of the treaty (Wijnstekers 2003). It has, for example, set up a Standing Committee to oversee the operation of the agreement between COPs as well as other committees that assist the parties in making decisions on the classification of species. It has also developed a compliance and enforcement mechanism operated by the Secretariat and the Standing Committee. This mechanism includes the possibility of banning all wildlife trade with recalcitrant states. Throughout the 1990s, for example, the Standing Committee banned such trade with a number of countries, including Italy, Thailand, and Greece, until they came into compliance (Lanchbery 1995; Reeve 2002).

No description of CITES, or almost any wildlife treaty, is complete without a description of the role of the IUCN. Founded on October 5, 1948, as the International Union for the Protection of Nature (IUPN), the organization changed its name to the International Union for the Conservation of Nature and Natural Resources (IUCN) in 1956. In 1990 this was shortened to IUCN–The World Conservation Union. It called for many of the conservation agreements and helps considerably in their operation, by providing information concerning endangered species and by providing services such as secretariats, often with UNEP (Lanchbery 1995). Indeed, the IUCN's "Red Lists" of endangered species of wild animals and plants that are produced by the Species Survival Commission of the IUNC (http://www.redlist.org) largely drive the listing of species in CITES appendixes.

The IUCN is a complex and unusual international organization in that it has a large and varied membership of both states and nongovernmental organizations (NGOs). In 2002, its membership comprised 675 national NGOs, 68 international NGOs, 72 states (i.e., governments), and 107 government agencies. This unique combination of members makes it both a source of excellent, reliable information and, because of its governmental membership alone, a powerful force to be reckoned with. It has a large permanent staff, of in excess of 1,000, with 10,000 expert volunteers (http://www.iucn.org).

CITES and the other wildlife conservation treaties also have strong links with the more conventional wildlife NGOs, almost all of which are members of the IUCN. Notable among these are the World Wide Fund for Nature (WWF), the World Conservation Monitoring Centre (WCMC), Trade Records Analysis of Fauna and Flora in Commerce (TRAFFIC), and, especially in the case of treaties with a significant wild-bird interest (such as the CMS and Ramsar), BirdLife International. Both the WCMC and TRAFFIC were originally set up by WWF but are now independent of it. The WCMC has in the meantime been incorporated in UNEP.

These organizations play a key part in the operation of CITES and the CMS. Indeed, the IUCN, WCMC, and TRAFFIC are formally recognized as the "technical partners" in CITES. They provide much of the information about science and about infractions that the regime needs in order to operate effectively. The IUCN's "Red Lists" of endangered species are based heavily on information from organizations such as BirdLife International and WWF and misbehavior by parties is often reported to the CITES Secretariat by TRAFFIC (Lanchbery 1995; Reeve 2002).

## Interactions and Synergies with Other Institutions

CITES has been involved in many interactions with other international institutions and EU legal instruments. Fourteen such interactions between CITES, involving seven other international institutions and the EU, are summarized in table 2.3.1. This list is not exhaustive but covers many pertinent cases. In most cases, extensive and lasting cooperation and exchanges between CITES and the other institutions have developed in response to the initial interinstitutional influence indicated in the table.

**Table 2.3.1** Interactions of CITES

| | |
|---|---|
| Convention for the Conservation and Management of the Vicuña (CCMV) | • CCMV has asked CITES for help in limiting trade in vicuña products and CITES has responded positively with a COP Resolution. |
| International Convention on the Regulation of Whaling (ICRW) | • The ICRW has asked for help in restricting trade in whale products and CITES has responded positively with a COP Resolution. |
| Convention on Migratory Species of Wild Animals (CMS) | • In response to a call for action by CMS, CITES passed a COP Resolution in support of CMS concerning the houbara bustard. |
| Convention on Biological Diversity (CBD) | • CITES supports implementation of the CBD; several decisions and resolutions in both institutions promote cooperation and synergy. |
| World Trade Organization (WTO) | • CITES restricts free trade and thus is in potential conflict with the WTO; it allows for trade with nonparties complying with its obligations. |
| World Customs Organization (WCO) | • CITES asked the WCO for help in implementation.<br>• In response, WCO supports implementation of CITES by helping coordinate CITES enforcement and training via its members (national customs organizations). There is a CITES/WCO memorandum of understanding on cooperation.<br>• CITES asked WCO to change customs codes (e.g., for shark products). |
| International Criminal Police Organization (ICPO, Interpol) | • CITES asked Interpol for help in implementation and enforcement.<br>• In response, Interpol supports implementation of CITES. There is a CITES/ICPO memorandum of understanding on cooperation, a CITES/ICPO Wildlife Crime Working Group, and work on joint training. |
| EU Regulation on trade in endangered species | • The EU (then: the EEC) adopted a regulation to control wildlife trade in 1982 in response to CITES, although it was not a party to CITES.<br>• CITES concerns about abolition of internal border controls caused the EU to strengthen its CITES Regulation in 1997 (revised in 2001).<br>• CITES Regulation of the EU supports the implementation of CITES. |
| EU Single Market Program | • Abolition of intra-EU border controls for goods and persons endangers effective implementation of CITES trade restrictions in the EU. |

## Horizontal Interactions with Other International Institutions

While it is hard to generalize about all CITES interactions from what is not an exhaustive list, all the horizontal interactions between international institutions were synergistic or neutral, or they were managed successfully so that tensions were prevented from turning into open conflict. The interaction with the WTO is the only one in which the underlying relationship was disruptive because the WTO promotes free trade, which is restricted by CITES. The commitments of both institutions are potentially at odds (Interaction through Commitment). This is not to say that political conflict did not occur about the political responses to interinstitutional influence. For example, a minority of parties (the remaining nations that conduct whaling) vigorously opposed the CITES decision to restrict trade in whale products in response to a request by the International Convention on the Regulation of Whaling and lodged reservations to it (for an account of the changes in the whaling regime and its impacts elsewhere, see Andresen 1998). The request as such, however, was fully in line with the conservation objective of CITES.

With the exception of the interaction with the WTO, all other cases of interaction followed the causal mechanisms of Cognitive Interaction and Behavioral Interaction. All cases in which CITES asked other institutions for support, or vice versa, constituted Cognitive Interaction because the decision on whether to respond favorably to the request for help was made completely voluntarily by the targets. The request as such included no substantive carrots or sticks that could have motivated the target, but drew the latter's attention to the needs of the requesting institution. The positive response of the WCO and Interpol as well as the UN Food and Agriculture Organization (FAO; see chapter 6) to the request by CITES then contributed to a more effective implementation of CITES (Behavioral Interaction). The implementation of CITES itself contributes to achieving the objective of the Convention on Biological Diversity (CBD) to protect biological diversity (see also chapter 4).

CITES has "natural" synergies with many other environmental institutions, particularly those concerning wildlife conservation. These arise from the fact that these treaties often have either the same or overlapping aims, basically to conserve wildlife and, more generally, biological diversity. These treaties include global agreements such as the Convention on Migratory Species, the CBD, and a host of regional agreements, such as that on the conservation of the vicuña. This synergy tends to be reinforced by the fact that they typically employ different means to achieve their ends: CITES restricts wildlife trade, the CMS provides for protection measures "on the ground," and so on. Rather than compete, the regimes therefore usually complement each other, often with one regime asking another to support it in attaining a particular goal, as in the case of the interactions recounted later.

That CITES has been a prominent target for requests for help from other regimes may be due to the fact that it has the largest membership, possibly the greatest influence, and certainly the highest public profile of the wildlife regimes.

The interactions of CITES with nonenvironmental institutions are quite different from those with wildlife treaties. Because CITES seeks to influence international trade it clearly should, in order to be effective, attempt not to come into conflict with and, if possible, benefit from other bodies concerning trade, notably the World Customs Organization (WCO), the International Criminal Police Organization (ICPO, Interpol), and the WTO.

Because of the institutions' different modes of operation, the potential for conflict between CITES and the WTO is greater than with the WCO and Interpol. The WCO and Interpol tend to act in many ways as trade associations whereas the WTO, like CITES, aims to regulate and control behavior—that is, international trade. The WCO and Interpol mainly aim to foster cooperation among their members, for example by providing education and training programs. The request for help in implementation originally issued by CITES to both WCO and Interpol was thus compatible with their overall aims, although it also did not promise to facilitate achieving their primary aims. Both organizations responded positively and have since supported the effective implementation of CITES, for instance by providing focused training to national customs and police officers (Reeve 2002). CITES has also long had memoranda of understanding with the WCO and Interpol, which were updated in 1999 in the drive for greater effectiveness by CITES. The CITES Secretariat sits on Interpol's Wildlife Crime Working Group.

As indicated above, the relationship between CITES and the WTO has been more problematic but has been managed successfully so as to avoid open conflict so far. Like other trade-related multilateral environmental agreements (chapter 8), CITES restricts international trade, but it promotes compatibility of its provisions with international trade rules by allowing parties to trade products regulated by CITES with nonparties that essentially comply with CITES requirements. While not all tensions may have been removed, no dispute related to CITES has yet arisen under the WTO. A cooperative and amicable relationship between both institutions is further promoted by the CITES Secretariat that sits on the WTO's Committee on Trade and Environment (CTE).

CITES has actively promoted synergy with other international agreements in order to maximize its effectiveness, and has had a formal policy of doing so since the early 1990s. The need to promote synergy, in general, was first formally raised at the ninth meeting of the Conference of the Parties (Fort Lauderdale 1994) in the Strategic Plan of the Secretariat (CITES 1994). At the tenth Conference of the Parties, this need was reiterated in the context of a review of the effectiveness of the Convention, and a decision was adopted calling for intensified and extended cooperation with other conventions (CITES Decision 10.110). This led the Secretariat to produce a document for the CITES Standing Committee at its forty-second meeting in 1999 titled *Synergy Between the Biodiversity-Related Conventions and Relations with Other Organizations* (CITES 1999), which contains various recommendations spanning a wide scope. In practice, members of the secretariats of wildlife agreements regularly attend others meetings. Also, CITES and the CMS concluded a memorandum of understanding concerning the need to work more closely together in September 2002.

Nevertheless, cooperation is often far from perfect, as the CITES Secretariat pointed out in the 1999 synergies paper:

> The need now to develop synergy and provide better policy coordination among existing and future agreements is obvious. This particularly applies to the so-called biodiversity-related MEAs: CITES, the Convention on Biological Diversity (CBD), the Convention to Combat Desertification (CCD), the Convention on Migratory Species (CMS) and the Convention on Wetlands (Ramsar). Although these Conventions address different aspects of the same issue, the risk of some overlap and duplication of effort is evident. (CITES 1999, 1)

## Vertical Interactions with EU Legal Instruments

Although the EU is not a party to CITES, its legislation has interacted "vertically" with CITES in several ways. The interaction has relied on the fact that most EU member states have always been parties to CITES and have in large part relied on the EU for the implementation of their commitments. Even though CITES was officially amended in 1984 to allow for membership of regional economic integration organizations (i.e., the EU), the EU has not been in a position to join CITES because the amendment still awaits sufficient ratifications for entry into force. In the meantime, Ireland was the last EU member state to join CITES in 2000. Since all ten states that joined the EU in 2004 are also parties to CITES, all EU member states are now CITES parties.

Facilitated by the fact that (most) EU member states were committed to implementing CITES controls (Interaction through Commitment), the EU acted, synergistically, in many ways as though it were a member by implementing CITES in EU legislation. As early as 1982 it developed a Regulation (EEC No. 3626/82) for implementing CITES within the EU, which came into force in 1984. As elaborated below, it has since revised and updated this legislation to ensure compliance with CITES requirements. It set up a CITES Committee and an Enforcement Working Group and established a common reporting format. It also imposed trade sanctions against states for noncompliance with CITES, for example by banning trade in endangered species with Indonesia in 1992 (Reeve 2002, 126).

The significance of this EU implementation of CITES is that it activates the particularly effective supranational enforcement powers of the EU that subsequently support an effective implementation of CITES in the EU (Behavioral Interaction). Evidence for this synergistic effect of the EU implementation is found in enforcement activities of the European Court of Justice. In 1990, for example, the Court found that France had unlawfully issued import permits for 6,000 wildcat skins from Bolivia (Reeve 2002, 113).

Another part of the EU's "acquis communautaire," however, increasingly endangered the effective implementation of CITES since the 1980s and thus had a disruptive effect at the behavioral level. The Single European Act of 1987 introduced a legislative program that aimed at the complete abolition of internal border controls. This added to concerns raised by other parties because it would endanger an effective implementation of CITES in the EU. The effectiveness of CITES enforcement within the EU would essentially be determined by the member state with the most lax external import and export controls. CITES responded to this challenge by adopting a number of resolutions calling on the EU and its member states to ensure a more effective implementation of CITES (Reeve 2002, 112–120).

The EU's eventual response (after fifteen years) was new Council Regulation (EC) No. 338/97 and Commission Regulation (EC) No. 939/97, which came into effect on June 1, 1997. These conceded that the new regulations were needed to "adequately reflect the current structure of trade" and "cope with the abolition of internal border controls which resulted from the Single Market. The abolition of internal borders has made necessary the adoption of stricter trade control measures at the Community's external borders." In 2001 Commission Regulation (EC) No. 939/97 was replaced by Commission Regulation (EC) No. 1808/2001.

## The Interaction between CITES and the CMS Concerning the Houbara Bustard

### The Origins and Operation of the CMS

In the 1960s, the IUCN General Council drew international attention to the plight of many migratory animals and called for a treaty to protect them. As in the case of CITES, this call was reinforced by the 1972 Stockholm Conference, in its Recommendation 32 (CMS 2002). After a long gestation period, the treaty was concluded in Bonn in 1979 and entered into force in November 1983.

As in the case of many postwar wildlife treaties, the CMS was constructed as a framework agreement that allows its commitments to be expanded or changed over time. Like CITES, it achieves this by having two revisable appendixes that list species needing protection. Species can be listed on both appendixes. The first lists species having "unfavorable conservation status," which countries within the natural range of a migratory animal (range states) are obliged to protect. The second lists species for which completely new subagreements are required. In other words, the CMS is deliberately designed to spawn new agreements. There are now agreements on African-Eurasian migratory waterbirds, small cetaceans of the Baltic and North Seas, European bats, and the Great Bustard and six other species or sets of species (see the CMS website at http://www.cms.int for the latest information on agreements).

Originally, it was intended that only full, legally binding new subagreements (Agreements with a capital A) would be set up, but it soon became apparent that nonbinding memoranda of understanding could be usefully employed as well, and so both are now used. Which is employed is largely a practical decision. Where few parties with a record of cooperation are involved, memoranda are commonly used, because they can be agreed on more quickly and avoid the need for formal ratification.[4]

Both Agreements and memoranda are usually developed with one party taking a lead in drafting it. The party selected should be both a range state for the species involved and have knowledge of and expertise in it. In the case of the interaction covered here, the lead on the houbara bustard was taken by Saudi Arabia.[5]

In the context of this study, it is significant that the CMS has more limited participation (by states) than some other wildlife conservation agreements that are also, nominally, global in scope. Notable absentees from the list of CMS parties are the United States, Russia, Canada, Mexico, and Brazil. The reasons for lack of participation vary. The United States, for example, claims that existing arrangements with its neighbors make participation unnecessary. However, many states that are not parties to the CMS itself still participate in its Agreements and memoranda. The United States and Russia are, for example, parties to such agreements. Nevertheless, it can still assist the CMS in achieving its aims if it can elicit the support from other institutions with wider participation, such as, in this case, CITES.

## The Interaction

The houbara bustard (*chlamydotis undulata*) is a rare and endangered species of large terrestrial bird (IUCN 2002). There are two subspecies: the Asiatic, which is migratory, and the North African, which is not (BirdLife International 2000). Only the former, migratory population (*chlamydotis undulata macqueenii*) therefore potentially qualifies for inclusion in the CMS although both populations are eligible for inclusion in, and are included in, the CITES appendixes. The Asiatic subspecies of the houbara bustard is included in Appendix I of CITES.

*Chlamydotis undulata macqueenii* breeds mainly in Central Asia and migrates to the Arabian peninsula during the period October to March. Throughout most of their vast range the houbara's numbers have long been in decline. The reasons for this decline appear to be habitat destruction, through overgrazing and intensive farming in their breeding areas, coupled with overhunting, human disturbance, and overtrapping in countries through which they migrate (BirdLife International 2001).

The Asiatic subspecies of the houbara bustard has long been on the IUCN "Red Lists" and therefore, within the CMS, it was recognized as having "unfavorable conservation status" and requiring either an Agreement or a memorandum of understanding between range states. The first institutional call for concerted action was made at the third Conference of the Parties of the CMS (COP Resolution 3.2) in 1991. The call was repeated at the fourth COP in 1994 (Resolution 4.4). CMS Resolutions are less targeted than its Decisions, and generally intended to provide long-standing guidance. They are politically important because they indicate a strong desire by the COP for parties to take action.

As a result of these Resolutions, Saudi Arabia offered to take the lead in drafting an agreement, either binding or nonbinding. Saudi Arabia is both a range state for the houbara bustard and has considerable knowledge of it. It was also the Asia representative on the Standing Committee of the CMS, which provides policy and administrative guidance between regular COPs. The Standing Committee consists of seven representatives of the main regions and includes the depositary (Germany) and the host of the next COP (http://www.cms.int). It was generally accepted that drafting an action plan would probably not be hard, given Saudi Arabia's expertise on the bustard.[6]

The status of the bustard was then raised, again, at the fifth COP of the CMS in April 1997 (Recommendation 5.4), by which time Saudi Arabia had prepared a draft agreement. Without specifically mentioning CITES, the Recommendation merely reiterated the need to conserve the bustard and for range states to assist Saudi Arabia with the agreement. In addition, IUCN's World Conservation Congress had highlighted the poor conservation status of the houbara bustard in 1996 (Recommendations 1.27 and 1.28). Recommendation 1.27 was a general call for the protection of two species of the houbara bustard and mentions the CMS and CITES in the context of many countries being obliged to protect it under these agreements (it being listed in the appendixes of both). Recommendation 1.28 specifically calls on range states to conclude an agreement under the CMS quickly and to assist Saudi Arabia in doing so.

Shortly after the CMS COP 5, CITES met for its tenth COP in June 1997. The parties to CITES were already familiar with the plight of the Asiatic species of the bustard: it had long been included in the IUCN's Red Lists and had been listed in CITES Appendix I. A number of countries that were parties to both CITES and the CMS (and the IUCN) now used the call for action passed by the CMS COP, as reinforced by the IUCN's World Conservation Congress, to raise the issue within CITES and bring it to the attention of other CITES parties. Realerted of the need for urgent action, the majority of CITES parties had no direct stake in the Asiatic houbara bustard and were thus sympathetic to further supporting its protection, as suggested by the initiators.

As a result, the CITES COP passed Resolution 10.11 on the houbara bustard that responded to the call for action by the CMS, as reinforced by the IUCN, without having been specifically asked to do so. The resolution mentioned all three of the CMS and IUCN resolutions and called on range states to take domestic action to protect the bustard. This was not particularly unusual, because CITES often echoes calls both from other nature conservation conventions and the IUCN. However, in its Resolution 10.11, CITES also "calls upon all range states of the Asiatic subspecies of the houbara bustard (chlamydotis undulata macqueenii) to review the Draft Agreement officially circulated by the Government of Saudi Arabia and communicate their comments to the National Commission for Wildlife Conservation and Development (NCWCD), Riyad, Saudi Arabia." This was a remarkable action for CITES to take because it called on CITES parties to take a highly specific action in support of a decision taken by another institution.

Following the CMS and CITES resolutions in 1997, there was a long delay and little progress was made on the CMS agreement. Indeed, in 1999, COP 6 of the CMS passed a further recommendation (6.4) on the subject. However, by COP 7, in 2002, matters were moving along more satisfactorily, as Resolution 7.7 states:

> i. [The COP] *Takes note* of the information provided by the representative of the Kingdom of Saudi Arabia that an updated text of an Agreement and Action Plan on the Asiatic populations of the Houbara Bustard is ready for official dissemination and comment;

ii. *Takes further note* that an informal meeting to review the updated text will be held some time in early 2003; and

iii. *Welcomes* the information that the Kingdom of Saudi Arabia will hold a meeting of the Range States to conclude the Agreement and Action Plan in late 2003.

## Discussion and Conclusions

Although the CMS had not issued a formal request for help to CITES, it was still influential in bringing about the action by CITES supporting the protection of the houbara bustard under the CMS. Having been alerted by several parties and the IUCN who employed the related CMS call for action (as reinforced by IUCN), CITES was cognizant of the CMS decisions about the houbara bustard, mentioning the most recent one in the preamble to its resolution. Even without a formal request, the knowledge about the need for urgent action as expressed in the CMS decisions changed the situation within CITES by raising awareness and enhancing support for action by CITES. The ensuing CITES resolution was thus a result of Cognitive Interaction (figure 2.3.1).

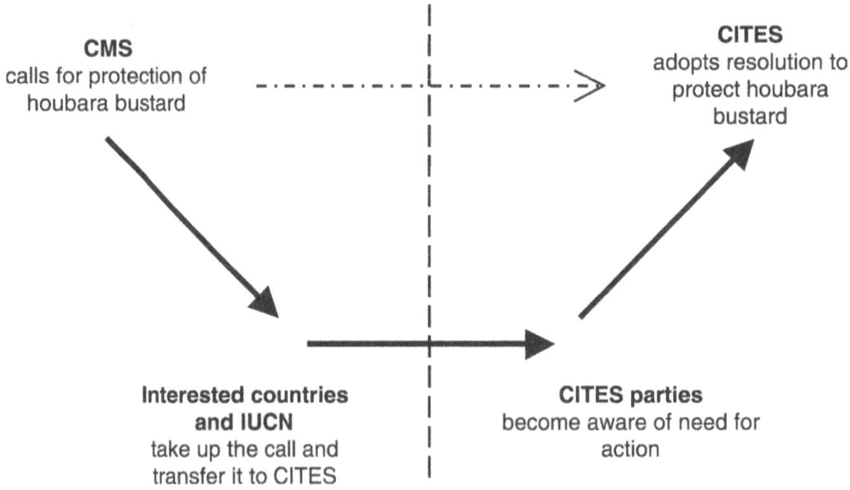


**Figure 2.3.1** Convention on Migratory Species triggers CITES action on Houbara Bustard

Interestingly, the CITES resolution calls on both CMS parties and nonparties (in the form of range states) to take action under the CMS, rather than CITES. In most cases of one institution assisting another, the supporting institution would call for action within its own sphere of competence or influence. CITES might, for example, call for trade sanctions in support of another regime. In this case, the houbara bustard was already subject to trade regulation (being listed in CITES Appendix I) and CITES was calling for action under the auspices of the CMS, rather than itself.

Furthermore, the interaction demonstrates the way nature conservation treaties act in support of one another, with the IUCN facilitating such support both with scientific information and via its access to both parties and institutions. It was the IUCN Red Listing that first alerted CITES and the CMS of the need for action on the houbara bustard. The recommendations of the IUCN World Conservation Congress then reinforced the calls for action of the CMS and helped transmit them to CITES, which responded by asking for action in the CMS.

The question remains, however, why CITES should bother to help the CMS in this case, when the bustard was already protected by CITES. The answer, most probably, lies in the fact that CITES has a far larger membership than the CMS. In particular, more of the range states for the Asiatic houbara bustard are parties to CITES than are parties to the CMS. Given that it is common for states that are not parties to the CMS to join Agreements or memoranda of understanding concluded under it, CITES asking for help from range states for the bustard makes considerable sense. As can be seen from table 2.3.2, only four of the twenty-four range states for the houbara were parties to the CMS at the end of 1997 (although several range states participate in CMS subagreements without becoming parties to the CMS itself, such as Iran, Russia, China, Oman, and Yemen). CITES membership in 1997 included more than three times as many range states (thirteen). The fact that there are so many range states for the bustard, many of which are parties to neither CITES nor the CMS and many of which are poorer developing countries with more pressing priorities than the environment, may also help to explain why it is taking so long to conclude an Agreement.

**Table 2.3.2** Membership of Range States of the Houbara Bustard in CITES and CMS at the end of 1997

| Range States of chlamydotis undulata macqueenii (from IUCN Red List) | Whether party to CMS | Whether party to CITES |
|---|---|---|
| Afghanistan | Not a party | Party |
| Armenia | Not a party | Not a party |
| Azerbaijan | Not a party | Not a party |
| Bahrain | Not a party | Not a party |
| China | Not a party | Party |
| India | Party | Party |
| Iran | Not a party | Party |

*(Continued)*

**Table 2.3.2** *(Continued)*

| Range States of chlamydotis undulata macqueenii (from IUCN Red List) | Whether party to CMS | Whether party to CITES |
|---|---|---|
| Iraq | Not a party | Not a party |
| Israel | Party | Party |
| Jordan | Not a Party | Party |
| Kazakhstan | Not a party | Not a Party |
| Kuwait | Not a party | Not a party |
| Lebanon | Not a party | Not a party |
| Mongolia | Not a Party | Party |
| Oman | Not a party | Not a party |
| Pakistan | Party | Party |
| Qatar | Not a party | Not a Party |
| Russian Federation | Not a party | Party |
| Saudi Arabia | Party | Party |
| Syria | Not a party | Not a party |
| Tajikistan | Not a Party | Not a party |
| Turkmenistan | Not a party | Not a party |
| United Arab Emirates | Not a party | Party |
| Uzbekistan | Not a Party | Party |
| Yemen | Not a party | Party |

*Source*: http://www.cites.org and http://www.cms.int.

## The Interaction with the Convention for the Conservation and Management of the Vicuña (CCMV)

### The Vicuña and the Convention Covering It

The vicuña (*vicugna vicugna*) is the smallest species of the South American Camelidae, which include the llama, guanaco, and alpaca (Torres 1987). It lives on the high Andean plateaus. At the time of the Incas, vicuñas were an important source of wool and meat. The main product was, however, their wool and so they were normally captured, shorn, and released into the wild again, maintaining the population at an estimated 1.5 million (Grizmek 1990). Vicuña numbers dropped with the coming of the Spanish. During the nineteenth and twentieth centuries, there was a huge commercial demand for the wool, which is very soft and can be woven into delicate fabrics. Because the vicuña was then killed for its wool, rather than being "farmed" as in the time of the Incas, by 1960, vicuña numbers had fallen to only 6,000 (Torres 1987; Mendoza 1987).

Since the conclusion of the vicuña protection treaties and increased domestic efforts to conserve them in their range states, the vicuña population had risen to 125,000 by 1990 (Nowak 1991). By 2002 numbers stood at about 150,000 (http://www.iucn.org). The vicuña was until recently classified as vulnerable by the IUCN in its Red Lists but has recently been downgraded to lower risk. It was originally listed in Appendix I (endangered) of CITES although, as numbers have risen, populations have increasingly been transferred to Appendix II (threatened).

The origins of the vicuña convention are in a bilateral treaty concluded in 1969 between Bolivia and Peru, in La Paz. The agreement declared that the vicuña was a "species on the way to extinction" (Preamble) and all commercial exploitation of the species or products made from it was prohibited for a period of ten years. During the following decade, Chile and Argentina joined the agreement. In October 1979 a meeting was held in Lima at which the four parties to the agreement were joined by Ecuador. On December 20, 1979, the treaty was amended to include the five countries at the meeting, whose territories include all of the current natural range of the vicuña. While the vicuña does not occur naturally in Ecuador, it was introduced later on. The agreement was also extended indefinitely and named the Convention for the Conservation and Management of the Vicuña (Torres 1987).

The treaty prohibits hunting of the vicuña and their live export, with exception of those used for scientific purposes or for display in legally established zoological gardens. It also bans trade in vicuña wool, hair, skins, and items manufactured from them and the manufacturing itself within the territories of the parties, except under special license. Licensed products nowadays bear a special CCMV logo. The parties are obliged to establish and maintain reserves and centers for raising the vicuña. In addition, they are obliged to conducting awareness raising and training activities.

As in the case of other wildlife agreements, the CCMV works closely both with environmental regimes (including CITES) and with environmental groups. Cooperation with the IUCN's Species Survival Commission Specialist Group on South American Camelids—which serves CITES as well—is particularly close.[7] The CCMV also works closely with WWF and with UNEP, which funds some of the IUCN work on vicuñas. Indeed, a compendium of resolutions of the Conference of the Parties to the CCMV has an entire section devoted to relationships with the IUCN, WWF, and TRAFFIC (Government of Argentina 2004). Over the years, the CCMV has cooperated closely with CITES. Indeed, between 1980 and 2000 the CCMV passed twenty-four resolutions concerning and involving CITES. Many of them concerned listings in the CITES appendixes, but the CCMV has also repeatedly tried to improve its effectiveness by having CITES ask its parties to restrict trade in vicuña products, particularly cloth made from vicuña wool (Government of Argentina 2004).

## The Interaction

Although territories of the parties to the CCMV cover the entire natural range of the vicuña, most demand for the valuable vicuña wool, and products made from it, comes from highly developed countries that are not parties to the CCMV. The very long, often extremely rugged borders of the CCMV parties, coupled with the fact that these countries are not wealthy, makes it hard for them to effectively control the illegal export of vicuña wool and cloth. Controlling their import into highly developed countries may provide effective complementary protection. Since the 1980s, the CCMV has thus repeatedly called on CITES to ask its members, which include all relevant importing developed countries, to help it to restrict trade in vicuña products (Government of Argentina 2004).

Interaction between the CCMV and CITES concerning vicuña wool and cloth began in 1987 when the CCMV passed Resolution 56/87. It asked the CITES Secretariat to recommend to all CITES parties that had stocks of vicuña cloth and wool to submit a list of those stocks, as soon as possible, to the CITES Secretariat, which would forward them to the CCMV. The CITES Secretariat acted accordingly by issuing a notification (number 472) to CITES parties asking them to respond. The idea was to enable an accurate assessment of globally, and legitimately, held stocks so as to better be able to track which trades were of legally held stocks and which were likely to be illegal.

This call was apparently not effective because, at its twelfth meeting in 1990, the CCMV issued a reminder to CITES about declaring stocks, CCMV Resolution 97/90. This also pointed out that all legally exported wool and cloth should bear CCMV official markings (logos). The logo was to enable a clear distinction between legal and illegal trades in wool and cloth. CITES responded by passing Resolution 8.11 concerning notification of stocks of wool and cloth, and markings, at its eighth COP in Kyoto in 1992.

This too was apparently not completely effective because in 1994 the CCMV fired off two more resolutions (133/94 and 137/94) to CITES, reminding it of CCMV resolutions 56/87 and 97/90, again concerning stocks of wool or cloth and their marking. The CCMV COP also passed two additional resolutions on listings in CITES appendixes and another on wool. The former two resulted in an amendment to CITES Resolution 8.11 at the tenth CITES COP in Harare in 1997.

Eventually, the CCMV's point about declaring stocks of wool and cloth seem to have been heeded, but the point about using the official CCMV logo on all cloth would appear not to have been acted on by all parties. At CITES COP 11 in Kenya in 2000, yet another resolution (11.6) was passed, essentially reiterating the previous resolutions. After first reminding the CITES parties of previous CCMV and CITES resolutions, it recommends that parties should "only authorize the import of vicuña cloth if the reverse bears the logotype corresponding to the country of origin and the trade mark VICUÑA—COUNTRY OF ORIGIN or if it is cloth containing pre-Convention wool of vicuña."

## Discussion and Conclusion

This case shows how wildlife conservation treaties often interact so as to support each other in pursuit of common goals. The goal of the CCMV is the conservation of the vicuña and, to the extent that the vicuña is endangered or threatened as a species, this is also part of the objective of CITES. The main reason for the request by the CCMV was that the developed-country parties to CITES are the importers of vicuña products, both legal and illegal. Their controlling imports thus helps considerably in the enforcement of the CCMV, particularly because tight control over exports from the countries of origin is hard. Improving information on stocks of vicuña wool and cloth helped to clarify in which countries they had ended up after export, thereby facilitating the tracking of further trade. Gaining recognition of the CCMV logo helped in the practical enforcement of restrictions on both imports and exports.

The interaction between the CCMV and CITES followed the causal mechanism of Cognitive Interaction (figure 2.3.2). The requests of the CCMV were not supported by any carrot or stick so that CITES was completely free in its choice of whether and how to respond. The request was easily brought to the attention of CITES parties because it was explicitly directed at them. The secretariats and CCMV members that were also parties to CITES transmitted the relevant CCMV decisions. These decisions drew the attention of CITES parties to the enforcement problem concerning the protection of the vicuña, which they may otherwise have ignored. Once alerted, most CITES parties had little reason to oppose the request that implied action only by a limited number of developed countries.

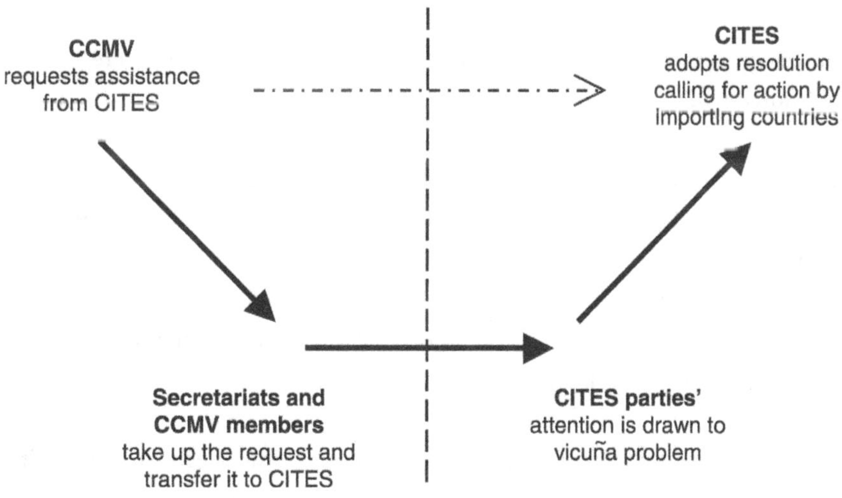


**Figure 2.3.2** Vicuña Convention requests CITES assistance

Ostensibly, the interaction between the CCMV and CITES appears to have been effective because assistance by CITES occurred as requested and vicuña numbers rose. However, numbers were rising prior to the interaction, and the resurgence of the vicuña appears to have been primarily due to domestic measures to protect and manage them. Having said this, the trade measures pursued by CITES in response to the CCMV have probably made a limited positive contribution, but it is hard to quantify their practical effect.

## Conclusion

CITES actively and systematically strives to improve synergy with other institutions. The Convention works particularly closely with other international nature conservation regimes, as facilitated by several international and nongovernmental organizations. This is partly because the nature conservation regimes were designed to complement each other and share the common goal to conserve nature, and partly because they have evolved closer links over time. The role of the IUCN in forging these links has been considerable by, for example, providing information on which species are endangered and threatened by means of its Red Lists, which are used by all wildlife treaties.

In this study, horizontal interactions between CITES and other international institutions were either found to be synergistic or managed successfully so as to prevent tensions from turning into open conflicts. There have notably been tensions between CITES and the WTO, but CITES carefully manages its relationships so as to avoid conflict and promote synergy. This is facilitated by the fact that the overlap in membership between such large global institutions is considerable, and it seems unlikely that states would knowingly pursue one course of action in one forum and an opposing course of action in another.

There have been political conflicts between CITES and the EU, mainly as a result of CITES trying to improve enforcement. However, these conflicts have been handled in productive ways so as to eventually create synergistic effects. As early as 1982, the EU passed legislation that enhanced the effective implementation of CITES in the Union by subjecting it to the supranational EU enforcement powers. When the EU abolished internal border controls in the 1980s and 1990s, however, this potentially endangered effective implementation and enforcement of CITES restrictions on wildlife trade, leading to rising concerns of CITES and considerable political conflict. Eventually, the EU responded by strengthening its internal legislation and other implementation measures. In the end, the interaction thus produced synergistic results.

A common cause of the synergistic interactions between CITES and other wildlife treaties is that the latter try to use the greater membership of CITES to increase the effectiveness of their enforcement, as was at least partially the case in both interactions detailed here. However, in spite of the efforts by the institutions concerned, the interactions of CITES with the CMS and the CCMV demonstrate that interaction is often less successful in achieving tangible results "on the ground." It usually results in institutional action in the form of a COP decision or recommendation, but these do not necessarily have the desired practical effect.

This is because there is, perhaps, too much belief in the extent to which interactions between international regimes, or action by the regimes themselves, can achieve concrete, practical outcomes, especially regarding enforcement. This is particularly so in the case of organizations such as the WCO, which is designed to foster cooperation rather than enforcement. Ultimately, enforcement must mainly occur domestically, as seems to be demonstrated by the CITES/CCMV case concerning vicuña wool and cloth, where it appears to be domestic action—rather than regime interactions—that has caused vicuña numbers to increase.

## Endnotes

1. Throughout this chapter, the term *wildlife* includes both wild fauna and wild flora.
2. Personal communication from Wolfgang Burhenne of the IUCN's International Law Centre in Bonn.
3. The World Heritage Convention had 177 parties in spring 2004 but is not exclusively concerned with wildlife conservation since it covers both cultural and natural heritage.
4. CMS 2002, and personal communications with Arnulf Muller-Helmbrecht, CMS Coordinator.
5. Personal communications within the BirdLife Partnership.
6. Personal communications from the BirdLife Partnership. The Saudi Arabian government representative in the CMS—the National Commission for Wildlife Conservation and Development, NCWCD—is the Saudi Arabian BirdLife Partner.
7. For more details on the group see the IUCN Species Survival Commission website at http://www.iucn.org/themes/ssc/sgs/sgs.htm#SACSR.

## References

Andresen, Steinar. 1998. The Making and Implementation of Whaling Policies: Does Participation Make a Difference? In David G. Victor, Kal Raustiala, and Eugene B. Skolnikoff, eds., *The Implementation and Effectiveness of International Environmental Commitments: Theory and Practice*, 431–474. Cambridge, MA: IIASA/MIT Press.

BirldLife International. 2000. *Threatened Birds of the World.* Barcelona and Cambridge: Lynx Edicions/BirdLife International.

BirdLife International. 2001: *BirdLife's Online World Bird Database: The Site for Bird Conservation.* Version 1.0. Cambridge: BirdLife International.

Burns, William C. 1990. CITES and the International Regulation of International Trade in Endangered Species of Flora: A Critical Appraisal. *Dickinson Journal of International Law* 8 (2): 203–223.

CITES. 1994. CITES Secretariat. *Strategic Plan of the Secretariat.* 9th Conference of Parties, Fort Lauderdale, Florida, 1994. CITES Doc. 9.17.

CITES. 1999. CITES Standing Committee. *Synergy Between the Biodiversity-Related Conventions and Relations with Other Organizations.* Forty-second meeting of the Standing Committee, Lisbon (Portugal), September 28–October 1, 1999. CITES Doc. SC.42.17.

CMS. 2002. CMS Secretariat. *Guide to the Convention on the Conservation of Migratory Species of Wild Animals,* January 2002. Available at http://www.unep-wcmc.org/cms/pdf/CMS_Guide_Jan02_en.pdf.

Government of Argentina. 2004. *Resoluciones de la Comisión Técnico-Administradora del Convenio de la Vicuña, Reuniones Ordinarias (Analizadas y Extractadas) 1980–2000.* Available at http://www.medioambiente.gov.ar/fauna/programas/manejo/proyecto_vicuna/convenio/default.htm.

Grizmek, Bernhard. 1990. *Grizmek's Encyclopedia of Mammals.* Volume 5. New York: McGraw-Hill.

IUCN. 2002. *The IUCN Red List of Threatened Species.* IUCN Species Survival Commission, Gland, Switzerland: IUCN–The World Conservation Union. Available at http://www.redlist.org/search/details.php?species=4702.

Lanchbery, John. 1995. Reviewing the Implementation of Biodiversity Agreements. In John B. Poole and Richard Guthrie, eds., *Verification 1995*, 327–350. Boulder, CO: Westview Press/VERTIC.

Lanchbery, John. 1998. Long-Term Trends in Systems for Implementation Review in International Agreements on Fauna and Flora. In David G. Victor, Kal Raustiala, and Eugene B. Skolnikoff, eds., *The Implementation and Effectiveness of International Environmental Commitments: Theory and Practice*, 57–87. Cambridge, MA: IIASA/MIT Press.

Lyster, Simon. 1985. *International Wildlife Law.* Cambridge: Grotius.

de Mendoza, Luis Hurtado. 1987. Notas Arqeológicas y Etnohistoricas acerca de la Vicuña en el Antiguo Perú (Notes about the Vicuna in Old Peru). In Hernàn Torres, ed., *Tecnicas para el Manejo de la Vicuna*, 13–23. IUCN Species Survival Commission, South American Camelid Specialist Group, UNEP. Cambridge: IUCN.

Mulliken, Teresa. 2002. Wildlife and Livelihoods. *World Conservation* 3 (special issue on "The Species Trade—CITES in the New Millennium"), 14–15.

Nowak, Ronald M. 1991. *Walker's Mammals of the World.* 5th ed. Baltimore: Johns Hop-kins University Press.

Reeve, Rosalind. 2002. *Policing International Trade in Endangered Species: The CITES Treaty and Compliance.* London: Earthscan.

Sand, Peter H. 1997. Commodity or Taboo? International Regulation of Trade in Endangered Species. In Helge Ole Bergesen, Georg Parmann, and Øystein B. Thommessen, eds., *Green Globe Yearbook 1997*, 19–36. Oxford: Fridtjof Nansen Institute and Oxford University Press.

Torres, Hernàn. 1987. Preface. In Hernàn Torres, ed., *Tecnicas para el Manejo de la Vicuna*, 5–7. IUCN Species Survival Commission, South American Camelid Specialist Group, UNEP. Cambridge: IUCN.

Wijnstekers, Willem. 2003. *The Evolution of CITES: A Reference to the Convention on International Trade in Endangered Species of Wild Fauna and Flora.* 7th ed. Geneva: CITES Secretariat.

## DISCUSSION QUESTIONS

1. CITES seeks to protect wild species by regulating trade in both the species themselves and products made from them. It has natural synergies with many other environmental institutions. What are the institutions? Why are they proved to show synergy effects despite their overlapping aims for wildlife conservation?
2. EU developed a Regulation (EEC No. 3626/83) for implementing CITES within the EU, which came into force in 1984. Why is it significant for the EU to implement CITES concerning the efficacy of CITES?
3. Environmentalists believe that the interactions of CITES with the CMS and the CCMV demonstrate that interaction is often less successful in achieving tangible results "on the ground." Using either the interaction between the CITES and the CMS or the interaction between CITES and the CCMV, explain the mechanisms for interactions and limitations to cooperation.

UNIT III

# Contemporary Issues and Toward Sustainable World

READING 3.1

# Public Participation and Environmental Justice

## Access to Federal Decision Making

By Dorothy M. Daley and Tony G. Reames

Executive Order 12898 on Environmental Justice (EO 12898) directs federal agencies to develop broad strategies to identify and address any disproportionate, negative impacts stemming from agency activities and affecting minority and low-income communities. It aims to integrate environmental justice considerations into the standard operating procedures of federal agencies, and in doing so, mitigate the likelihood that minority and low-income communities experience concentrated environmental burdens. By their very nature, environmental justice concerns are not uniformly distributed across the country. Rather, they tend to be local or regional in scale, and the specific details of the environmental justice situation may be unique. For example, contaminated drinking water in the Appalachians, poor air quality in Southern California, or traffic congestion in Houston may disproportionately affect low-income communities, minority communities, or both, but these problems occur on a local or regional scale. Therefore, a "one size fits all" approach to environmental justice is unlikely to be efficient or effective. The diversity and distribution of environmental justice problems pose a considerable challenge to federal agencies charged with implementing the executive order.

Public participation is one mechanism to address this challenge. Effective public participation could not only help identify and characterize environmental justice concerns, but it could also inject critical local knowledge and inform policies and programs to solve environmental justice problems (Dietz et al. 2008). EO 12898 emphasizes the need for widespread public participation to better identify, understand, and tackle environmental justice concerns. Consequently, the definition of environmental justice by the Environmental Protection Agency (EPA) underscores the importance of public participation by calling for "meaningful involvement of all people" in every aspect of environmental decision making.

At the federal level, cultivating and maintaining widespread and diverse public participation to prevent and combat concentrated environmental risk requires significant agency commitment (Dietz at al 2008; Innes and Booher 2004; Foreman 1998). Although EO 12898 tasks federal agencies to increase public participation, to date, there has been limited evaluation aimed at understanding how—after twenty years of implementation—agencies have addressed that charge. This chapter evaluates the ways in which federal agencies utilize public participation to address environmental justice in minority and low-income communities in response to EO 12898.

The chapter begins by examining the research on public participation and environmental decision making in general. Based on this, we highlight the opportunities and challenges of using participation to address environmental justice problems. To better understand how EO 12898 has influenced public participation in federal agencies, we examine the EPA, the agency responsible for leading the federal government's approach on environmental justice. In addition, the chapter compares and contrasts how the EPA, the Department of Energy (DOE), and the Department of Transportation (DOT) utilize public participation to advance environmental justice. Our assessment of these agencies is based upon examining a range of government documents and electronic sources that detail each agency's environmental justice strategy in 1995 and subsequent revisions. In addition, we compiled annual reports from the three agencies, along with any existing evaluations of agency efforts related to implementing the executive order. Material from these sources is integrated with findings from existing research on civic engagement, public participation, and social equity to provide a general assessment of how well each agency has expanded opportunities for public participation in light of the executive order. Finally, the chapter concludes with policy prescriptions for federal agencies as they move forward with their reaffirmed commitment to environmental justice and public participation.

## Public Participation and Environmental Decision Making

Public participation is woven into the fabric of American democracy and it can take a variety of forms. Voting, letter writing, attending public meetings, forming an interest group, or serving on advisory committees are all examples of public participation. In recent decades, public participation has been an increasingly important element of environmental governance (Bulkeley and Mol 2003; Daley 2013; Dietz et al. 2008). Public participation in environmental decision making can be *process-oriented*. For example, public comment periods for permitting, setting standards, and writing and revising regulations are all avenues to engage the public in the process of environmental decision making. In addition, when the EPA or other agencies are in the midst of a particularly controversial environmental issue, they may hold listening sessions, workshops, and seminars to provide additional opportunities to gauge public sentiment on potential changes in advance of a final decision. Public participation can also be more *outcome-oriented*. This type of participation tends to focus on existing environmental hazards resulting from past decisions. Examples include protesting the existence of multiple polluting facilities within one community or serving on a community advisory board for a hazardous waste site that needs to be remediated. Outcome-oriented participation can also advocate for strict enforcement and compliance with existing environmental laws by reporting facilities that might be in violation of those laws.

Environmental decisions tend to be highly technical, complex, and value-laden. Scientific and technical expertise is critical to foster better understanding of the nature of environmental problems and potential solutions. But even when scientific and technical knowledge is combined to inform environmental decisions, conflict and gridlock can remain, particularly when public preferences on the nature and distribution of environmental risks and benefits are poorly understood or not carefully considered (Dietz et al. 2008; Weber 2003; Webler and Tuler 2006). Public participation provides an avenue to gauge public preferences and insert public values into environmental decision making. Recent research suggests that when done well—an important caveat—public participation can increase equity, reduce conflict and gridlock, and lead to improved environmental decision making (Dietz et al. 2008; Klyza and Sousa 2013; Pellow and Brulle 2005). There are a number of ways that public participation could result in these desirable outcomes. Widespread and meaningful participation can add legitimacy to any final decision and enhance overall levels of trust in government. Local knowledge could provide more detailed information on the nature of a problem, along with identifying locally appropriate solutions that capitalize on community norms and in doing so, increase the chances of successful policy implementation (Bulkeley and Mol 2003; Daley 2013; Dietz et al. 2008; Reed 2008).

Conversely, when done poorly, public participation can reduce overall levels of trust in government, increase conflict and gridlock, and highlight weaknesses in both the decision-making process and outcomes from that process. Thus, the promise of public participation hinges on both the quality of the participatory process and the overall ability of stakeholders to engage in the process. Effective or high quality participatory processes tend to have a clear goal, adequate financial and human capital, consistent institutional commitment, an ability for participatory action to influence all stages of decision making, and an emphasis on implementation and evaluation (Beierle and Cayford 2002; Charnley and Engelbert 2005; Dietz et al. 2008; Leach 2006; Reed 2008; and Sirianni 2009).

Most environmental legislation calls for some form of public participation, and EO 12898 is no exception. Traditional participatory mechanisms used in environmental legislation include public hearings and public comment periods for permits, regulations, and other environmental decisions. One-time seminars and workshops, occasional roundtables, and advisory committees are increasingly being utilized to improve the scope and impact of public participation (Innes and Booher 2004; Kellogg and Mathur 2003; Spyke 1999; Beierle 1998; Coglianese 1997). Although some of these approaches to public participation can be more innovative than others, research suggests that as currently implemented, all of these mechanisms tend to result in top-down, expert-driven decision making, despite consistent calls for more bottom-up approaches to public participation (Agyeman and Angus 2003; Dietz et al. 2008; Laurian 2007). Therefore, in their present form, these participatory mechanisms would not be *effective* participatory processes to reduce conflict and gridlock or improve equity (Beierle 1998; Brion 1988; Buchanan 2010; Fine and Owen 2005; Hernandez 1995; Webler and Tuler 2006).

In many instances, both the quality of the participatory process and the ability of stakeholders to engage in that process are compromised (Klyza and Sousa 2013). Determining who represents the affected public and how to broaden the scope of public participants in a decision-making process remains difficult. Government agencies commonly recruit people from organized groups who have expressed interest or are active around a particular issue (Larson and Lach 2008). Although this seems like an efficient strategy, it raises concern about the degree to which organized interests represent the views of a broader community. Relying on this approach to insert public values into decision making may not expand access to new participants, as it tends to result in a similar set of engaged stakeholders taking part in the decision-making process (Coglianise 2006; Agyeman and Angus 2003; Beierle 1998). Comparatively, business interests are much easier to identify and engage in the decision-making process. They have considerable incentive to remain involved in environmental decision making, particularly when decisions directly regulate their behavior. Moreover, these concentrated interests tend to have more resources than other stakeholders, and they are in a better position to shape environmental decision making in their favor (Furlong 2007; Kamieniecki 2006; Yackee and Yackee 2006).

Federal agencies face a complicated decision-making environment: While regulated interests are motivated and likely to remain active in any and all aspects of decision making, engaging the public is far more challenging. Overall levels of civic engagement and public participation in the United States are declining (Macedo et al. 2005). Inconsistent public participation directly limits the ability of this tool to give voice to a diverse public (Dietz et al. 2008; Foreman 1998). Meaningful public participation within federal agencies requires creativity, resources, and a consistent commitment to a participatory process. Since the Reagan era, the federal government has experienced near-constant pressure to devolve responsibilities to state and local government whenever possible. While devolution to subnational governments may provide more opportunity for public participation in state and local institutions (Macedo et al. 2005), it significantly complicates the ability of federal agencies to maintain well-resourced public participation processes.

## Public Participation and Environmental Justice: Opportunities and Challenges

Successfully incorporating public participation into any environmental decision-making process remains a significant opportunity and a challenge. These opportunities and challenges are magnified with environmental justice concerns. Because public participation can increase equity and reduce conflict and gridlock in decision making, it holds tremendous promise for both ameliorating existing environmental justice problems and preventing future concentrated risks. However, this promise is situated in a broader context of racial, economic, and political inequality (Brulle and Pellow 2006; Cole and Foster 2001; Schlozman, Verba, and Brady 2012). Minority and low-income communities are less politically active overall (Rosenstone and Hansen 1993; Schlozman, Verba, and Brady 2012), and historically, they have mobilized less around environmental issues than wealthy, white communities have (Brulle and Pellow 2006; Gauna 1995). The modern environmental movement is largely comprised of white, middle class Americans concerned with natural resource degradation (Baber and Bartlett 2013; Gauna 1995); often, social justice and equity are not on the agenda (Mohai, Pellow, and Timmons Roberts 2009). In contrast, the environmental justice movement is distinctly shaped by the history of civil rights in the United States, as well as grassroots anti-toxics activism stemming from environmental disasters like Love Canal. As a result, there tends to be more outcome-oriented public participation in minority and low-income communities that focus on existing environmental risks in their communities.

Some within the environmental justice community view the disproportionate impact of environmental hazards on minority and low-income communities as a product of the same social structure that produces racial oppression. Others view the concentration of burdens as an intended consequence of dominant economic forces (Brulle and Pellow 2006; Cole and Foster 2001; Foreman 1998). Regardless, either of these causal stories creates significant hurdles in using public participation to advance equity in environmental decision making. Successful public participation in environmental decision making is predicated on trust. As with any collaborative relationship, high levels of trust facilitate productive interactions (Lubell et al. 2005). When that trust is frayed, the promise that public participation would increase equity and reduce conflict and gridlock in decision making becomes more difficult to realize.

Despite this difficulty, public participation can provide critical information regarding the ways in which local residents experience concentrated environmental burdens. From a pragmatic point of view, the expansive geography of the United States and the local or regional scale of environmental justice concerns combine to highlight the need for public participation as an important mechanism to advance environmental justice in federal agencies. But patterns of public participation directly affect the ability of this tool to ameliorate environmental justice concerns. In fact, some contend that public participation in a decentralized political system actually contributes to environmental justice problems (Foreman 1998; Gauna 1995; Munton 1996).

Local grassroots mobilization, described as "Not In My Backyard" or NIMBY, has been a powerful response to environmental risks (Fletcher 2003; Kraft and Clary 1991). Over the years, politically active communities have mobilized successfully to block power plants, hazardous waste sites, landfills, and other locally unwanted land uses (LULUs) from being established in their vicinity. This participatory activity increases the likelihood that LULUs are instead located in communities with lower levels of political mobilization and public participation, which often are minority and low-income neighborhoods. NIMBY can extend beyond siting; local groups may advocate stringent enforcement of laws governing existing facilities within their communities and demand swift action in response to accidents (Gauna 1995), while less organized communities receive less attention. Thus, this type of grassroots activism can facilitate the concentration of environmental risks in minority and low-income communities in multiple ways.

The past several decades have witnessed a consistent increase in opportunities for public participation in almost all aspects of environmental decision making. However, there is little evidence of a corresponding increase in widespread, diverse public involvement. In fact, evidence suggests that levels of civic engagement and public involvement in the United States have declined (Coglianese 2006; Putnam 2000; Sander and Putnam 2010), and existing patterns of participation tend to represent white, wealthy, and educated citizens (Macedo et al. 2005; Schlozman, Verba, and Brady 2012). Minority and low-income communities may face higher barriers to entry for public participation. Public participation requires some general understanding of how agency decisions affect citizens' interests. Lower levels of educational attainment, language barriers (Larson and Lach 2008; Fine and Owen 2005), and limited knowledge about federal decision-making processes or how decisions affect their lives are likely to constrain citizens' motivation to participate (Coglianese 2006).

Despite these challenges, public participation remains an important tool in advancing environmental justice considerations within federal agencies. In 2011, the seventeen agencies covered under EO 12898 declared, "the continued importance of identifying and addressing environmental justice considerations in agency programs, policies and activities"[1] by signing a Memorandum of Understanding on Environmental Justice and Executive Order 12898.

## The EPA, Public Participation, and Environmental Justice

The EPA is the one of the most active federal agencies in terms of incorporating environmental justice into agency activities, and it is also responsible for convening and leading the Interagency Working Group on Environmental Justice. Despite a concerted effort to integrate environmental justice and public participation into agency activities, progress remains uneven (GAO 2011; CCR 2003). In part, this reflects the nature of the participation challenges outlined above, as well as highlighting the challenge of changing bureaucratic behavior. The EPA is a large bureaucracy charged with implementing a wide variety of environmental legislation, including the Clean Water Act (CWA), the Clean Air Act (CAA), the Resource Conservation and Recovery Act (RCRA), the Toxic Substance Control Act (TSCA), and several others, in addition to EO 12898. The agency's duties are scientifically complex and administratively difficult, with decision making often generating conflict across a range of interests, including environmental justice stakeholders. Environmental justice issues may arise in a number of activities for which the agency is responsible, including setting standards, permitting facilities, awarding grants, issuing licenses and regulations, and reviewing proposed actions by other federal agencies.

Public participation is a key element underpinning the EPA's environmental justice strategy as the agency seeks to "work with communities through communication, partnership, research and the public participation process" and also "help affected communities have access to information which will enable them to meaningfully participate in activities" (EPA 1995, p. 3). Shortly after EO 12898 was signed, the agency acknowledged that a host of stakeholders are directly affected by the agency's environmental decisions and therefore "must have every opportunity for public participation in the making of those decisions" (EPA 1995, p. 4). Environmental justice problems tend to be local in nature; therefore, participation and outreach efforts need to be tailored to the specific problem and community context. But this type of customization is complicated. In the first ten years following EO 12898, EPA regional offices relied on different approaches to identifying minority and low-income communities; this variation created significant implementation and evaluation hurdles (EPA 2004). As research on public participation suggests and the EPA's experience highlights, identifying the affected community is challenging (Daley 2013; Dietz et al. 2008; Larson and Lach 2008), and absent this identification, public participation is not likely to yield increases in equity.

Environmental justice staff within the agency have a challenging mission: to integrate environmental justice considerations into all aspects of a major bureaucratic organization and create systemic change, including increasing opportunities for meaningful public participation. Historically, the EPA has been a "stove-piped" organization with separate offices for air, water, and toxics, each operating largely in their own silos. The agency has no overarching legislative agenda, but rather a series of diverse environmental problems to address. Without clear guidance on how to prioritize among divergent environmental efforts, the agency has been criticized as engaging in turf battles (Rosenbaum 2002). Creating meaningful change in a large hierarchical organization requires significant time (up to a decade or longer), consistent commitment from all levels of personnel, considerable resources, and multiple, overlapping strategies (Bardach 1998; Brehm and Gates 2002; Mazmanian and Sabatier 1989; Wilson 1989).

In November 1992, an Office of Environmental Equity (later renamed the Office of Environmental Justice (OEJ)) was created within the agency, and each regional office has environmental justice coordinators to integrate environmental justice into its policies, programs, and activities. Over the last two decades, the agency has relied upon a range of participatory mechanisms to engage minority and low-income communities in environmental decision making. These include public meetings, public notice and comment periods, developing partnerships, conducting seminars and workshops, and convening the National Environmental Justice Advisory Council (NEJAC). Since 1993, NEJAC has been providing independent advice and recommendations to the agency on environmental justice issues. The approximately 26 members of the committee represent stakeholders from academia, business and industry, state and local governments, tribal governments, environmental organizations, community groups, and nongovernmental organizations.

Agency and NEJAC documents note the importance of public participation, and several also highlight successful collaborative relationships, but it is difficult to determine if these success stories are representative of the norm (EPA 1997). Similarly, it is difficult to determine if EPA's general approach to participation has consistently resulted in increased diversity of participation. In 2006, the agency released a series of environmental justice accomplishment reports on their website to highlight environmental justice integration, including public participation, into the agency's decision-making processes.[2] Notably, two (out of ten) regional offices and three (out of nine) offices within the agency's headquarters do not provide accomplishment reports. The available reports provide detailed tables listing the region's or office's activity, output, outcome, and results in relationship to a set of goals and objectives. They provide an excruciating level of detail, but this actually makes understanding the overall progress toward integration more difficult.

For example, one objective from the Office of Air and Radiation (OAR) report included providing opportunities for meaningful involvement between agency staff and affected community members. OAR listed six activities they developed to achieve this goal, one of which was the development of training modules to facilitate public participation in air quality permitting in environmental justice communities. Another activity included year-round monitoring and reporting of the Air Quality Index (AQI). The training module to enhance engagement in air quality permitting was not funded and therefore had no impact on participation. But year-round monitoring and reporting of the AQI led to the development of an e-alert system. This allows individuals to receive electronic air quality information, which can be particularly useful for limiting exposure to air pollution. The report does not indicate if the agency engaged environmental justice communities to encourage participation in the e-alert program. They may have done so, and it is simply not listed in this report. Absent more context about which activities are critical in achieving meaningful involvement, it is hard to evaluate the accomplishments listed in these reports.

Along with using traditional participatory approaches such as public notice and comment periods, the agency has invested considerable effort in capacity building by improving access to environmental and demographic information. Providing information to affected communities and interested citizens is one mechanism to level the playing field and facilitate effective participation. EJView, for example, is an interactive mapping tool on the EPA's website (http://epamap14.epa.gov/ejmap/entry.html) which allows users to see how environmental burdens may be concentrated within a geographic area. Any facility reporting to EPA can be identified on a map, along with water-monitoring stations. This includes current hazardous waste transfer, storage and disposal facilities, Superfund sites, Brownfield areas, Toxics Release Inventory (TRI) facilities, and air and water dischargers. This tool overlays demographic information as well, making it relatively easy to identify if low-income or minority communities have a large number of EPA-permitted facilities compared to wealthy, white communities. EJView also provides critical health outcomes, such as information on infant mortality rates, birth rates, and cancer risk. This is a powerful diagnostic tool that communities and advocacy groups could use to identify potential environmental justice issues. In its current form, however, it falls short. While the agency has devoted considerable resources to create this level of access to information, EJView lacks any corresponding information about how to *act* on this information. This is a missed opportunity for the agency to facilitate participation. If people use EJView to better understand the density of permitted facilities within their community, what next steps could they take to engage in environmental decision making? Currently, there is no guidance connecting the information provided in EJView to information on the agency's permitting process, rulemaking, or other elements of environmental decision making.

In comparison, the EPA's Community Action for a Renewed Environment (CARE) program exemplifies a model initiative to provide information and empower communities while also facilitating public engagement (Hansell, Hollander, and John 2009; Sirianni 2009; EPA 2011). This competitive grant program aims to reduce toxic pollution by (1) working collaboratively with local communities to reduce exposure to toxic pollutants, (2) helping communities understand individual and cumulative sources of toxic exposure, (3) working with communities to identify and prioritize risk-reducing activities, and (4) creating long-term, community-based partnerships to improve and protect the local environment.[3] While many federal agencies, including the EPA, struggle with how best to work with local communities, CARE demonstrates that national-local partnerships can be effective and have considerable spillover benefits. For example, two different CARE communities identified exposure to solvents and other chemicals used in auto body shops as an environmental risk that could—and should—be minimized. On the local level, environmental groups, the EPA, and local auto body shops worked collaboratively to identify alternative, less toxic chemicals for paint stripping, along with exploring opportunities for improved disposal practices. This experience, in turn, prompted the EPA to work closely with these CARE grantees to develop national emission standards regulating paint strippers and other solvents used in auto body refinishing (Hansell, Hollander, and John 2009). These regulations broaden the impact of the CARE program because they apply to auto body shops across the country.

The focus of the CARE program often results in investment in environmental justice communities, but any community can apply for support from this program. The Environmental Justice Small Grants program, administered by the EPA since 1994, is specifically designed to support environmental justice communities. These grants provide a tangible way to identify local issues, support community groups, and build trust between the agency and affected community members. Reflecting the diversity of environmental justice concerns, grants have focused on a wide range of environmental issues, such as radon, lead, farmworker safety, recycling, water quality, and children's health.[4] But the commitment to investing in communities has varied greatly over time. Figure 3.1.1 shows the number of Environmental Justice Small Grants awarded by year. The number of grants peaked shortly after EO 12898 was signed, and while there were increases around the time of the American Recovery and Reinvestment Act, more recent years have witnessed a decline. It is not possible to conclude if the variability in grants awarded reflects drastic changes in the applicant pool, changes in agency priorities, or is simply the result of federal budgetary constraints.

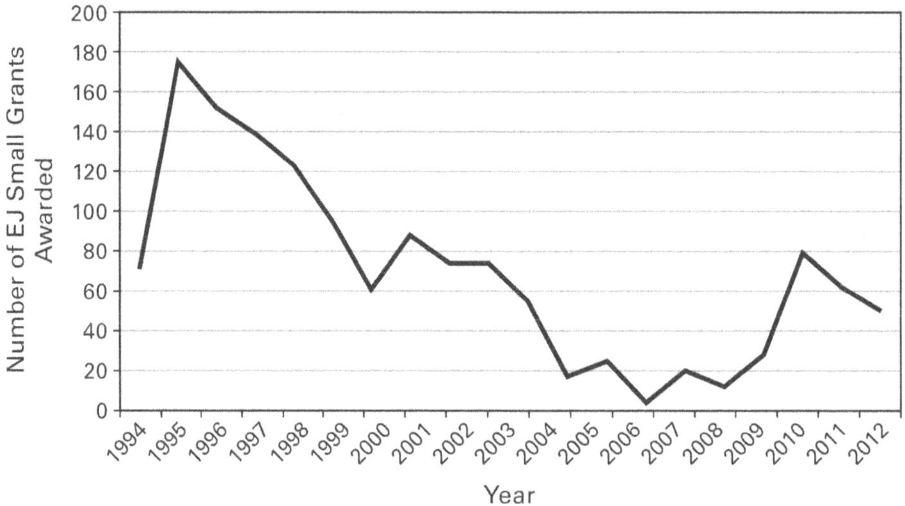


**Figure 3.1.1** Number of Environmental Justice (EJ) Small Grants Awarded by Year (1994–2012)
*Source*: Data in this chart are drawn from reports available at http://www.epa.gov/environmentaljustice/grants/ej-smgrants.html

Moreover, recent research comparing all Environmental Justice Small Grants awarded between 1994 and 2004 suggest some challenges in targeting environmental justice communities. During this time period, the majority of the funds distributed were not directed toward minority and low-income communities with higher than the nation's average TRI emissions (Vajjhala 2010). It is impossible to determine if this pattern is due to a selection effect, meaning that those minority and low-income communities with above-average TRI emissions did not apply for a grant, or if in fact, there are problematic patterns in the distribution of funds. The Environmental Justice Small Grants program could be an innovative tool that builds trust and increases participation, but inconsistent support or biased implementation will limit its reach; effective participatory mechanisms require consistent commitment.

Environmental justice problems are diverse and may require that the EPA devote a range of expertise within its agency to understand and address community concerns. Agency leadership and commitment to high-quality participatory practices are necessary to tackle most environmental justice problems. Many in the environmental justice community worried that in 2001, under President George W. Bush, that EO 12898 would be repealed. This, in fact, did not occur. But the change in presidential administration did result in a shift in emphasis within environmental justice at the EPA. Christine Todd Whitman, the first administrator of the EPA under President Bush, issued a memo restating the agency's commitment to environmental justice. Rather than highlighting the significance of minority and low-income communities in environmental justice, the agency opted to focus on environmental justice for everyone (EPA 2004; Mohai, Pellow, and Timmons Roberts 2009). This change in focus, deemphasizing minority and low-income communities, adds additional challenges to expanding meaningful access for public participation within agency decision making. It strains trust in public institutions with stakeholders who were likely already suspicious of the federal government's commitment to social equity and environmental justice.

Under President Barack Obama, the EPA has renewed its focus on environmental justice and reiterated the importance of engaging minority and low-income communities to achieve environmental justice. In 2010, EPA administrator Lisa Jackson listed environmental justice as one of the agency's top priorities, and the following year, the agency published its blueprint to achieve environmental justice, *Plan EJ 2014*. This plan is an innovative strategy, and its structure suggests that agency leadership have clearly received the message: agency fragmentation is a significant hurdle in advancing environmental justice. *Plan EJ 2014* emphasizes cross-agency responsibility for advancing environmental justice into all aspects of environmental decision making. The plan also aims to improve the scientific and technical tools available to better diagnose and prevent the concentration of environmental risk in any community, along with evaluating more carefully the way that the agency's current initiatives can be tailored to support environmental justice goals.

Public participation looms large in this plan; the three main goals include to "protect the environment and health in overburdened communities; empower communities to take action to improve their health and environment; and establish partnerships with local, state, tribal, and federal governments and organizations to achieve healthy and sustainable communities." (EPA 2011, p. 1). *Plan EJ 2014* highlights the need to strengthen community-based programs with a particular focus on identifying "scalable and replicable" programs to more effectively address concentrated environmental burdens. For example, successful programs like CARE should be replicated and expanded whenever possible, and as the agency proceeds with implementing *Plan EJ 2014*, it intends to evaluate its progress regularly, along with producing information on "lessons learned" to facilitate communication about strategies that are effective in addressing environmental justice problems.

Some of the more innovative participatory approaches have emerged in recent years as the agency reinvigorates its commitment to environmental justice. In advance of developing *Plan EJ 2014*, the agency held a series of community forums and listening sessions across the country. It has also integrated communication technology to expand public participation, holding quarterly community outreach teleconference calls to gather and respond to community concerns. The OEJ hosts these calls, and agency staff from other programs and offices are present to respond to concerns that were submitted beforehand, as well as answer questions from the public during the call. Once a call is completed, the

EPA provides both an audio version and a written transcript of it on the agency's website. Putting aside any consideration of the digital divide, this type of community outreach has the ability to expand access to a wide range of interested citizens. Recently available transcripts suggest that fragmentation within the agency and between the EPA and its state counterparts remains frustrating for community members trying to engage in environmental decision making. One caller noted that existing rules from the Superfund program, combined with longstanding agreements between the EPA and a state environmental agency, were contributing to the concentration of drinking water risk in a community, rather than protecting community members and providing a platform for a safe environment.[5]

While a renewed commitment to environmental justice is clear in agency documents, advancing a streamlined collaborative approach in a large organization remains difficult. *Plan EJ 2014* holds tremendous promise for advancing environmental justice. With an emphasis on cross-cutting implementation and improved access to information, *Plan EJ 2014* could enhance the diversity of public participation in environmental decision making. It aims to strike a balance between creating some standard operating procedures—like a national approach to identifying environmental justice communities—and providing discretion and flexibility to ensure that solutions are tailored to local problems.

As with all innovative plans promising change, the devil is the implementation details (Mazmanian and Sabatier 1989; Pressman and Wildavsky 1984). In the coming years, the challenge within EPA includes maintaining this renewed focus on environmental justice. Working across the breadth of programs within the agency and with stakeholders outside the agency to more successfully integrate public participation and environmental justice into the agency's decision-making processes will require resources and dedication. And, although the agency has had some success in expanding the conversation, improving access to information, and forging new partnerships with communities, more work remains, as the scope of environmental justice problems is large and public participation provides one potential mechanism for successful resolution of conflict and improved decision making.

## Federal Agencies, Public Participation and Environmental Justice

While the EPA is a lead agency in advancing environmental justice within the federal government, it is by no means the only federal agency that struggles to integrate EO 12898 (including its focus on public participation) into daily routines. To compare and contrast the approach of other federal agencies to the EPA, we examine environmental justice and public participation in two other agencies: the DOE and the DOT. Table 3.1.1 compares the original participatory goals for the three agencies immediately after EO 12898 was signed, along with current participation goals. Material for this table is drawn exclusively from the government documents cited in the text. The table also highlights some of the participatory approaches commonly used by the agencies to address environmental concerns.

**Table 3.1.1** Comparison of Environmental Justice and Public Participation across Federal Agencies

| Agency | EPA | DOE | DOT |
|---|---|---|---|
| Agency mission | Protect human health and the environment. | Ensure the nation's security and prosperity using science and technology to address energy, environmental, and nuclear challenges. | Ensure fast, safe, efficient, accessible, and convenient transportation systems. |
| Public participation goal (1995 EJ strategy) | To achieve widespread opportunity for participation in environmental decision making. An informed and involved community must underpin environmental protection. | Improve DOE's credibility and trust by enhancing public participation in agency activities. | Bring government decisions closer to the communities affected by them; expand opportunities for public participation in decisions relating to human health and the environment. |
| Public participation goal (updated strategy) | Public participation underpins two of the three main goals in *Plan EJ 2014*. | In more recent documents, the DOE's public participation goals remain unchanged. | To ensure the full and fair participation by all potentially affected communities in the transportation decision-making process. (DOT 2012 EJ strategy) |
| Participatory tools used | • Notice and comment periods<br>• Advisory boards (NEJAC and community advisory boards)<br>• EJ Small Grants<br>• Translated documents and interpreter<br>• Hot lines/reporting links<br>• Conference calls | • Notice and comment periods<br>• Site-specific advisory boards<br>• Partnerships with minority organizations<br>• Cooperative agreements to provide funding to communities | • Notice and comment periods<br>• Seminars/ workshops<br>• Directs states, MPOs, and transit operators to engage citizens in project planning |

## The Department of Energy

The DOE's mission is to "ensure America's security and prosperity by addressing its energy, environmental, and nuclear challenges through transformative science and technology solutions."[6] DOE has approximately 16,000 employees based around the country at its various offices, laboratories, and field sites. Among other duties, DOE is responsible for cleaning up the environmental legacy from the nation's nuclear weapons program. This is an extraordinarily technically complex program that must confront very long time horizons, as the half-life on some of the spent nuclear material will remain radioactive for many decades to come. DOE is responsible for more than 80 federal facilities throughout the country that are contaminated and are currently undergoing environmental cleanup. In addition to developing its own environmental justice strategy, EO 12898 tasks the Secretary of Energy or a designated officer to serve on the Interagency Working Group.

Interestingly, DOE's public participation goal is to "enhance the credibility and public trust of the department by making public participation a fundamental component of all program operations, planning activities, and decision making" (DOE 1995). While the strategy emphasizes community participation and empowerment, it seems to suggest that this is done to improve the agency's profile, as opposed to improving or resolving conflict between the department and its stakeholders. Indeed, when the department first published its environmental justice strategy in 1995 following EO 12898, it noted that no stakeholder comments were included in the document because the department did not provide adequate time for public review prior to publishing the strategy.[7] Certainly, this is not an ideal way to establish positive relationships with stakeholders (Dietz et al. 2008). To its credit, DOE noted in early documents that the department's environmental justice strategy is a living document, and there would be ample opportunity for stakeholder contribution and change in the future.

Improving trust and credibility through participation may be the part of the department's approach to environmental justice, but it has not been easy. DOE acknowledges that minority, low-income, and tribal communities have traditionally lacked access to information and technical advisers to be informed participants in complex environmental decisions. NEJAC released a report noting, among other things, the strained relationships between DOE and the affected communities near the federal facilities the department manages (NEJAC 2004). National security and confidentiality issues surrounding activities at DOE facilities directly hamper the ability of the department to build trust and engage stakeholders. Despite this challenge, NEJAC recommended continued investment in public participation.

Currently, the Office of Legacy Management within DOE provides leadership for environmental justice programming. Environmental justice concerns may arise in relation to the treatment, storage, and disposal of hazardous, radioactive, and mixed waste. DOE is responsible for a number of federal sites throughout the nation that are currently undergoing cleanup processes, such as the Hanford site in Washington and the Savannah River site in South Carolina. Environmental justice issues may also arise during the National Environmental Policy Act (NEPA) planning process when the agency is upgrading existing energy projects or constructing new facilities.

DOE utilizes typical participatory mechanisms to engage the public, including public notice and comment periods, along with relying on citizen advisory groups and site-specific advisory boards. The department attempts to ensure that advisory boards reflect the communities they represent, but identifying and engaging an affected community can be difficult. For example, the Nevada Test Site Advisory Board has lacked broad representation for decades. The department attempted to recruit a wide cross section of potential stakeholders, but has had little success. In 2010, the Nevada Site office conducted a membership recruitment drive, advertising in the Las Vegas valley, rural communities, and a Spanish-language newspaper; however, no applications for the advisory board were received (DOE 2011). On the other hand, the Hanford Advisory Board reflects the diverse viewpoints in the affected community and region, including minorities and members of tribal nations (DOE 2011).

While the EPA relies on small grants to invest broadly in communities and environmental justice solutions, DOE takes a different programmatic approach. Many of their public participation initiatives seem to hinge on building technical capacity in affected communities (DOE 2011). This likely reflects both the department's mission to rely on "science and technology" to meet energy challenges, along with the highly technical nature of the cleanup at DOE facilities. The department supports efforts by historically black colleges and universities to build the science, technology, and engineering workforce and fills a variety of intern positions with minority students. In 2009, DOE entered into fifteen cooperative agreements with tribal nations, totaling approximately $6 million. This financial support is designed to build local communities' capacity to increase participation in DOE decision making (DOE 2011). Communities can use the funds to hire scientific and technical staff to help examine site cleanup strategies in order to educate community members on the more technical nature of DOE's responsibilities, as well as building trust by increasing access and transparency to site documents and the decision-making process.

In some cases, tribal nations have succeeded in affecting the department's decision making through cooperative agreements. For example, at the Hanford site, the inclusion of tribal input resulted in the protection of cultural, religious, and natural resources relating to Gable Mountain (DOE 2009). DOE's Los Alamos Pueblos Project in New Mexico relies on tribal governments to manage pollution monitoring programs and tribal governments also actively participate in generating the Los Alamos and National Laboratory Site-Wide Environmental Impact Statement by reviewing and commenting on the document (EPA 2013; DOE 2008). Despite success in many areas relating to environmental justice, DOE progress reports note that much work remains (DOE 2009; 2011).

## The Department of Transportation

The DOT's mission is to "serve the United States by ensuring a fast, safe, efficient, accessible and convenient transportation system that meets our vital national interests and enhances the quality life of the American people, today and into the future."[8] DOT is the largest of the three agencies compared here, with over 57,000 employees across the country. Within DOT, there are thirteen agencies, ranging from the Federal Highway Administration to the Federal Transit Administration to the Pipeline and Hazardous Material Safety Administration, working to accomplish DOT's broad mission. In addition to developing its own environmental justice strategy, EO 12898 tasks the Secretary of Transportation or a designated officer to serve on the Interagency Working Group.

In its 1995 environmental justice strategy, DOT expressed its commitment to "bringing government decision making closer to the communities and people affected by [its] decisions and ensuring opportunities for greater public participation in decisions relating to human health and the environment" (DOT 1995). DOT published its draft strategy in the Federal Register and mailed approximately 3,000 copies to constituent groups and representatives of the environmental justice community. They received approximately 50 comments and modified the final version to incorporate suggestions. In 1997, DOT issued an internal order on environmental justice as key component of the department's strategy.[9] In the internal order, the department reaffirmed its commitment to establishing or expanding procedures that enhance the participation of minority and low-income communities during all stages of the department's decision making. DOT updated its strategy in 2012, stating that its guiding principle on public participation is "to ensure the full and fair participation by all potentially affected communities in the transportation decision-making process" (DOT 2012).

Most of DOT's work involves setting policies and procedures to be followed by state and local governments in planning and constructing transportation facilities that receive federal funding. Stakeholder involvement, as required by DOT guidelines, is often carried out by state and local agencies responsible for the process. Environmental justice issues arise most frequently when some communities get transportation benefits, while others experience fewer, or when some communities suffer disproportionate negative impacts from transportation programs. DOT, like the EPA and DOE, struggles with representation in public participation, as some communities are consistently less well represented than others during policy and decision making concerning transportation resources (Cairns et al. 2003).

In the late 1990s, DOT acknowledged increasing public concerns regarding compliance with environmental justice provisions during metropolitan and statewide transportation planning (DOT 1999). In response, the department requested that administrators within DOT raise a litany of questions during state, metropolitan planning organization (MPO), and transit operator certifications pertaining to equity and public involvement in particular. Recognizing room for improvement in engaging low-income and minority communities in the public participation process, the department directed administrators to review public participation plans for agencies receiving federal funds and to address the strengths and deficiencies (DOT 1999).

In recent years, DOT has released "Environmental Justice Implementation Reports" available on the agency's website.[10] Like EPA and DOE, DOT engages in the typical range of public participation processes, including public notice and comment periods, convening advisory groups, and holding seminars and workshops. DOT is also using technology to increase public participation. In advance of finalizing its most recent environmental justice strategy, the department held traditional public notice and comment periods but added to this approach with a novel electronic participatory mechanism called EJ Ideascale. This electronic comment feature allowed the public to contribute their ideas *and* also view and respond to public comments made by others.[11]

According to the department's website, a considerable number of comments have been received on their updated environmental justice strategy. The department's response to public comments are also available online.[12] Yet again, the public comments highlight the challenges of advancing environmental justice in a large-scale, multifunctional bureaucracy. Some public comments strongly support the need for increased harmonization and integration of a unified environmental justice strategy within the department, while others advocate for more flexibility to ensure that decision making can accurately take into account unique, place-based features. Under these conditions, implementing agencywide environmental justice strategies remain challenging: federal agencies receive virtually no guidance on how to proceed when a diverse public provides conflicting input.

## Conclusion

There is tremendous variation across federal agencies; for instance, they have divergent missions, different professional norms, and diverse agency cultures. EPA operates not only through its national offices, but also through its ten regional offices, DOE functions through various offices, laboratories, and field sites, while DOT works through hundreds of state transportation departments, MPOs, and local transit authorities, each of which enjoys substantial decision-making discretion. Such an overlay of arrangements leads to considerable variations in policy approaches across jurisdictions, especially since cities, states, and regions vary widely in their environmental problems. Thus, in many instances, environmental justice must contend with a fragmented and decentralized policy process.

Our assessment is based on examining a range of existing government documents and electronic sources. We compare information from these sources to existing research on civic engagement, public participation, and social equity to examine how well federal agencies meet the participation challenges embedded in EO 12898. Overall, the environmental justice movement and this executive order have increased opportunities for public participation in federal decision making. But despite the increased opportunity, participation from minority and low-income communities remains uneven. Perhaps this should not be surprising, given what we know about both the challenges inherent in generating diverse participation, particularly in communities that have been historically disenfranchised, and the challenges of creating systemic change in large bureaucracies.

The three federal agencies examined here have all experienced some success in using public participation to address environmental justice concerns, and they have also faced significant challenges.

These challenges stem from multiple sources: (1) a complex decision-making environment at the federal level, complicated by devolution and privatization; (2) the capacity of large public organizations to incorporate public participation is variable; (3) the technical nature of environmental problems, which demands some level of competence on the part of the affected public, and the capacity of citizens to engage in scientific and technical decision making; and (4) the general decline in public engagement over time.

While there is significant promise in using public participation to address environmental justice concerns, this promise hinges on developing and maintaining effective public participation mechanisms. Prior research highlights that effective participation is characterized by clear goals, adequate human and financial capital investment, consistent institutional commitment, and an ability for participation to affect change in all stages of decision making (Beierle and Cayford 2002; Charnley and Engelbert 2005; Dietz at al 2008; Leach 2006; Reed 2008; Sirianni 2009). In the years since EO 12898 was signed into law, the EPA, DOE, and DOT have experienced challenges across the range of characteristics that describe effective participatory mechanisms. In the years ahead, if federal agencies want to increase opportunities for public participation, they should consistently invest more staff time and agency resources in a range of community outreach efforts. This can help build trust and establish a framework for effective participation if environmental justice problems arise. Federal agencies face a diverse and decentralized political system. Building agile organizational capacity to partner with state and local governments will remain essential in the years ahead. Similarly, federal agencies addressing environmental justice challenges would be well served by building the technical capacity of affected communities. This provides the affected communities more opportunity to partner with government agencies when tackling environmental justice problems. Across all of these efforts to engage the public, it is also imperative to design systematic interventions to allow for clear identification of what works and why when addressing environmental challenges.

## Endnotes

1. Memorandum of Understanding on Environmental Justice and Executive Order 12898 (August 2011).
2. The accomplishment reports can be found at http://www.epa.gov/compliance/environmentaljustice/resources/reports/actionplans.html.
3. http://www.epa.gov/air/care/basic.htm.
4. http://www.epa.gov/environmentaljustice/resources/publications/grants/ej_smgrants_emerging_tools_2nd_edition.pdf contains a full description of EJ Small Grant projects.
5. This example is drawn from the following transcript: http://www.epa.gov/environmentaljustice/multimedia/transcripts/2012-09-20-community-outreach-call.pdf.

6. See the DOE website: http://energy.gov/mission.
7. http://energy.gov/sites/prod/files/EJStrategy_EO12898.pdf.
8. See the DOT website: http://www.dot.gov/about.
9. http://www.fhwa.dot.gov/environment/environmental_justice/ej_at_dot/order_56102a.
10. http://www.fhwa.dot.gov/environment/environmental_justice/ej_at_dot/dot_ej_strategy.
11. http://www.fhwa.dot.gov/environment/environmental_justice/ej_at_dot/2011_implementation_report.
12. http://www.fhwa.dot.gov/environment/environmental_justice/ej_at_dot/dot_ej_strategy/public_comment/index.cfm.

## References

Agyeman, Julian, and Briony Angus. 2003. The Role of Civic Environmentalism in the Pursuit of Sustainable Communities. *Journal of Environmental Planning and Management* 46 (3): 345–363.

Baber, Walter F., and Robert V. Bartlett. 2013. Green Political Ideas and Environmental Policy. In *The Oxford Handbook of U.S. Environmental Policy*, ed. Sheldon Kamieniecki and Michael E. Kraft, 48–66. New York: Oxford University Press.

Bardach, Eugene. 1998. *Getting Agencies to Work Together: The Practice and Theory of Managerial Craftsmanship*. Washington, DC: Brookings Institution Press.

Beierle, Thomas C. 1998. *Public Participation in Environmental Decisions: An Evaluation Framework Using Social Goals*. Washington, DC: Resources for the Future.

Beierle, Thomas C., and Jerry Cayford. 2002. *Democracy in Practice: Public Participation in Environmental Decisions*. Washington, DC: Resources for the Future.

Brehm, John, and Scott Gates. 2002. *Working, Shirking, and Sabotage: Bureaucratic Response to a Democratic Public*. Ann Arbor, MI: University of Michigan Press.

Brion, Denis J. 1988. An Essay on LULU, NIMBY, and the Problem of Distributive Justice. *Boston College Environmental Affairs Law Review* 15: 437–504.

Brulle, Robert J., and David N. Pellow. 2006. Environmental Justice: Human Health and Environmental Inequalities. *Annual Review of Public Health* 27: 103–124.

Buchanan, Sariyah S. 2010. Why Marginalized Communities Should Use Community Benefit Agreements as a Tool for Environmental Justice: Urban Renewal and Brownfield Redevelopment in Philadelphia, Pennsylvania. *Temple Journal of Science, Technology, & Environmental Law* 29: 31–52.

Bulkeley, Harriet, and Arthur P. J. Mol. 2003. Participation and Environmental Governance: Consensus, Ambivalence, and Debate. *Environmental Values* 12 (2): 143–154.

Cairns, Shannon, Jessica Greig, and Martin Wachs. 2003. *Environmental Justice & Transportation: A Citizen's Handbook.* Berkeley, CA: ITS Berkeley.

Charnley, Susan, and Bruce Engelbert. 2005. Evaluating Public Participation in Environmental Decision-Making: EPA's Superfund Community Involvement Program. *Journal of Environmental Management* 77 (3): 165–182.

Coglianese, Cary. 1997. Assessing Consensus: The Promise and Performance of Negotiated Rulemaking. *Duke Law Journal* 46 (6): 1255–1349.

Coglianese, Cary. 2006. Citizen Participation in Rulemaking: Past, Present, and Future. *Duke Law Journal* 55 (5): 943–968.

Cole, Luke W., and Shelia R. Foster. 2001. *From the Ground Up: Environmental Racism and the Rise of the Environmental Justice Movement.* New York: New York University Press.

Commission on Civil Rights (CCR). 2003. *Not In My Backyard: Executive Order 12,898 and Title VI as Tools for Achieving Environmental Justice.* http://www.usccr.gov/pubs/envjust/ej0104.pdf.

Daley, Dorothy M. 2013. Public Participation, Citizen Engagement, and Environmental Decision Making. In *The Oxford Handbook of U.S. Environmental Policy,* eds. Sheldon Kamieniecki and Michael E. Kraft, 487–503. New York: Oxford University Press.

Department of Energy (DOE). 1995. *Environmental Justice Strategy: U.S. Department of Energy.* http://energy.gov/sites/prod/files/nepapub/nepa_documents/Red-Dont/G-DOE-EJ_Strategy.pdf.

Department of Energy (DOE). 2009. *Environmental Justice Five-Year Implementation Plan: First Annual Progress Report.* http://energy.gov/sites/prod/files/EJ_Progress_Report.pdf.

Department of Energy (DOE). 2011. *Environmental Justice Five-Year Implementation Plan: Second Annual Progress Report.* http://energy.gov/sites/prod/files/20110825%20EJ%20report%20WEB.pdf.

Department of Transportation (DOT). 1995. *Department of Transportation Environmental Justice Strategy.* http://www.epa.gov/environmentaljustice/resources/publications/interagency/dot-strategy-1995.pdf.

Department of Transportation (DOT). 1999. *Implementing Title VI Requirements in Metropolitan and Statewide Planning.* http://www.fhwa.dot.gov/environment/environmental_justice/facts/ej-10-7.cfm.

Department of Transportation (DOT). 2012. *Department of Transportation Environmental Justice Strategy.* http://www.fhwa.dot.gov/environment/environmental_justice/ej_at_dot/dot_ej_strategy.

Dietz, Thomas, Paul C. Stern, and the National Research Council. 2008. *Panel on Public Participation in Environmental Assessment and Decision Making, and National Research Council (U.S.) Committee on the Human Dimensions of Global Change. Public participation in Environmental Assessment and Decision Making.* Washington, DC: National Academies Press.

Environmental Protection Agency (EPA). 1995. *The EPA's Environmental Justice Strategy.* http://www.epa.gov/environmentaljustice/resources/policy/ej_strategy_1995.pdf.

Environmental Protection Agency (EPA). 1997. *Environmental Justice: 1996 Annual Report Working Toward Solutions.* Document no. EPA/300-R-97-004.

Environmental Protection Agency (EPA). 2004. *EPA Needs to Consistently Implement the Intent of the Executive Order on Environmental Justice.* Document no. 2004-P-00007. http://www.epa.gov/oig/reports/2004/20040301-2004-P-00007. pdf.

Department of Energy (DOE). 2008. *Final Site-Wide Environmental Impact Statement for Continued Operation for Los Alamos, New Mexico.* http://energy. gov/sites/prod/files/EIS-0380-FEIS-Summary-2008.pdf.

Environmental Protection Agency (EPA). 2011. *Plan EJ 2014.* http://www.epa.gov/environmentaljustice/resources/policy/plan-ej-2014/plan-ej-2011-09.pdf.

Environmental Protection Agency (EPA). 2013. *Plan EJ 2014 Progress Report.* Document no. EPA/300-R-13-001.

Fine, James D., and Dave Owen. 2005. Technocracy and Democracy: Conflicts between Models and Participation in Environmental Law and Planning. *Hastings Law Journal* 56 (5): 901–982.

Fletcher, Thomas H. 2003. *From Love Canal to Environmental Justice: The Politics of Hazardous Waste on the Canada-U.S. Border.* Peterborough, Canada: Broadview Press.

Foreman, Christopher H. 1998. *The Promise and Peril of Environmental Justice.* Washington, DC: Brookings Institution Press.

Furlong, Scott R. 2007. Business and the Environment: Influencing Agency Policy-making. In *Business and Environmental Policy: Corporate Interests in the American Political System*, ed. Michael E. Kraft and Sheldon Kamieniecki, 155–184. Cambridge, MA: MIT Press.

Gauna, Eileen. 1995. Federal Environmental Citizen Provisions: Obstacles and Incentives on the Road to Environmental Justice. *Ecology Law Quarterly* 22:1–87.

Government Accountability Office (GAO). 2011. *Environmental Justice: EPA Needs to Take Additional Actions to Help Ensure Effective Implementation.* Document no. GOA-12-77

Hansell, William H., Elizabeth Hollander, and Dewitt John. 2009. *Putting Community First: A Promising Approach to Federal Collaboration for Environmental Improvement.* Washington, DC: National Academy of Public Administration.

Hernandez, Willie G. 1995. Environmental justice: Looking Beyond Executive Order No. 12,898. *UCLA Journal of Environmental Law & Policy* 14:181.

Innes, Judith E., and David E. Booher. 2004. Reframing Public Participation: Strategies for the 21st Century. *Planning Theory & Practice* 5 (4): 419–436.

Kamieniecki, Sheldon. 2006. *Corporate America and Environmental Policy: How Often Does Business Get Its Way?* Stanford, CA: Stanford University Press.

Kellogg, Wendy A., and Anjali Mathur. 2003. Environmental Justice and Information Technologies: Overcoming the Information-Access Paradox in Urban Communities. *Public Administration Review* 63 (5): 573–585.

Klyza, Christoper McGrory, and David J. Sousa. 2013. *American Environmental Policy: Beyond Gridlock.* Cambridge, MA: MIT Press.

Kraft, Michael E., and Bruce B. Clary. 1991. Citizen Participation and the NIMBY Syndrome: Public Response to Radioactive Waste Disposal. *Western Political Quarterly* 44 (2): 299–328.

Larson, Kelli L., and Denise Lach. 2008. Participants and Non-Participants of Place-Based Groups: An Assessment of Attitudes and Implications for Public Participation in Water Resource Management. *Journal of Environmental Management* 88 (4): 817–830.

Laurian, Lucie. 2007. Deliberative Planning through Citizen Advisory Boards—Five Case Studies from Military and Civilian Environmental Cleanups. *Journal of Planning Education and Research* 26 (4): 415–434.

Leach, William D. 2006. Collaborative Public Management and Democracy: Evidence from Western Watershed Partnerships. *Public Administration Review* 66 (1): 100–110.

Lubell, Mark, Paul A. Sabatier, Arnold Vedlitz, Will Focht, Zev Trachtenberg, and Marty Matlock. 2005. Conclusions and Recommendations. In *Swimming Upstream: Collaborative Approaches to Watershed Management*, ed. Paul A. Sabatier, Will Focht, Mark Lubell, Zev Trachtenberg, Arnold Vedlitz, and Marty Matlock, 261–296. Cambridge, MA: MIT Press.

Macedo, Stephen. 2005. *Democracy at Risk: How Political Choices Undermine Citizen Participation and What We Can Do about It.* Washington, DC: Brookings Institution Press.

Mazmanian, Daniel A., and Paul A. Sabatier. 1989. *Implementation and Public Policy: With a New Postscript.* Lanham, MD: University Press of America.

Mohai, Paul, David Pellow, and J. Timmons Roberts. 2009. Environmental Justice. *Annual Review of Environment and Resources* 34: 405–430.

Munton, Don, ed. 1996. *Hazardous Waste Siting and Democratic Choice.* Washington, DC: Georgetown University Press.

National Environmental Justice Advisory Council (NEJAC). 2004. *Environmental Justice and Federal Facilities: Recommendations for Improving Stakeholder Relations between Federal Facilities and Environmental Justice Communities.* http://www.epa.gov/compliance/ej/resources/publications/nejac/ffwg-final-rpt-102504.pdf.

Pellow, David N., and Robert J. Brulle. 2005. *Power, Justice, and the Environment: A Critical Appraisal of the Environmental Justice Movement.* Cambridge, MA: MIT Press.

Pressman, Jeffrey L., and Aaron B. Wildavsky. 1984. *Implementation: How Great Expectations in Washington Are Dashed in Oakland: or, Why It's Amazing that Federal Programs Work At All, This Being A Saga of the Economic Development Administration as Told by Two Sympathetic Observers Who Seek to Build Morals on a Foundation of Ruined Hopes.* 3rd ed. Berkeley, CA: University of California Press.

Putnam, Robert D. 2000. *Bowling Alone: The Collapse and Revival of American Community.* New York: Simon & Schuster.

Reed, Mark S. 2008. Stakeholder Participation for Environmental Management: A Literature Review. *Biological Conservation* 141 (10): 2417–2431.

Rosenbaum, Walter A. 2002. *Environmental Politics and Policy.* 5th ed. Washing-ton, DC: CQ Press.

Rosenstone, Steve J., and John M. Hansen. 1993. *Mobilization, Participation, and Democracy in America.* New York: Longman.

Sander, Thomas H., and Robert D. Putnam. 2010. Still Bowling Alone? The Post-9/11 Split. *Journal of Democracy* 21 (1): 9–16.

Schlozman, Kay L., Sidney Verba, and Henry E. Brady. 2012. *The Unheavenly Chorus: Unequal Political Voice and the Broken Promise of American Democracy.* Princeton, NJ: Princeton University Press.

Sirianni, Carmen. 2009. *Investing in Democracy: Engaging Citizens in Collaborative Governance.* Washington, DC: Brookings Institution Press.

Spyke, Nancy Perkins. 1999. Public Participation in Environmental Decisionmaking at the New Millennium: Structuring New Spheres of Public Influence. *Boston College Environmental Affairs Law Review* 26: 263–314.

Vajjhala, Shalini P. 2010. Building Community Capacity? Mapping the Scope and Impacts of EPA's Environmental Justice Small Grants Program. *Research in Social Problems and Public Policy* 18: 353–381.

Weber, Edward P. 2003. *Bringing Society Back In: Grassroots Ecosystem Management, Accountability, and Sustainable Communities.* Cambridge, Mass.: MIT Press.

Webler, Thomas, and Seth Tuler. 2006. Four Perspectives on Public Participation Process in Environmental Assessment and Decision Making: Combined Results from 10 Case Studies. *Policy Studies Journal: the Journal of the Policy Studies Organization* 34 (4): 699–722.

Wilson, James Q. 1989. *Bureaucracy: What Government Agencies Do and Why They Do It.* New York: Basic Books.

Yackee, Jason Webb, and Susan Webb Yackee. 2006. A Bias towards Business? Assessing Interest Group Influence on the U.S. Bureaucracy. *Journal of Politics* 68 (1): 128–139.

## DISCUSSION QUESTIONS

1. Most environmental legislation calls for some form of public participation, and government agencies commonly recruit people from organized groups who have expressed interest or are active around a particular issue. Do you think the agencies' strategy to facilitate public participation is effective? Why? If not, why?
2. The U.S. EPA seeks to "work with communities through communication, partnership, research, and the public participation process" and also "help affected communities have access to information which will enable them to meaningfully participate in activities, to the end". The EPA has adopted Executive Order 12898 and the Office of Environmental Justice (OEJ)? How do the EO12908 and the creation of the OEJ affect the public participation process? In what capacity did they engender an effective public participation system?
3. Federal agencies have used public participation to address environmental justice concerns. Despite some successes, they also face significant challenges. What are they? How could federal agencies minimize the potential challenges? Do you believe building trust-based networks with decentralized political systems would play a role in mitigating the challenges?

READING 3.2

# The Mapping of Local Knowledge

By Jason Corburn

*Tell me, I forget.*
*Show me, I remember.*
*Involve me, I understand.*

—Anonymous

Community scientists often map what they know about environmental health in order to communicate to both local people and professionals. Maps ranging from cartoon sketches by young people to sophisticated GIS images can powerfully display and communicate *street science*. Maps may not influence professionals, though, even when community knowledge is joined with advanced technologies such as GIS. Maps, as a medium for communicating *street science* about community environmental health problems, are crucial tools for community members. But like other modes of communication, maps can distort as much as they can reveal.

## The Toxic Avengers

The Toxic Avengers was founded in 1988 by a group of high school students who organized themselves to raise community awareness about environmental pollution. The name came from a comic book of the same name, whose characters were crusaders against toxic waste.[1] The students were from the El Puente Academy high school and the community organization's program on community health, youth service, and leadership. What began as a science-class project turned into an organization that raised environmental awareness in the community and helped galvanize a community coalition that would be instrumental for taking action against neighborhood environmental hazards.

The young people who formed the Toxic Avengers were part of a science class that was doing a unit on understanding the neighborhood environment. The class researched local hazards by gathering readily available information from local, state, and federal environmental agencies on the environmental performance of facilities in the community. The students also searched through newspaper archives to find references to environmental pollution in their neighborhood. They discovered, for example, that the Radiac Corporation—a storage and transfer facility for toxic, flammable, and low-level-radioactive waste located in the neighborhood—was the only facility of its kind in the entire city.

The class instructors, with the help of local environmental activists and agency professionals, organized environmental "tours" of the neighborhood. Environmental professionals and activists often led these "toxic tours" in which students visited the local sewage-treatment plant, natural-gas tank farm, waste-transfer station, scrap-metal recycling facility, Superfund site, depot for sanitation trucks, and other locally noxious industries. Students also identified the "green" spaces in the neighborhood. On the tours, the gravity of each environmental insult often was felt immediately because of fumes, odors, or noise levels. While on the tours, students took photos and recorded their observations, feelings, and perceptions about each site.

The students returned to the classroom and were tasked with developing a "community-risk map." Community-risk mapping is a process adapted from the practices of labor organizers, often in farming and other industries, where potential health and safety risks exist in the workplace (Hesperian Foundation 1998; Mujica 1992; Smith, Barret, and Box et al. 2000). In workplace-risk mapping, workers identify and categorize risks they face then plot them on maps of their work environments. Workers are encouraged to use symbols and other nontraditional mapping devices to display the locations of areas or tasks in the workplace where they have experienced or perceived dangerous or noxious conditions (Mujica 1992). Community-risk mapping emulates the workplace mapping process and generally involves a group brainstorming session to list hazards, code and symbolize these hazards, and then map them on large poster-board. The process, also analogous with community "visioning" sessions commonly used for planning purposes, can be particularly effective when used in communities where residents may be uncomfortable with public speaking or technical information, are not fluent in English, and seek a means for creatively expressing how they perceive their neighborhood (Aberley 1993; Ames 1998).

The Toxic Avengers used what they learned in science class to develop a map of the community for the explicit purpose of organizing residents. After learning that an upcoming public hearing would be reviewing the operating permit of the Radiac waste storage and transfer facility, the students decided to use their map of the neighborhood to draw attention to the poorly maintained and, in their eyes, dangerous facility. The Avengers came up with a map that became affectionately known as the Skulls map (figure 3.2.1). The map was turned into a poster and used to publicize the Radiac hearing throughout the neighborhood. The risk-mapping process created more than a new image of the community. The process itself helped build a new network of young activists, created a new organization for young people to express their knowledge, and helped galvanize other community members to consider the environmental-health challenges in front of them.

**Figure 3.2.1** Toxic Avengers skulls map
*Source*: El Puente Toxic Avengers

## What Maps Do

Maps perform at least three political functions in relation to knowledge. First, maps always *aggregate and select data* and how they do this can lead to enormous differences in interpretive outcomes. Second, maps are *identity forming* devices since the symbols used to visually present information give "life" and persuasiveness to certain representations. Third, maps are always *boundary makers* by including some information and excluding others.

### Aggregation

How maps aggregate information for visual presentation may lead to enormous differences in interpretive outcomes. The maps and images that are used as standard ways of seeing a problem tell us whose vision matters, what should be rendered visible, and what should be made invisible. Maps are also always made for certain purposes, such as to convince an audience of a certain point of view, and they provide rules for real-world decisions. A particular map "wins" or becomes the dominant image of the day by resonating with those in political power (Scott 1998). For example, *National Geographic* often is cited for generating maps during the Cold War with an explicitly Western perspective; the Soviet Union was portrayed as a large (and presumably dangerous) land mass compared to Europe and the United States. Similarly, maps of the world often have portrayed Africa as smaller and less prominent (and thus less important) compared to Europe and North America (Monmonier 1996).

Yet, the power of maps for (mis)representing reality remains a contentious subject in planning, science, and policymaking. Harley (1989) notes that maps represent hypothetical generalizations and are always, to some degree, inaccurate. They model a reality known to be more complex than any map can portray. Yet, at the same time, maps exert a compelling persuasiveness; they are designed to look real—particularly to those beyond the mapmaking community (Monmonier 1996).

## Boundary Making

Mapmaking also can be understood as a scientific process, where some information is selected and others excluded in order to make the project legible (Lynch and Woolgar 1990). For example, Gieryn (1995) notes how mapmaking acts as a powerful metaphor for understanding the production of scientific knowledge itself. Science often is portrayed as an "empty map" that becomes filled in by certain groups or institutions in order to have influence over a particular audience. The "mapmaking" of science is the decision to include and exclude certain information, and thereby to create boundaries around what counts as science. In other words mapping, like science, always shows a limited representation of a complex reality and generates provisional, contextual, and always amendable information (Gieryn 1995, 406).

Yet, the production of visual images can extend the influence of science, often taking on a life of its own. For example, Latour (1988) introduces the idea of the "immutable mobile," which is an image such as a map that is a fixed display of information and is used in different times and contexts to represent ideas or facts. One common example is the picture of the earth suspended in space, which has come to represent such things as environmentalism, holism, peace, and a number of other things. The meaning of the image, how it was produced, and by whom often is taken for granted or even ignored when it is used.

Ultimately, the legitimacy and credibility of a map is judged by what the cartographers choose to include in the physical rendering and the trustworthiness of the cartographers themselves. By creating boundaries around what is and is not important to see, maps can encourage viewers to "see like the state" or suggest some other imagined vision (Anderson 1991; Scott 1998). As Harley notes, mapmaking is a political process that deserves a critical analysis:

> All maps strive to frame their message in the context of an audience. All maps state an argument about the world and they are propositional in nature. All maps employ the common devices of rhetoric such as invocations of authority

> and appeals to a potential readership through the use of colors, decoration, typography, dedications, and written justifications of their method. Rhetoric may be concealed, but it is always present, for there is no description without performance. (Harley 1989, 11)

Thus, the mapmaking "performance" should be recognized as a political process that can reveal much about the society within which the image is created.

## Identity Formation

Ultimately, while maps are models of reality, they also shape that reality. In environmental planning, maps often reflect the views of scientists and policy makers about what knowledge and whose perspectives are authoritative, whether one or a plurality of plausible interpretations are legitimate, and at what scale a problem ought to be addressed (i.e., local, state, federal). For example, land-use maps are often de facto "base maps" used to describe the attributes of a place, implicitly suggesting that making physical changes to the land-use of a place is the principal means to address local issues (Hayden 1995). Peter Hall (1994) argues that the widespread institutional acceptance of land use mapping has helped perpetuate the "functionalist" view of city planning as the dominant paradigm in the field. In the functionalist view, planning is defined by how professionals label, demarcate, and separate land uses into zones and classify these areas by their function. In this case, mapping and particular types of standardized maps, have defined an entire field.

One of the most common tools used to model reality in urban planning today is the geographic information system (GIS). The GIS technology is a means of integrating spatial and nonspatial information into a single computer system for analysis and graphical display. The technology allows users to input vast amounts of information, perform statistical spatial analyses, and generate images of data analyses that extend the vision of the modern geographer. However, the reliance on computer-generated maps has been criticized for raising obstacles for public participation in and understanding of the mapping process. For instance, lay publics, especially those from disadvantaged groups, may have limited knowledge of and access to computers. Since the assumptions underlying computer-produced maps are buried within the computer application itself, GIS may further hinder lay understanding of the mapping process. Yet, at the same time, the increased availability of computing power also might lead to the democratization (or at least accountability) of map-making, precisely because citizen groups may be able to offer their own computer-generated maps.

The "GIS revolution" in planning has perpetuated an almost unfettered trust by both users and consumers of planning information in quantitative data as the most legitimate information for generating accurate spatial analyses, making maps, and ultimately characterizing places. Another emerging implication is that the technology is beginning to frame social problems as spatial research questions. In a note of irony and precaution, Monmonier (1996) reveals that the errors, inaccuracies, and imprecision inherent in GIS devolve from one of the technology's greatest strengths: the ability to collate and cross-reference many types of data and discrete data sets by location, called "geo-coding," in a single system. As new data sets are imported, the GIS also can inherit its errors and combine these with errors already in the system. Users of GIS must concern themselves as much with "cleaning" disparate data sets to match one another as with devising strategies to visually display the data.

As professionals increasingly rely on GIS in their work, some are making efforts to incorporate public stakeholders, especially community members, into the spatial mapmaking process (Aberley 1993). Efforts at public participation in GIS often include processes to incorporate local knowledge into data sets (Craig and Elwood 1998; Robbins 2003). As community members increasingly become both producers and consumers of GIS, planning processes and participants will continue to be shaped by this and other professional mapping technologies.

## Maps as Organizers of Attention

The Toxic Avengers' Skulls map (figure 3.2.1) describes the neighborhood as "NYC's toxic nightmare." It shows skulls describing numerous local hazards and uses both graphic visuals and text. The background, or base map, is a photocopied tax-surveyor map made to look like an X-ray, enhancing the sense of urgency that pollution is compromising personal health. Photographs of industrial facilities used to identify the locations of particular polluters personalize the map for local residents since most would recognize the facilities. However, the pictures were slightly "whited out" to look almost ghostly.

The Toxic Avengers brought the map to Luis Garden-Acosta, El Puente's founder and executive director, in an effort to encourage him to personally invite the neighborhood's Hasidic Jewish population to the Radiac hearing. After seeing the map, Acosta was convinced that all the community's ethnic groups would need to work together to improve environmental conditions (Hevesi 1994). According to Garden-Acosta:

> It was nothing but confrontation [with the Hasidim] before young people from the Toxic Avengers came to me and said, "Isn't it time to ask the Hasidim to join forces with us in reclaiming our environment?" It was their request and their graphic map gave me the "ah ha" that we all breathe the same air. (quoted in Hevesi 1994)

Acosta sent an invitation to Rabbi David Niederman, executive director of the UJO of Williamsburg, to come to a planning meeting for the Radiac event. Niederman agreed to meet with El Puente and bring other Hasidim with him after El Puente agreed to hire police to guarantee their security. As Garden-Acosta recounts those events in May 1991:

> It was a historic moment when a Hasidic rabbi, a leader of the Satmar, walked through the doors of El Puente. We were planning a march to a hearing on Radiac emergency procedures, and Rabbi Niederman volunteered to help lead that march through Latino streets. I can't describe what a change that meant. It was a clear act of courage on the part of David Niederman. (quoted in Hevesi 1994)

The multiethnic march raised interest in the issues, and over 200 people attended the hearing. The success of the event encouraged the two groups to organize an "environmental town meeting" to raise awareness about local hazards and specifically to educate residents about a proposed municipal waste incinerator in the Brooklyn Navy Yard. According to Niederman, the meeting was necessary because no group alone could confront the multiple environmental threats the community faced: "We were facing the incinerator, lead poisoning, garbage transfer stations, chemicals from abandoned factories around here, sandblasting from the bridge and Radiac. We had to come together" (quoted in Hevesi 1994).

The incinerator proposal galvanized the community, which saw the project as treating their homes as the dumping ground for unwanted garbage. The incinerator was supposed to be the most cost-effective way for the City to dispose of municipal solid waste. In the 1980s, after closing all but one landfill and most of its incinerators, New York City feared a garbage-disposal crisis. The possibility of a crisis made headlines in 1987 when a garbage barge called the "Mobro," carrying 32,206 tons of NY refuse, left Islip on a six-month journey in search of a place to unload. The barge, turned away by several states and three countries, eventually returned to New York; most of its garbage was burned at the Southwest Brooklyn incinerator (Miller 2000). Soon thereafter, the City devised a comprehensive solid-waste management plan that would close the 22 City-operated incinerators and the over 1,200 private apartment-building incinerators. In order to handle its waste, the City planned to build eight new incinerators and the Williamsburg facility was planned as the first and largest (Miller 2000).

The Brooklyn Navy Yard incinerator was proposed as a "state of the art" facility that could burn nearly one-third of the city's daily municipal waste (approximately 3,000 tons per day at the time of the proposal) and was supposed to ease the burden on the only operating landfill site in the city, Fresh Kills on Staten Island (Waldman 1997). At the time, the largest incinerator in the city was burning 550 tons per day. Neighborhood residents, along with city, state, and national environmental groups sued the City to stop the proposed project based on the expected increased truck traffic and unsafe air emissions (Liff 1992; Sullivan 1995). Barry Commoner, who emerged as a vocal opponent of the project, claimed that dioxins from the incinerator would poison local residents (Commoner 1992, 109–119).

The town meeting brought together community leaders representing different issues and ethnic groups to speak about hazards in the community and the need to organize together to stop the incinerator. According to Elizabeth Colon, executive officer of the Brooklyn Navy Yard corporation, the meting was as much about the future direction of community development, particularly concerns over the changing economic realities in the neighborhood, including "unemployment and a deteriorating economic base," as about environmental issues (Hevesi 1994). Residents also feared that if the City was allowed to build an incinerator on the property of one obsolete industrial site, a similar fate would await the hundreds of other decaying and abandoned industrial properties scattered around the neighborhood.

The Toxic Avengers helped develop another map of the community. The "Our Town" map (figure 3.2.2) was intended to show that the community was under multiple environmental stressors, not just the proposed incinerator. Like the Skulls map, the Our Town map used graphic displays of death and danger to portray the neighborhood. Skulls and crossbones were used to label toxic storage sites, a large nuclear symbol identified the Radiac facility, and black smoke was shown coming from stacks to identify the proposed incinerator sites around the community. The Our Town map also was filled with descriptive information about the amount of pollution emitted from local facilities.

Over 1,200 residents attended the environmental town meeting, which ended with a commitment from leaders of the Latino, Hasidic, African-American, and Polish communities to form the Community Alliance for the Environment (Greider 1993).[2] The first action CAFE planned was a multiethnic march over the Williamsburg Bridge during rush hour to protest the proposed incinerator (Hevesi 1994).[3] The Toxic Avengers' map helped educate and organize the new multiethnic environmental coalition. The 1992 march has been credited as one of the key turning points that eventually convinced the City to mothball the incinerator proposal (Sullivan 1995).

Both the Skulls and Our Town maps reveal the creativity and awareness young people can bring to an environmental issue. They suggest that, as Mumford noted, the planning process often begins "with a dynamic emotional urge, springing out of a sense of frustration on one hand and a renewed vision of life on the other" (1938, 359). The maps acted as powerful representations of a "dying neighborhood" inundated with hazards. On each map, almost no space was left for viewers to see what else was in the neighborhood besides the polluting facilities. The maps help "pattern attention selectively," or reveal what some residents' value. They publicly express allegiances and prepared residents "to recognize new issues and attend creatively and responsively to particular struggles at hand" (Forester 1999, 139). The maps accomplished their mission of organizing and galvanizing an important multiethnic environmental coalition in the neighborhood.

Students were able to combine local knowledge and professional data into powerful visual information. Visualizing local knowledge, whether through community maps, murals, or theater, allows local people to express what they know, share it with other community members in a way that is understandable for all, focus discussion, and propose options for action. As tools for educating community members, sharing experiences, and mobilizing action, maps can be as or more important than local knowledge as text, particularly in communities with disparate levels of formal education, common language, symbols, and traditions. But while the student maps showed that mapping local

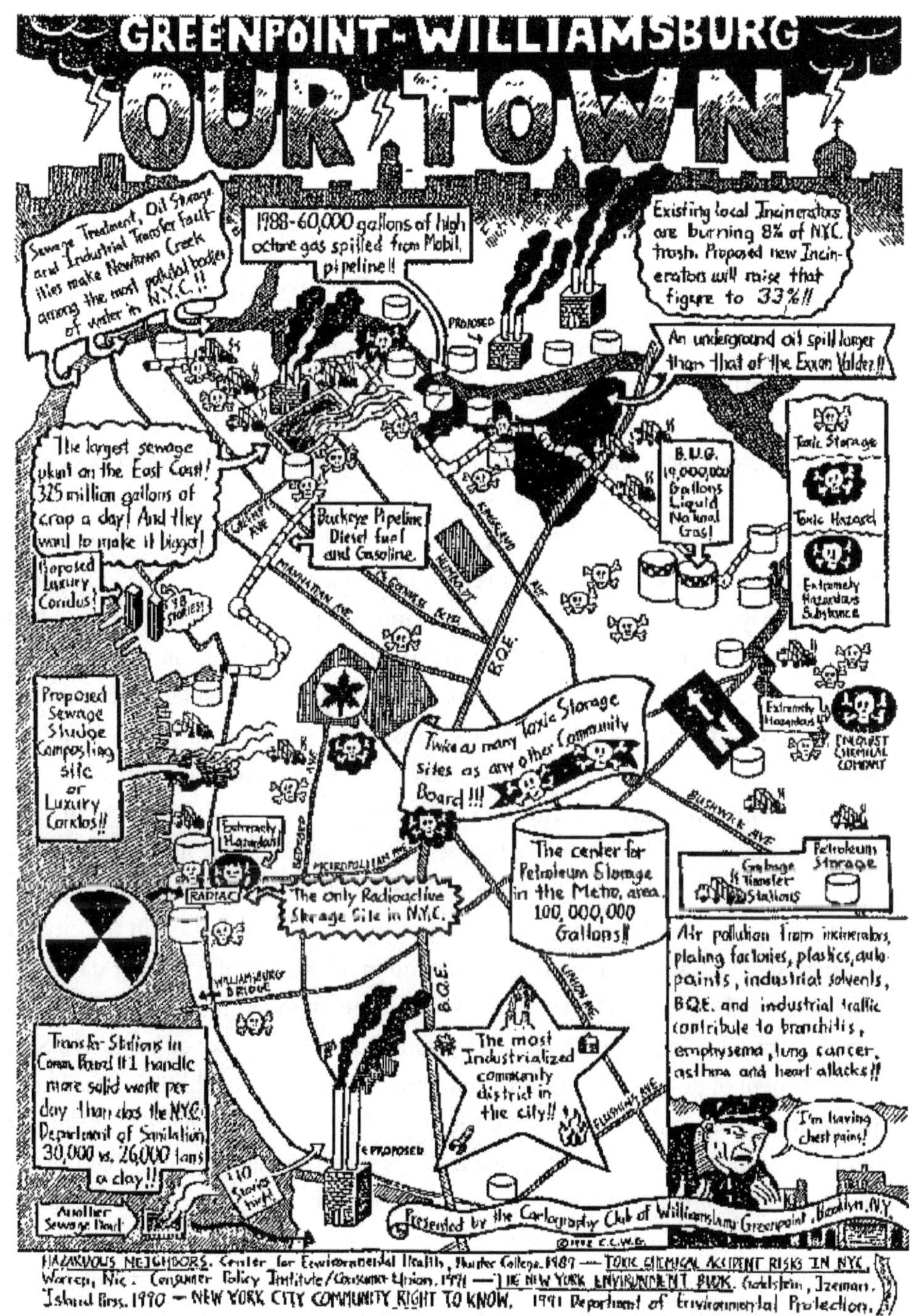


**Figure 3.2.2** "Our Town" community map
*Source*: Cartography Club of Williamsburg/Greenpoint

knowledge can be important for influencing people *within* the community, it is less useful for relating to outside professionals.

The student maps gave "voice" to those previously silent about environmental hazards and showed how residents perceived local pollution and its impacts on different groups within the neighborhood. And while the maps did not help extend professional science, they stimulated community interest in developing other visual portraits of neighborhood pollution.

## Contested Images: Community and Professional Maps

The student maps were low-tech images that contained a lot of detail but were cartoonlike. Community groups realized during the incinerator battle that they would have to start generating maps to compete with technical experts in order to make their point of cumulative environmental impacts in the neighborhood (Swanston 1999). Soon after CAFE formed, the Watchperson Project was created. Part of the Watchperson Project's charter included developing GIS and making it accessible for community members (ICLEI 1993; Sweeney et al. 1994). Beginning in 1993, the Watchperson Project partnered with Hunter College to gather electronic data to enter into a community-based GIS. A key goal for the community was to use the GIS for analyzing the proximity of polluters to residents and to develop sophisticated and "official looking" maps (Hanhardt 1999). The Watchperson Project initially used GIS to produce maps displaying the relationship between hazards and residents, schools, and other sensitive receptors. One of the first published maps displayed the proximity of the Radiac facility, an electroplater, and a sugar factory to a school, day care center, and neighborhood playground (figure 3.2.3). The community first used the GIS to challenge a City-backed project during a public hearing over the permitting of a controversial waste-transfer station in the neighborhood.

In April 1998, the city Department of Sanitation (DOS) and the state Department of Environmental Conservation (DEC) approved the siting of the largest waste-transfer station in the city's history.[4] The transfer station, which was permitted to process up to 5,000 tons of waste per day on the Kent Avenue site known as Eastern District Terminal, would be operated by the USA Waste Services Corporation (Saltonstall 1998).[5] The 60,000-square-foot facility was approved by the DOS and DEC without an assessment of potential environmental, traffic, and public health impacts. The agencies granted the facility a "Neg Dec," declaring that the facility posed no potential significant impact on the community. A coalition of community organizations sued the state claiming that the size of the facility required an environmental impact statement.[6] A public hearing, the required final step in the permitting process, was held in April after the facility's approval.

Representatives from a number of community groups testified against the proposed facility. From restaurant owners, who said the noise, dust, and smell of the facility would destroy their business, to community leaders such as Rabbi Niederman, who claimed that the trucks and pollution would put all community residents at risk. The testimonials of over 200 residents occupied almost the entire hearing

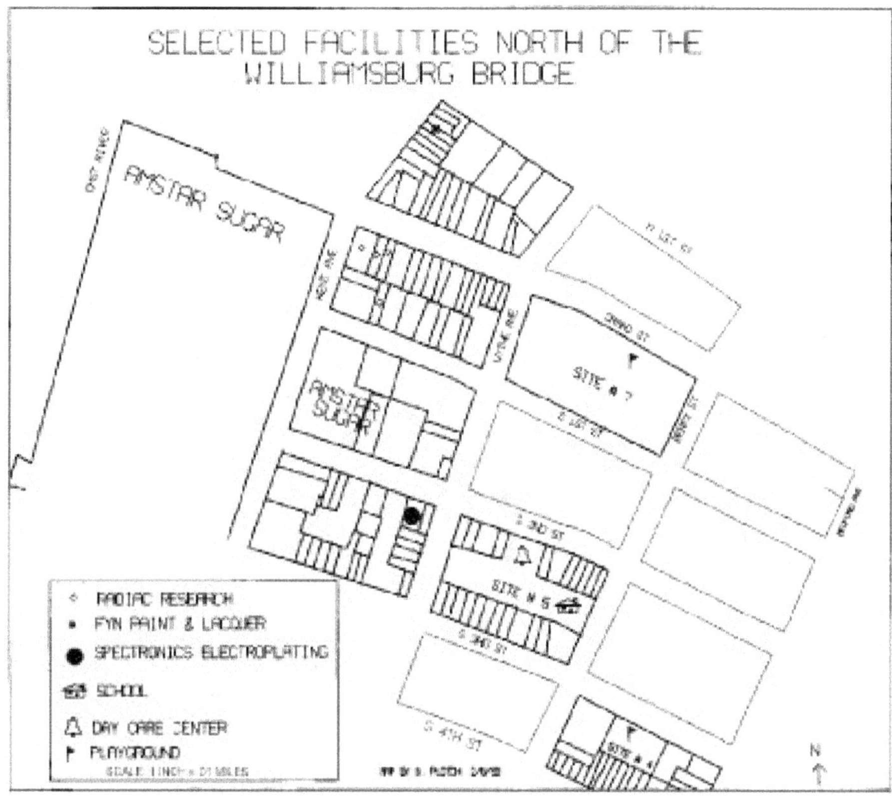


**Figure 3.2.3** GIS map depicting selected facilities north of the Williamsburg Bridge
*Source*: Watchperson Project

and carried the proceeding well past midnight.[7] An administrative law judge presided over the hearing. Samara Swanston, presented a series of maps showing the areas in the community that would be impacted, such as those along truck routes. The maps also showed the number of existing waste-transfer stations and their proximity to low-income and minority-group populations. According to Swanston:

> We tried to make the case that not only was this mammoth facility going to hurt business, it was also part of a pattern of environmental injustice in the neighborhood. When community folks start talking about environmental justice, regulators tend to cringe, and that is what the DEC did. But, the ALJ [administrative law judge] was more open. I think he hadn't really heard of the issue before. When we put up the map of the cumulative hazards and I asked him if he'd want his kids to live here, he kind of did a double take. (Swanston 1999)

The cumulative hazard map showed the truck routes, the locations of the neighborhood's transfer stations, school and park properties, and sites where toxins were used and released (figure 3.2.4).

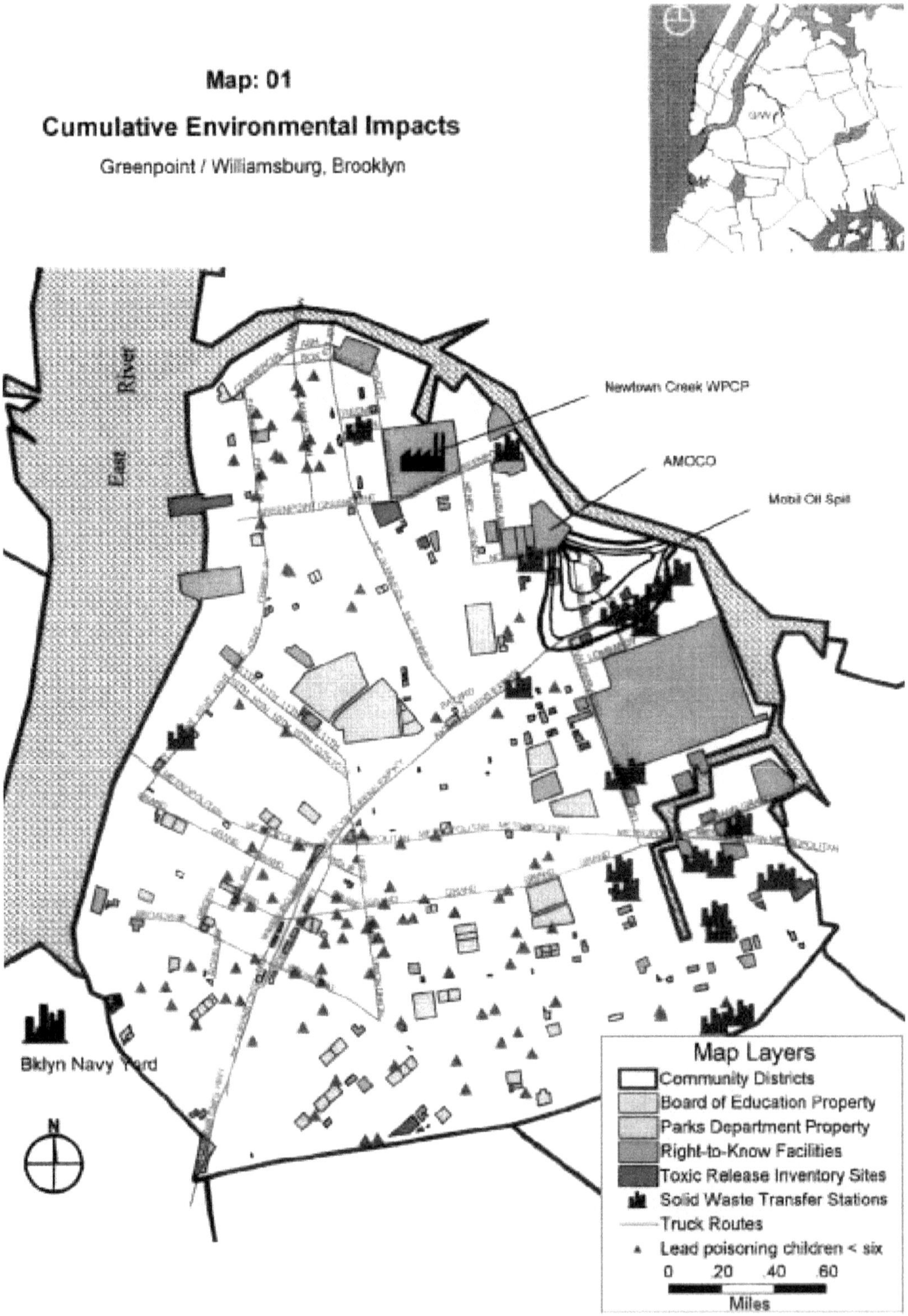

**Map: 01**

**Cumulative Environmental Impacts**

Greenpoint / Williamsburg, Brooklyn

East River

Newtown Creek WPCP

AMOCO

Mobil Oil Spill

Bklyn Navy Yard

N

Map Layers

- Community Districts
- Board of Education Property
- Parks Department Property
- Right-to-Know Facilities
- Toxic Release Inventory Sites
- Solid Waste Transfer Stations
- Truck Routes
- Lead poisoning children < six

0 .20 .40 .60

Miles

**Figure 3.2.4** Cumulative environmental impact map
*Source*: Watchperson Project

The map also plotted the locations where elevated lead levels were found in neighborhood children, an oil plume underneath the neighborhood, and the sewage treatment plant. According to Heather Roslund, an activist with Neighbors Against Garbage (NAG), the map was significant because:

> It gave us legitimacy. We not only gave our testimony, but we showed them [DEC and DOS] that we also did our homework and had technical skills. The community maps showed that we were not just about NIMBY, but that this was a much larger issue about environmental hazards and social justice. We showed that we were prepared and could go head-to-head with the city, state and even a big corporation like USA Waste.

The DOS countered the community's presentation with maps of their own. The DOS argued that this was a siting case and that the facilities were necessary to avoid a garbage-disposal crisis. The issue, according to the DOS, was about available appropriately zoned land. The City displayed a map of the neighborhood's zoning and land use. The only other environmental features on the map were truck routes and the location of existing transfer stations (figure 3.2.5). The City argued that the only legal location for transfer stations was in areas zoned for heavy manufacturing, labeled "M-zones," and G/W happened to have more of this land than almost any other community district in the city. According to James Doherty, sanitation commissioner at the time:

> The only clustering we might see of transfer stations is because these facilities are limited to industrial areas and these tend to be concentrated in certain parts of the city. In fact, we even exempted the light-industrial, M-1 zones, which tend to be closest to residential areas. We [DOS] have no control over where these things get sited. They go where the zoning allows them to go. (quoted in Martin 1998)

The City's maps were used as a justification for the permitting of the waste-transfer station and were used to deflect concerns about injustice and whether G/W was a community already overburdened with hazards.

In the eyes of most community members, the maps were an indication of the City's refusal to acknowledge the cumulative toxic burden facing the neighborhood. The City's maps became known by residents as the "toxic donut" maps. They showed the oval-shaped community surrounded on all sides by manufacturing land uses and industrial zones, with residents living in the center of the industrial ring.

The administrative law judge overseeing the hearing ruled that the community's case was compelling and required USA Waste to provide more information to show that their facility would not have a significant environmental impact on local residents. The judge ruled that it seemed "unreasonable"

**Brooklyn**
**Community Board 1**

□ Residential or commercial
Manufacturing Zone M1
Manufacturing Zone M2 & M3
■ School
Park

○ Non-putresible transfer station
Putresible transfer station
Ⓕ Fill transfer station

D.O.T. truck rout

**Figure 3.2.5** New York City zoning map and locations of transfer stations in Greenpoint/Williamsburg
*Source*: New York City Department of City Planning

for a facility of such a size not to have some impact on the community, and, in light of the background environmental conditions in the community, more information would be necessary before any permits granted (Shin 1999). In June of 1998, both the New York State Assembly and Senate passed bills (S7610/A11084), introduced by Brooklyn representatives, requiring USA Waste to perform an EIS. And, just two months after the hearing, on June 23, 1998, Governor Pataki signed the bill and announced that the State would require USA Waste to prepare the environmental assessment.[8] However, after a year of study, the EIS concluded that there would again be "no significant impacts" from the facility but, at the urging of Congresswoman Nydia Velazquez, the White House Council on Environmental Quality and the EPA began an examination into whether G/W had been targeted for garbage-transfer stations because residents were poor and minorities (Shin 1999). According to Brad Campell, a CEQ associate director:

> The problems we see here have a huge influence on policy and legislation. We were very disappointed that the City Housing, Sanitation and Environmental Protection departments are not joining us in this effort. The best chance for solutions is when we have a partnership between federal, state and local governments. (quoted in Shin 1999)

As the federal investigation went ahead, the DOS granted the waste-transfer station its permit. It wasn't until May 2000, after the NY Lawyers for the Public Interest (representing the community) convinced a Manhattan Supreme Court judge to block the permit, that the facility finally stopped operating (Liff 2000).

By combining agency data with residents' experience of hazards, the community hazard map was attempting to extend the work of professional science. The community map also tried to shift the debate from facility siting and zoning to cumulative impacts and environmental injustice. However, the City perceived the map as a threat and countered that it was "irrelevant" for siting decisions that were based on zoning. The map did help residents gain attention from the environmental justice movement, and this visibility played a significant role in getting the federal government and eventually the administrative law judge to pay attention to the community's claims. Community mapping played a key role organizing attention but ultimately only supplemented the legal arguments that influenced professional action.

## Mapping Small-Source Air Polluters

As environmental justice claims continued to surface in the neighborhood,[9] community groups continued expanding the capabilities of their own GIS. The Watchperson Project used its mapping technology to influence the EPA's Cumulative Exposure Project (CEP), the same project that assessed risks from subsistence fish diets discussed in chapter 3. This time, the community mapped polluters that an EPA exposure model in the community would have overlooked.

While the relationship between air pollution and public health long has been studied (ATS 1996; Holgate et al. 1999), definitive conclusions about air pollution's effects on urban residents are limited. In addition to gaps in understanding regarding the biologic mechanisms responsible for the morbidity and mortality associated with increased air pollution, a lack of consistent ambient monitoring in urban areas has prevented scientists from capturing pollution at the local or microenvironment level. Yet, high concentrations of air pollutants are suspected of being common in many poor urban neighborhoods. The lack of microenvironment air monitoring also has prevented study of intra-urban or neighborhood differences that also might help better understand distributions of health effects associated with urban air pollutants. Additionally, combining point, area, and mobile sources to characterize pollution in microenvironments has proved difficult. Thus, dispersion models are used to estimate micro-scale urban pollution.

The CEP's first task of the air toxic exposure assessment involved gathering data inputs for the hazardous-air-pollutant (HAP) dispersion model called, Assessment System for Population Exposure Nationwide (ASPEN). The ASPEN model estimates long-term outdoor concentrations of 148 of the 188 HAPs listed in the Clean Air Act of 1970 for every census tract in the contiguous United States, based on 1990 data (totaling 60,803 census tracts) (EPA 1999a; Rosenbaum et al. 1999; Woodruff et al. 1998). ASPEN is a Gaussian dispersion model that estimates outdoor concentrations of HAPs on the basis of their emission rates, frequency of various meteorologic conditions, and the effects of atmospheric processes such as decay, secondary formation, and deposition.

The EPA planned on using the ASPEN model in G/W and adding any relevant local emission sources. However, the agency was content on basing the model on pollution data from the one NYS DEC air monitor in the neighborhood and the roughly fifty Toxic Release Inventory (TRI) sites registered with the EPA that were known to emit some hazardous air pollutants (EPA 1999a). During meetings presenting the project to the community, EPA heard from residents that their proposed methodology, particularly the census-tract aggregation and the reliance solely on state and federal data, was going to miss some potentially hazardous exposures. According to a local resident attending one of the meetings:

> If you just walk around here you can see that we've got polluters mixed in with residents; some small and other large factories. To tell us that everyone in the census tract was exposed more or less the same missed the variations on the street.

More specifically, representatives from the Watchperson Project noted that the air-dispersion model was going to miss hundreds of potential polluters because they did not show up in any state or federal air-quality database. These polluters were registered, since they had to file for permits with the NYC DEP, but their emissions were not monitored. According to community members commenting on the EPA analysis, the census-tract aggregation of the ASPEN model was going to "wash out" the block-to-block pollution differences that existed in the neighborhood. The Watchperson Project noted that the air toxic model made no mention of indoor air pollution, specifically perchloroethylene ("perc"), a known carcinogen suspected of affecting residents living above dry cleaners (Swanston 2000).

In making their case to the EPA, community residents once again developed their own set of maps. The Watchperson Project used their GIS to develop maps comparing the state hazardous sites the EPA used as data inputs for the model to the DEP-regulated air polluters that the model was slated to ignore (figure 3.2.6). The Watchperson Project had spent over two years trying to obtain environmental information from the City, including air-permit information, environmental complaints records, and parcel-by-parcel tax information from the City's Department of Finance. The DEP data was from the Bureau of Air Resources Administration Management Information System and included permit data on over 3,000 facilities in the neighborhood that were required to file for an air-emission permit but were not regulated, such as apartment-building boilers, auto-body paint shops, and printers. The Department of Finance data set included details about the history of every land parcel in the neighborhood for tax assessment purposes, and included information such as building type, property value, fire department inspections, and property owner. After a lengthy battle with the City, including numerous Freedom of Information Act requests, the community group obtained the electronic data (Swanston 1999). The Watchperson Project was the only community organization in the City that obtained these disparate data sets and, since these data were not housed at any one agency, no agency had compiled this information into one computer system capable of graphically displaying the information (Hanhardt 1999). With the help of computer specialists from Hunter College, the group began manipulating the data in their own GIS.

The Watchperson Project's map showing the block-by-block variation of air polluters was aimed at convincing the EPA that their model's aggregation was not fine-grained enough to accurately characterize air pollution in the neighborhood. According to Robert Lewis, director of the Watchperson's Office GIS project:

> To capture data only by census tract or block group averaged-out significant localized emissions. A data-set that aggregated by census-tract or even block would miss important distinctions between city blocks and even within one block. We had the data to show this. So we produced maps of the entire neighborhood and presented them to EPA showing just how many small-sources there are in the neighborhood and how the state and federal databases missed all these. (Lewis 2000)

The Watchperson Project mapped 15,167 distinct land parcels in the community and produced maps comparing the facilities used in the EPA model with facilities regulated by the DEP but which the dispersion model was not going to include (e.g. figure 3.2.6). The group found over 1,000 potentially toxic air polluters that the EPA would miss in its census-tract level assessment (Swanston 2000).

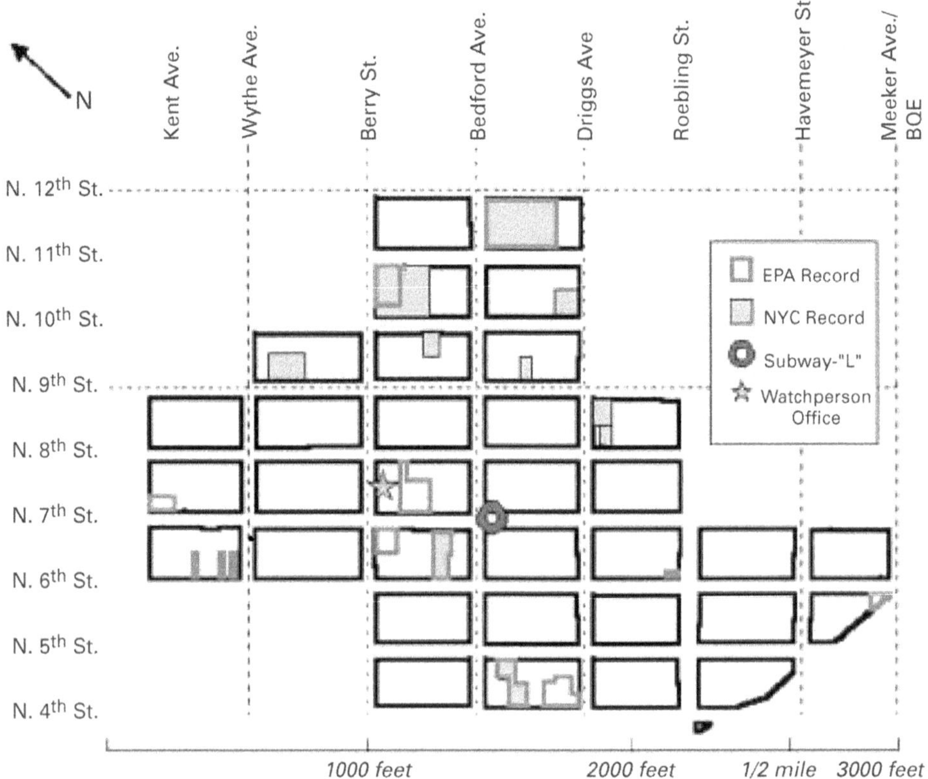


**Figure 3.2.6** Community generated block-by-block map comparing EPA and DEP modeling sites
*Source*: Watchperson Project

The Watchperson Project's maps were convincing to EPA scientists, but the agency struggled with how to treat the information in their dispersion model. According to one EPA scientist:

> The community maps made sense, especially after some of us had toured the neighborhood with some residents. We had a sense there were lots of small sources, but we didn't realize the full extent until we saw the community's maps. We struggled for a long time considering what to do with their data set. We tweaked the model some but we just couldn't aggregate all those sources at a block by block level without loosing accuracy in the dispersion model. What

> we did do, however, was take the area sources we could get enough data for, plot them, and model them as point sources.[10]

The community-generated map forced EPA to rethink whether its dispersion model was an accurate characterization of on-the-ground exposures, but it ultimately did not significantly alter the agency's dispersion model.

A second map produced by the Watchperson Project's GIS was also used to try to influence the EPA modelers. As part of their GIS program, the community group used volunteer high-school students to canvass the neighborhood in teams to follow up on community complaints of air, noise, and odor pollution registered by residents with the DEP. The community group plotted the location of the complaints on GIS-generated maps and students "investigated" the areas near the complaints to look for any obvious sources of pollution that might need attention. One finding from the student's "street survey" was that a large number of complaints were coming from residents living in buildings with dry cleaning establishments (Swanston 2000).

After learning about the findings of the student canvass, the Watchperson Project organized a special project focused on documenting the location of all neighborhood dry-cleaning establishments and the specific type of buildings in which they were located. The survey found 54 dry cleaners in the neighborhood, with 23 of the 54 performing dry-cleaning in a residential building (EPA 1999a). Using the GIS and census data, the community group estimated that as many as 183 apartments and approximately 550 residents were living above dry-cleaning establishments (EPA 1999a). Again the group mapped these findings and presented them to the EPA modelers (figure 3.2.7).

The Watchperson Project's dry-cleaning survey raised a particular concern to EPA since a number of recent studies in New York City had found concentrations of perc inside apartments, at up to three floors above a dry cleaner in the same building, averaging 150 ppm (parts per million), with some measurements exceeding 1,000 ppm (Wallace et al. 1995; NYS DOH 1993).[11] In one study by the NYS DOH, 39 of 40 apartments above dry cleaners tested had concentrations of perc in the air exceeding the 100 ppm state guideline for noncancer effects. One measurement in this study found perc levels at 197,000 ppm. Another study by the Consumers Union found that 24 of 29 apartments above dry cleaners had four-day average concentrations of perc above the DOH guideline and 8 had average concentrations above 1,000 ppm (Wallace et al. 1995).

The EPA ASPEN model estimated the expected *outdoor* concentration of perc at less than 2 ppb (part per billion), with a maximum-modeled census-tract outdoor concentration of 39 ppb (EPA 1999a). According to Fred Talcott, Project Director of the CEP at EPA:

> The average concentration found in apartments above dry cleaning establishments was on the order of 1,000 times higher than the outdoor concentration of "perc" as predicted by the ASPEN model in G/W. That to me is an illustration of a

**Figure 3.2.7** Community plots of neighborhood dry cleaners
*Source*: US EPA 1999a, chapter 6, p. 23

> micro-level problem that would be completely obscured if you only looked at daily walking around concentration. Without the community group data set, we would have missed this. (Talcott 1999)

EPA considered performing a separate assessment for this subpopulation, but eventually decided to document the findings only in the CEP report (EPA 1999a, 6–24).

These two examples of community mapping reveal that local knowledge can bring important insights to sophisticated technological assessments. The community GIS organized information that no other agency had compiled and then mapped these data to reveal what daily experience already told most residents: that pollution exposures differ from block-to-block and even along the same block. The community group also combined their computer-mapping capabilities with a student survey to find a hazard unanticipated by the EPA: potential toxic exposures from dry cleaners in residential buildings. In both instances, the community-mapping technology helped validate what residents already were experiencing (e.g., following up on air and odor complaints) and helped bring this knowledge to the attention of the EPA. While the community maps failed in the end to significantly alter the EPA air-dispersion model, the maps did challenge the EPA to address new questions, new sources of data, new exposures, and new groups claiming access to the assessment process—all of which had a significant impact on the way professionals viewed their role, if not their final decisions.

## How Community Maps Influence Professionals

Maps are an important tool for organizing and making publicly visible the *street science* performed in communities. The mapping of local knowledge in G/W ranged from student drawings on photocopied street maps to sophisticated computer-generated GIS outputs. In each instance, maps were used as counter expertise, opposing a noxious facility or challenging professional assumptions about how to assess the neighborhood's environment. In each case, residents eventually changed the way professionals viewed the environmental issue at stake, although the extent to which the community maps were responsible for these changes was mixed.

The Toxic Avenger's maps did not directly influence professionals but, by helping organize the community around environmental issues, the student maps helped build an important coalition that played a role influencing professional decisions. The community's cumulative burdens map was a key piece of a series of influential testimony that convinced the administrative law judge and other politicians to eventually demand that USA Waste perform an EIS. However, the community's hazard map was not convincing to the City, as they continued to permit the transfer station even after the federal government intervened. For the City, the issue was appropriate zoning, not cumulative environmental impacts or unfair siting practices. It took successful litigation two years after the initial public hearing to convince the City to revoke the transfer station's permit. Finally, the GIS maps that the Watchperson Project offered to the EPA modelers were compelling, even mapping information that no other agency could combine, but did not significantly alter the air dispersion model.

In this case, the student maps were explicitly aimed at building a community coalition, but the other maps were not. The student maps combined understandings from agency databases, environmental pollution information, and local experiences with pollution. However, the maps were more expressions of how a group of local people saw the conditions under which they lived and the cartoonlike use of symbols might have contributed to professionals not taking these maps seriously. The community's GIS-generated maps combined electronic information that agencies and scientists were themselves using with local knowledge of problems and experiences with hazards. These *street science* maps both extended the understanding of scientists and also radically challenged professional analyses. For example, the GIS maps identified small-source air polluters that the EPA model was going to miss and helped fill gaps in the agency's modeling inputs. The cumulative environmental impacts map radically challenged the fairness of the City's transfer-station-siting practices and attempted to shift the discourse from zoning to environmental justice.

The influence of expert intermediaries was less significant in these episodes because visual images tend to "speak for themselves." The community did use intermediaries to help them obtain some electronic data and build their GIS, however. In some ways, the GIS technology itself acted as the surrogate intermediary, since the technology was something both professionals and locals accepted as a legitimate means for displaying environmental information. The more the street scientists were able to make their knowledge resemble professional renditions, the more professionals took their work seriously.

As these episodes reveal, community-generated maps can challenge radically the way professionals are normally prepared to address environmental health problems. When community groups reframed the waste-transfer-station issue as one about fairness and justice by using their cumulative-hazard map, the City could not respond. Even when the federal government intervened to investigate whether waste-transfer stations were being targeted for poor and minority neighborhoods, the City refused to participate in this probe. Similarly, the EPA modelers could find no easy solution to the inadequacy of the census-tract-level aggregation of their air dispersion model, or for keeping the model from missing hundreds of small pollution sources, such as dry cleaners. The EPA was committed to the ASPEN model even when compelling community-generated information suggested that it might not accurately characterize local air toxics exposures. As street scientists generate maps that reframe and reorient definitions of "problems," and as these same scientists develop the sophisticated skills of computer-aided mapping, they will continue to blur the line between professional and local knowledge and whose evidence counts as credible in environmental health decision making.

## Endnotes

1. See: www.toxicavenger.com.

2. The main players in the multi-ethnic, multi-racial anti-incinerator coalition were El Puente, UJO, and the Polish and Slavic Center (PSC).

3. The march was called "CAFE con LECHE" because the Brooklyn CAFE coalition marched over the bridge to Manhattan to meet another community coalition opposing the incinerator called, Lower Eastside Coalition for Health and the Environment (LECHE).

4. Under a 1991 court order, DEC and DOS share responsibility for review of solid waste transfer stations under the State Environmental Quality Review Act. DEC leads in review of natural resource issues and DOS in issues of social and economic impact.

5. USA Waste Corporation was later acquired by Waste Management Inc. and the transfer station proposal was also pursued by Waste Management.

6. See: Howard S. Golden, et al. v. Michael Carpinello, et ano, Supreme Court of New York, Index Number 42723/98. Some of the community groups included Neighbors Against Garbage (NAG), Organization of Waterfront Neighborhoods (OWN), Red Hook Civic Association, El Puente, New York City Environmental Justice Alliance, The Watchperson Project, Organizations United for Trash Reduction and Garbage Equity (OUTRAGE) and Boroughs Allied for Recycling and Garbage Equity (BARGE). The case was submitted by the New York Lawyers for the Public Interest and Brooklyn Legal Services.

7. I attended the hearing as a member of the NYC DEP but was not involved in the review of the facility. The following accounts of the meeting are from my notes and observations unless cited otherwise.

8. State of New York, Executive Chamber, Press Office, June 23, 1998. "Governor Pataki, Mayor Giuliani Announce Environmental Review for Brooklyn Transfer Station." Governor Pataki notes in the announcement: "Given the location of both these actions under consideration by the State and the City, and after hearing the community's concerns about this project, we are requiring the preparation of an environmental impact statement."

9. In 2000, Congresswoman Nydia Velazquez filed a Title VI Civil Rights complaint with the EPA, asserting that G/W residents have been targeted for transfer stations. She also introduced the 2001 Community Environmental Equity Act (HR 4939), which prohibited disproportionate exposure to hazardous substances based on race, color, national origin, or economic status. See, www.house.gov/velazquez/PressReleases/2001/pr010420.htm.

10. EPA scientist interviewed on April 24, 2000, on the condition of anonymity.

11. Perc is a dry-cleaning solvent and at high exposures has been shown to have adverse effects on the central nervous system, liver and kidneys. The US EPA Cancer Benchmark Level for Perc is 1.7ppb. A report by the NYC Public Advocate, *Clothed in Controversy II: The Urgent Need to Protect New Yorkers from*

*Toxic Dry Cleaning Fumes*, March 18, 1997, noted that two flights above a dry cleaner in Tribeca, perc levels were measured at 5–16 times the State DOH guideline. See: publicadvocate.nyc.gov/padcdetail.cfm?id1=7&2=46.

## References


Aberley, D. 1993. *Boundaries of home: Mapping for local empowerment.* Gabriola Island: New Society Publishers.

American Thoracic Society (ATS). 1996. Committee of the Environmental and Occupational Health Assembly. Health effects of outdoor air pollution: Part 2. *American Journal of Respiratory and Critical Care Medicine* 153: 477–498.

Ames, S. 1998. *Guide to community visioning.* Chicago: American Planning Association Press.

Anderson, B. 1991. *Imagined communities: Reflections on the origin and spread of nationalism.* Rev. ed. London and New York: Verso.

Commoner, B. 1992. *Making peace with the planet.* New York: The New Press.

Craig, W. J., and S. Elwood. 1998. How and why community groups use maps and geographic information. *Cartography and Geographic Information Systems* 25 (2): 95–104.

Forester, J. 1999. *The deliberative practitioner.* Cambridge, MA: The MIT Press.

Gieryn, T. F. 1995. The boundaries of science. In *Handbook of Science and Technology Studies*, ed. S. Jasanoff et al., 393–443 Thousand Oaks, CA: Sage Publications.

Greider, K. 1993 Against all odds. *City Limits* (August/September): 34–37.

Hall, P. 1994. *Cities of Tomorrow.* Updated ed. London: Blackwell Publishers.

Hanhardt, E. 1999, 2000. Director of the Environmental Benefits Program, NYC Department of Environmental Protection. Personal communication.

Harley, J. B. 1989. Deconstructing the map. *Cartographica* 26 (2): 1–20.

Hayden, D. 1995. *The power of place: Urban landscapes as public history.* Cambridge, MA: The MIT Press.

Hesperian Foundation. 1998. Women's health exchange—Reducing workplace health hazards guide: Making a risk map. Berkeley, CA: Hesperian Foundation.

Hevesi, D. 1994. Hasidic and Hispanic residents in Williamsburg try to forge a new unity. *New York Times*, September 18, B47.

Holgate, S. T., J. M. Samet, H. S. Koren, and R. L. Maynard, eds. 1999. *Air pollution and health.* San Diego, CA: Academic Press.

International Council for Local Environmental Initiatives (ICLEI). 1993. Community-based environmental management: Greenpoint/Williamsburg Environmental Benefits Program. Toronto: ICLEI.

Latour, B. 1988. *Science in action.* Cambridge, MA: Harvard University Press.

Liff, B. 2000. Waste-transfer permit yanked: Ruling is another victory for Red Hook in trash war. *Daily News*, May 12.

Liff, S. 1992. State OKs City's solid waste plan. *Newsday*, October 29, p. 128.

Lynch, M., and S. Woolgar, eds. 1990. *Representation in scientific practice.* Cambridge: The MIT Press.

Martin, D. 1998a. Trash station proposal greeted by protest. *New York Times,* March 4.

Martin, D. 1998b. Boroughs battle over trash as last landfill nears close. *New York Times*, Nov. 16, sec. B; p. 1, col. 4, metropolitan desk.

Miller, B. 2000. *Fat of the land: Garbage of New York—The last two hundred years.* New York: Four Walls Eight Windows Press.

Monmonier, M. 1996. *How to lie with maps.* 2nd ed. Chicago: University of Chicago Press.

Mujica, J. 1992. Coloring the hazards: Risk maps, research, and education to fight health hazards. *American Journal of Industrial Medicine* 22: 767–770.

Mumford, L. 1938. *The culture of cities.* New York: HBJ.

New York City Department of City Planning. 1996. The newest New Yorkers 1990–1994: An analysis of immigration to New York City in the early 1990s.

New York State Department of Health (NYS DOH). 1993. New York State dry cleaner survey. Bureau of Toxic Substance Assessment. November. Albany, NY: NYS DOH.

Robbins, P. 2003. Beyond ground truth: GIS and the environmental knowledge of herders, professional foresters, and other traditional communities. *Human Ecology* 31 (2): 233–239.

Rosenbaum, A. S., D. A. Axelrad, T. J. Woodruff, Y. H. Wei, M. P. Ligocki, and J. P. Cohen. 1999. National estimates of outdoor air toxics concentrations. *Journal of the Air Waste Management Association* 49: 1138–1152.

Saltonstall, D. 1998. Down in the dumps: Greenpoint, Williamsburg fighting against proposed garbage site. *Daily News*, May 17.

Scott, J. C. 1998. *Seeing like a state: How certain schemes to improve the human condition have failed.* New Haven, CT: Yale University Press.

Shin, P. H. B. 1999. Waste probe launched: Garbage transfer is tops on fed's list. *Daily News,* March 9, suburban, p. 1.

Smith, K., C. B. Barrett, and P. W. Box. 2000. Participatory risk mapping for targeting research and assistance: With an example from East African pastoralists. *World Development* 28 (11): 1945–1959.

Sullivan, J. 1995. Plan to build incinerator faces delay; Navy Yard project is being postponed. *New York Times*, June 16, B4.

Swanston S. 1999, 2000, and 2001. Personal communication.

Sweeney, J., C. Shipman, and A. Tassi. 1994. The Environmental Benefits Program, Brooklyn, NY. The Mega Cities Project. Urban environment-poverty case study series. New York: United Nations Development Program.

Talcott F. 1999, 2000. Personal communication.

U.S. Environmental Protection Agency (US EPA). 1999a. Office of Policy, Planning, and Evaluation. Community-specific cumulative exposure assessment for Greenpoint/Williamsburg, New York. Washington, DC: US EPA.

Waldman, A. 1997. Concern grows on where trash will go after Fresh Kills. *New York Times*, Nov. 16, sec. 14, col. 3.

Wallace, D., E. Groth, E. Kirrane, B. Warren, and J. Halloran. 1995. Upstairs, downstairs: Perchloroethylene in the air in apartments above New York City dry cleaners. October 1995. Yonkers, NY: Consumers Union of the United States, Inc.

Watchperson Project. 1999. Maps and unpublished data.

Woodruff, T. J., D. A. Axelrad, J. Caldwell, R. Morello-Frosch, and A. Rosenbaum, 1998. Public health implications of 1990 air toxics concentrations across the United States. *Environmental Health Perspectives* 106: 245–251.

## DISCUSSION QUESTIONS

1. Local knowledge relying on community intuition about environmental-health problems is viewed critically to making new policies or revising existing regulations. Do you believe that local knowledge has been embraced when for key policy changes in environmental policy? Where are the instances the local expertise has been at the core of policy discussions initiated?
2. Despite the contributions of local knowledge to environmental health policy, there are several challenges for using local knowledge for environmental policymaking. What are the most significant challenges for integrating local and professional knowledge? How could they be overcome?
3. There are the four strategies introduced to ensure local knowledge to be accepted to improve environmental health research and policymaking. What are the four ways? Which strategy seems most desirable to you?

READING 3.3

# Mushroom Packages

## An Ecovative Approach in Packaging Industry

By Younsung Kim and Daniel Ruedy

## Introduction

Sustainability in the packaging industry has never been more important. A $400 billion USD industry globally, packaging includes the manufacture and transport of paperboard and plastics (Ernst and Young 2013). Most conventionally designed packaging is of low cost and spends little more than a year in a linear route from producer to consumer life cycle (Hopewell et al. 2009; Niero et al. 2017). In the United States, more than 35 million tons of packaging paperboard and 160 million tons of packaging plastic are produced annually to contain, cradle, and cushion goods as they make their way through the supply chain (Geyer et al. 2017; Richtel 2016). As these packaging materials are discarded and enter the waste stream, they are disposed of in landfills, recycled, or incinerated for waste-to-energy (WTE) recovery.

Being highly visible to consumers, the packaging industry receives intense scrutiny worldwide, along the entire supply chain, from raw materials to end-of-life processes, for reducing its societal and environmental impacts (Hillier et al. 2017). The increasing concerns about the rising volume of packaging wastes are also aligned with the unproductive use of resources and materials. Both packaging producers and their primary customers—original equipment manufacturers (OEM), ecommerce and brick-and-mortar retailers, and wholesalers—face pressures to reduce materials in packaging so as to mitigate packaging's price fluctuations linked to global commodities. As such, packaging producers are forced to seek out and manage stable supply chain sources due to the instability of conventional packaging feedstocks such as wood, pulp, and petrochemicals, which would lead to reduced environmental impacts (Ernst and Young 2013).

Enhancing resource efficiency has become a conventional approach when a firm attempts to address sustainability challenges for the packaging industry (Ernst and Young 2013; Hillier et al. 2017). Noticing emerging market potentials of bio-based alternatives, some other firms have considered a more innovative approach such as developing biomaterials that may have a potential for replacing conventional, petroleum-based materials (Haneef et al. 2017; Hillier et al. 2017). Once succeeded, sustainability-promoting innovations would help firms reap greater environmental benefits and create sustainable value for shareholders (Hart 2005). However, a few firms only consider the innovative approach positively, and prior literature has rarely discussed what factors would explain why a firm could undertake innovations for sustainability. Drawing on the case of Ecovative Design, a biomaterials company headquartered in New York, USA, this study explores key factors prompting the firm to innovate their package products. Founded in 2007, Ecovative Design develops an array of environmentally friendly packaging materials by growing fibers on waste like cotton seed, wood fiber, and buckwheat hulls.

In the following sections, we first introduce the Schumpeterian creative response framework as an eco-innovation, technology-based approach to contemporary social and ecological crises, which can result in ecological modernization (York and Rosa 2003; Janicke 2008; Mason 2011). Creative response framework has been used to explain the causes and the consequences of innovation in economics and in the economy. It deviates from the continuous improvement-based approach to adopting new ideas and systems within the assumption of static economic changes (Schumpeter 1947). In the subsequent section, we examine the unsustainability of packaging products. In doing so, we underpin the current waste treatment practices of packaging materials and describe the challenges for recycling packaging products. We then explain the product innovation procedures taken by Ecovative and identify key factors of its successful practices by taking an inductive reasoning approach. Our findings indicate that technical competence combined with systems-thinking skills would prompt a firm to undertake innovative sustainability changes in its products and processes. In addition, a firm's ability to engage with governments to garner financial support and market recognition would help a firm to pursue sustainability-driven innovations for the packaging industry.

## Creative Destruction for Sustainability

Global sustainability challenges present prodigious opportunities for creative responses from market disrupters. Current society-nature interactions are not sustainable in that they negatively affect both vital ecological systems and human welfare and induce irreversible, long-term damages. Achieving global sustainability then involves a sheer transition to economically revolutionary processes and routines that would be necessary to remain viable without overwhelming the society and environment. It particularly implies a structural realignment of our dominant economic development paths away from energy- and material-intensive processes relying on fossil fuels toward ecological modernization in which societies modify their institutions in order to internalize environmental impacts and ecologically transform material process and consumption processes (Mol 1995; Hajer 1995; Mason 2011).

Creative destruction was coined by Schumpeter (1947), as he noticed creative responses that brought economic developments with dynamic changes in economy. According to traditional economists, economic changes are explained by indicating specific conditioning or causal factors within a given historical development. For instance, classical economic theory predicted that an increase in population would result in a fall in per capita income, as population growth may have no other effect than that predicated by classical theory. However, this is not necessarily true in actual instances. Population growth may rather derive new developments with increasing income per capita. In other cases, a protective duty may have no other effect than to increase the price of the protected commodity and, in consequence, its output. Unlike the classical economists' prediction, however, it may also induce a complete reorganization of the protected industry which eventually results in an increase in output so great as to reduce the price below its initial level. In observation of such historical economic developments and societal changes, Schumpeter reported the neglected area of economic change, creative and energizing *reactions* to changes in "condition" that can cause novel achievements being outside of the range of existing practices (Schumpeter 1947).

As such, creative response is distinct from adaptive response. Adaptive response is the process by which an economy adapts itself to a change in its data by simply adding new resources or modestly modifying the currently existing practices. Creative response is something *beyond* the range of expanding existing practices or applying the ordinary rules. In general, the three fundamental characteristics would dictate creative response: (1) It can only be fully appreciated ex post, never being understood ex ante; (2) it shapes the whole course of subsequent events and their long-run outcomes; and (3) in terms of frequency, intensity, and success, it is influenced by the quality of the personnel available at a social and sector level and by decisions, actions, and patterns of behaviors of individuals or of groups. In this light, entrepreneurship aligned with creative response is the pivotal mechanism of inducing long-term sustained economic change in a capitalist society (Schumpeter 1947).

Creative response framework is a suitable theoretical approach to putting an emphasis on innovative responses to environmental and sustainability challenges in a society. Given the emergence and prevalence of wicked environmental problems (Lackey 2007) for the late twentieth and twenty-first centuries, different organizational responses from defiance to proactiveness have been observed (Kim and Darnall 2016). Scholars in the field of sustainability management have utilized a wide array of theoretical approaches advocated in the mainstream management sciences (Starik and Kanashiro 2013), and creative response framework has been uniquely poised to explore new ideas, experiments, or innovative sustainability practices such as biomimicry, leapfrog technology, sustainable technology, and closed loops (Braungart and McDonough 2002; Hart 2005; Larson 2000).

The social actor's energizing effects that induce new developments and exhaustive disruptions can be attributed to a different set of characteristics. Typically, sustainability responses involving modest changes for pollution involve rationalization in terms of the impact on the industry structure. That means firms' green initiatives would be flourished as long as they can yield relatively short-term benefits and appeal stakeholders that concern pollution prevention and product stewardship without restructuring the existing industry. However, the biggest leaps in performance may not be driven from firms' modest sustainability responses. Rather, firms pursuing emerging technologies, new markets, new partners, new customers not served before, and entirely new stakeholders would practice "beyond greening" initiatives that entail discontinuity (Hart 2005). For instance, the automobile industry looks nothing like it did 10–15 years ago, as companies aiming at designing sustainability mobility like Tesla pushed the industry divested from carbon-intensive, gasoline-based engine vehicles to electric ones (Jay and Gerand 2015). What makes re-invention and creative destruction possible will depend on a whole new set of skills and capabilities that have the potential of being inherently clean and sustainable (Hart 2005).

Some fundamental elements for sustainability-oriented innovation involve technical competency and stakeholder engagement for market innovation (Larson 2000; Hart 2005; Jay and Gerand 2015; Kim and Darnall 2016). Not all firms would equip with such capabilities, because the process of navigating a systems-based sustainability solution would not be appealing to most firms in the mainstream market. Some visionary companies can seize the opportunity to drive redefinition and redesign of their industries toward sustainability, and innovative upstarts can unseat established firms. The value of creative disruptive process would be reaped over the long term, as it would be able to exceed competitive gains from incremental changes in sustainability. Large incumbent firms would be less likely to shift their underlying portfolio away from what used to be its core competencies and move toward the entirely new skill sets to play a completely new, different game (Prahalad and Hart 2002; de Soto 2000; Christensen 1997).

## The Need for Ecological Modernization in the Packaging Industry

### Market-Oriented Sustainability Opportunity

*Unsustainability of plastics.* An estimated 9,150 million tons of plastics have been produced since large-scale production began around 1950, of which 30% remains in use, 9% has been recycled, and 60% is in landfills or the natural environment (Geyer et al. 2017). It is also projected that by 2050, the world will produce 28,600 million metric tons of plastic polymer resins based on observed trends (Geyer et al. 2017). The recent analyses of the global plastic packaging industry place production at 78 million tons annually at a total value of $260 billion USD (World Economic Forum et al. 2016), and it is expected to reach $490 billion by 2026 (BusinessWire 2018).

Plastic packaging does not biodegrade by design. Although exposure to sunlight is known to weaken and fragment plastic, the environmental impact of the resulting millimeter-sized fragments has not been well understood (Tudryn et al. 2018; Geyer et al. 2017). Plastic manufacturing is also dependent on nonrenewable petroleum resources for its feedstock, which indicates plastic prices fluctuating closely with the cost of petroleum (Tudryn et al. 2018). Energy consumption to sustain rising plastic demand extends past production. Transportation of plastic resins from manufacturers to downstream wholesalers also comes at a cost. The US Environmental Protection Agency (USEPA) estimates on average that plastic shipments travel 497 miles, consume 0.49 million British thermal units (BTUs) of energy, and emit 0.04 metric tons of $CO_2$ per short ton of plastic packaging waste (USEPA 2016a).

Approximately 50% of all plastics produced are manufactured into single-use items and packaging products among them (Hopewell et al. 2009). However, plastic recycling is increasing worldwide at 0.7% annually (Geyer et al. 2017), and the recycling practice is widely accepted to reduce lifecycle net $CO_2$ emissions by as much as 27% over plastic manufactured from virgin raw material feedstock (Hopewell et al. 2009). Recycling rates vary among plastic types. Polyethylene terephthalate (PET), which comprises plastic water bottles and some packaging components, is frequently recycled at a recovery rate of 19.5% by weight (USEPA 2015). However, polystyrene and its variants—expanded polystyrene (EPS) and extruded polystyrene (XPS, commonly known as Styrofoam™)—are the least recycled plastics, faring at just 0.9% recovery by weight. Polystyrene's high bulk (EPS is 95% air by weight) makes its transport costly and logistically difficult, and polystyrene's polymer structure makes it an unattractive candidate economically for primary and secondary recycling. When plastic recycling facilities are unavailable or the recovered plastic is of poor quality, waste-to-energy (WTE) incineration may be a preferred disposition option over landfilling. Yet when adjusted for the utility emissions WTE avoids, there remain net anthropogenic $CO_2$ emissions of 1.27 and 1.25 $MtCO_2$/ton for polystyrene and mixed plastics, respectively (USEPA 2015). Irrespective of treatment options, all plastic waste management practices (e.g., WTE incineration, recycling [including plastic fraction collection and transport to facility], landfill, etc.) have negative impacts on the environment and human health. However, it is evident that no perfect waste management solution exists, and finding the most optimal way is challenging (Rigamonti et al. 2014). In addition, on a global scale, the prospects of improving sustainability of plastics, ultimately in a hope to create a circular economy, seem to be bleak in large part due to increasing demand for consumer goods, change in consumers' lifestyle with rapid urbanization, and rising consumerism in emerging economies (De los Rios and Charnley 2017). Through a full life cycle assessment, only 5% of the value of recovered plastics is retained, costing the global economy between $80 and $120 billion USD in losses annually (World Economic Forum et al. 2016).

In response to the rigidity of the mature plastics market and its well-established supply and processing systems, plastics companies in the 1980s began blending plant starch-based polymers into environmentally friendly, theoretically biodegradable polyethylene blends (Iles and Martin 2013). When biodegradability of these bioplastics fell short of standards, they were instead remarketed as "renewably sourced," since they did replace a fraction of the petroleum-based feedstock of conventional plastics with plant-based material.

Bioplastic production is typically specialized to a single commodity feedstock, such as corn or sugarcane, and the production of which may carry its own environmental costs. Diversion of these commodities to industrial uses such as bioplastic manufacture also creates competition with stocks going to food supply, instigating complex socioeconomic policy problems. For example, North America and South America are already using 37% and 27% of domestic sugar crops for ethanol production, respectively (Golden et al. 2015). Further, though their manufacture is very similar to conventional plastics, significant infrastructure investment is required where plastics manufactured from petroleum-based feedstocks are already well-established. The wide adoption of bioplastics has failed to materialize, and prices of bioplastics remain higher than petrochemical-derived plastics (PricewaterhouseCoopers 2010), with a total production capacity of about 4 million metric tons per year (Geyer et al. 2017). Given these limitations, best-case projections predict bioplastics will at peak satisfy no more than 20% of global plastics demand (AT Kearnery 2012).

*Unsustainability of paperboard.* Paperboard containers travel an average of 675 miles from manufacturer to primary customer, consuming 0.67 million BTUs of energy and emitting 0.05 mT of $CO_2$ per short ton shipped (USEPA 2015). Though recycling is preferred to divert paperboard from landfill, paperboard that is contaminated or otherwise not suitable for recycling drives the retention rate down from an ideal 1:1 ratio (i.e., 100% of recovered paperboard is recycled) to an actual retention rate of 93.5% (USEPA 2016b). Though a paperboard product may be labeled as 100% post-consumer content, the increment not retained means long-term paperboard recycling operations will yield diminishing returns over time.

Compared to plastics, paperboard's recycling record is better at 89.5% in 2014 and, as testament to the market forces at play, up significantly from just 55% in 1993 (USEPA 2014). However, the majority of paperboard recycled is by retailers, as fewer than 50% of American consumers are estimated to utilize curbside paperboard recycling programs (Feiner 2017). This fraction of cardboard waste thus remains difficult to divert from landfill to recovery.

## Regulatory Demands for the Sustainable Packaging Industry

Aside from market forces, some government policy and regulatory actions have pushed packaging producers, OEMs, retailers, and consumers to adopt more sustainable business behaviors and models.

In the European Union (EU), the Registration, Evaluation, Authorisation and Restriction of Chemicals (REACH) Regulation passed in 2006 charges private industry to determine and register the physical, environmental, and toxicological properties of substances used in quantities greater than 1 ton annually in the manufacture of goods. Suppliers and manufacturers are then required to communicate this information to downstream users, empowering OEMs and consumers to account for sustainability in their purchase decisions. As a driver for minimization, diversion, and recovery of paperboard packaging, the 1999 EU Landfill Directive called for a 50% reduction by 2009, in landfilled biodegradable waste from 1995 levels, and a 65% reduction by 2016 (PricewaterhouseCoopers 2010).

In the United States, federal regulations pertaining to the packaging industry fall under the specialized Federal Food, Drug, and Cosmetic Act but are only relevant to packaging material that comes into contact with food. Other statutes include the Toxic Substances Control Act (TSCA), the Emergency Planning and Community Right-to-Know Act (EPCRA), the Clean Air Act (CAA), the Clean Water Act (CWA), and the Resource Conservation and Recovery Act (RCRA). Though these latter statutory authorities provide for reporting requirements and adherence to some emission limits at various points in the supply chain, none expressly regulates environmental or sustainability standards for packaging. An exception is the Federal Trade Commission's (FTC's) Guides for the Use of Environmental Marketing Claims which prohibit packaging producers from making deceptive claims about compostability, degradability, recyclability, and recycled content (16 C.F.R. 260).

In terms of recycling promotion policies, half of the states have data on curbside consumer recycling programs, totaling 4,371 and serving a population 87.9 million, roughly a quarter of whom live in California (Van Haaren et al. 2010). Nationwide, average per capita municipal solid waste generation is estimated at 1.28 tons annually, of which just over a quarter is recycled (Van Haaren et al. 2010). With the void of direct federal regulation, state and local governments have taken initiatives to implement their own policies; both Washington, DC, and New York have implemented bans on EPS. Acknowledging the increasing landfill volume that packaging waste occupies and in a significant step toward meeting an ambitious 80% waste reduction goal by 2032, the Washington, DC, Department of Energy and Environment banned the use of EPS in packaging effective January 1, 2016, for food containers and January 1, 2017, for all packaging containers (DOEE 2014). Pursuant to Local Law 142 of 2013, New York City's Department of Sanitation recently determined food-service foam cannot be effectively recycled and recommended a city-wide ban starting November 12, 2017, with enforcement beginning on May 14, 2018 (DSNY 2017).

## Eco-Innovation Opportunity Cumulated

In 2016 e-commerce giant Amazon delivered in excess of a billion packages (Green 2017), evidencing the tremendous success of e-commerce, but an ominous milestone from a sustainability perspective. As a whole, the e-commerce industry is valued at $350 billion and doubled in size between 2011 and 2016 (Richtel 2016). Leading online grocery markets are projected to double by 2020 (WEF 2016). Amazon for years has epitomized wasteful shipping and cardboard use—justified or not—based on its practices of packaging goods within cardboard shipping containers bearing its distinctive logo. Indeed, the successes of Amazon and ecommerce in general seem to suggest a boom in cardboard production and associated waste generation; e-commerce now accounts for 10% of all US retail (Howland 2017). But reports from the industry group Fibre Box Association (FBA) indicate that cardboard quantities shipped by US companies have actually decreased modestly since 1995 (Dove 2017).

However, a net decrease in cardboard shipped does not mean waste has been reduced or eliminated. When intrinsic costs of packaging materials are low and shipping fees are fixed, retailers and e-commerce sellers have little incentives to adopt sustainable business practices or materials into their operations and distribution. The rise of e-commerce and home delivery direct to consumers means more cardboard and plastic packaging—as well as more secondary shipping containers—can make their way directly to front stoops and business-receiving departments. The result is wasteful, producing environmentally costly over-packaging and growing waste streams.

Both consumers and shippers appear to have taken notice of this trend. Amazon's customer container feedback program has received more than 33 million responses—including comments, complaints, and photographs—from customers (Richtel 2016). In an effort to embrace an emerging positive marketing opportunity, Amazon introduced a "frustration-free packaging" option that its customers can select with their other shipping instructions (Gopaldas 2015). The option instructs Amazon's fulfillment services to forgo secondary shipping packaging to rely instead on carefully designed, minimalist OEM packaging and is credited with eliminating 83 million unnecessary cardboard boxes from shipments in 2016 alone (Pierce 2017). Further, Amazon has begun utilizing machine learning in the algorithms to determine packaging material and method (Green 2017). Informed by both cost data and customer comments, the algorithms seek to continuously optimize packaging configuration for reduced packaging and shipping costs and wastes at the consumer end (Green 2017).

Likewise, both UPS and FedEx have implemented billing systems based on dimensional weight—a measure of package volume relative to its actual weight (UPS 2017). Such measures are widely believed to incentivize OEMs and e-commerce retailers to optimize their packaging solutions to lightest and smallest possible.

While diversion of paperboard and plastic packaging waste to recycling or WTE incineration is certainly preferred over landfill disposal, many nuances influence the sustainability of this producer-to-consumer business model. Despite the good news of increased cardboard and plastic recycling or WTE rates, no matter how efficient or what material retention percent is reached, recycling at best delays waste disposal rather than eliminates it, and there remains not insignificant $CO_2$ emissions associated with conventional recycling and WTE incineration (Geyer et al. 2017; USEPA 2016a). Bioplastics then represents an important shift from traditional plastics manufacture, but it and other renewably sourced packaging—incrementally greener than conventional petrochemical plastics or paperboard sourced from virgin wood pulp—seem to constitute only adaptive responses to changing economic conditions (Schumpeter 1947).

Significant advances in sustainable packaging can be only made through source reduction—and ideally elimination. For example, USEPA estimates that source reduction of polystyrene from both current feedstock mixes and virgin inputs could reduce greenhouse gas (GHG) emissions by 2.5 $MtCO_2$ per short ton of source reduced (USEPA 2015). For paperboard, the reduction is more dramatic at 5.59 and 8.1 $MtCO_2$ for mixed recycled and virgin feedstock, respectively (USEPA 2015).

When upstream packaging suppliers are distanced from end users, sustainability in upstream manufacturing may not have much incentive to improve (Foerstl et al. 2015). However, as stakeholder interest in sustainability increases, as it has for Amazon, holdout firms place themselves at competitive risk by not adopting sustainable practices and may further fail to engage untapped customer bases with nascent interests in sustainably sourced materials and products (Foerstl et al. 2015). Facing pressure from expanding regulation and interest from primary and secondary customers for sustainable alternatives, the $400 billion USD packaging industry is therefore primed for disruption (Ernst and Young 2013). When assigned a monetary value, these regulatory- and altruistic-driven interests comprise a portion of a staggering $10 trillion USD in projected cumulative eco-innovation investment worldwide by 2020 (Boons et al. 2013).

## Defining and Developing Sustainable Package

### Sustainable Packaging Considering Business Performance and Environmental Concerns

Sustainable development and sustainability have become the focus of mainstream management studies and practices. However, the concept of sustainability has not yet been understood very clearly by corporate managers or the general public. This is in part because the concept of sustainability has been adapted to address very different challenges, ranging from the planning of sustainable cities to sustainable livelihoods, sustainable agriculture to sustainable fishing, and the efforts to develop common corporate standards in the UN Global Compact and in the World Business Council for Sustainable Development. Despite this creative ambiguity and openness to interpretation, sustainable development has evolved a core set of guiding principles and values, based on the Brundtland Commission's standard definition to meet the needs, now and in the future, for human, economic, and social development within the restraints of the life support systems of the planet (Kates et al. 2005).

As much as sustainability or sustainable development is vague in its definition, there is no clear understanding about what constitutes "sustainable packaging." A widely agreed-to and accepted understanding would be critical in the societal pursuit for promoting sustainability in the packaging domain and leading to associated business development (James et al. 2005).

As one of the semantic efforts to define sustainable packaging, Verghese and Lewis (2005) undertook a stakeholder survey in partnership with the Sustainable Packaging Alliance (SPA). The SPA's sustainable packaging definition took into consideration the role packaging plays in our social and economic systems. It also accounted for the need to meet environmental goals and reduce harm to humans and ecosystems. As such, the SPA's sustainable packaging definition includes four levels, which are society, packaging material, packaging system, and packaging component. It also identifies four different principles: *effective*, *efficient*, *cyclic*, and *safe*. The *effective* principle means that products should be packaged as they would be delivered from producers to consumers. The *efficient* principle seeks to maximize material and energy efficiency in every step of packaging, storage, transport, and handling. The *cyclic* principle is aligned with a closed-loop system, increasing recycling, reuse, and ease of disassembly and assembly. Lastly, the *safe* principle aims to minimize the human and ecological risks from packaging components, being subject to the precautionary principle (The precautionary principle is defined by Principle 15 of the Rio Declaration. Under the precautionary principle, if there are threats of serious or irreversible damage, lack of full scientific certainty shall not be used as a reason for postponing cost-effective measures to prevent environmental degradation (United Nations 1992).) (Pielke 2002; Raffensperger and Tickner 1999). Table 3.3.1 summarizes the four-level definition of sustainable packaging. Packaging is assumed to be *sustainable* and support sustainable development if the four principles are met. While this is an earlier attempt for conceptualization, the concept well represents the multifaceted dimensions of packaging in consideration of the elements of sustainability, economy, society, and the environment (Verghese and Lewis 2005).

**Table 3.3.1** SPA's sustainable packaging definition

| Principle | Description | Levels at which the principle is applied |
|---|---|---|
| Effective | It adds real value to society by effectively containing and protecting products as they move through the supply chain and by supporting informed and responsible consumption | Society |
| Efficient | Packaging systems are designed to use materials and energy as efficiently as possible throughout the product life cycle. This should include material and energy efficiency in interactions with associated support systems such as storage, transport, and handling | Packaging system |
| Cyclic | Packaging materials are cycled continuously through natural or (industrial) technical systems, minimizing material degradation and/or the use of upgrading additives | Packaging material |
| Safe | Packaging components do not pose any risks to human health or ecosystems. When in doubt, the precautionary principle applies | Packaging component |

*Source*: Adapted from James et al. (2005)

As another well-recognized definition, sustainable packaging is also defined by the Sustainable Packaging Coalition (SPC), a project of GreenBlue which is dedicated to the sustainable use of materials in society. The SPC's sustainable packaging concept highlights a closed-loop system and promotes the five principles of (1) responsible sourcing, (2) optimization for efficiency, (3) effective recovery, (4) nontoxic, and (5) low impact. Further outlining the five principles, eight criteria were developed to define sustainable packaging (Table 3.3.2).

**Table 3.3.2** SPC's definition of sustainable packaging

| Criterion | Characteristic |
|---|---|
| 1 | Is beneficial, safe, and healthy for individuals and communities throughout its life cycle |
| 2 | Meets market criteria for performance and cost |
| 3 | Is sourced, manufactured, transported, and recycled using renewable energy |
| 4 | Optimizes the use of renewable or recycled source materials |
| 5 | Is manufactured using clean production technologies and best practices |
| 6 | Is made from materials healthy throughout the life cycle |
| 7 | Is physically designed to optimize materials and energy |
| 8 | Is effectively recovered and utilized in biological and/or industrial closed-loop cycles |

*Source*: SPC (2011)

The eight criteria presented blend broad sustainability and industrial ecology objectives with business considerations and strategies that address the environmental concerns related to the life cycle of packaging. These criteria relate to the activities of the packaging value chain and define the areas in which we actively seek to encourage transformation, innovation, and optimization.

## Indicators for Sustainable Packaging Development

Sustainable packaging development would not be straightforward even with a clear definition. Translating the definition into more specific targets or performance indictors would be useful to implement sustainable development principles in product packaging development. The proposed key performance indicators for the SPA's four sustainability packaging principles underscore two focal points, to reduce product waste and to improve functionality. Table 3.3.3 provides 21 indicators that can assist in the process of reaching a state of sustainability in packaging.

Several sustainability packaging assessment tools have been used to evaluate and compare packaging with other options. The Packaging Impact Quick Evaluation Tool (PIQET), developed by SPA, is a tool for rapid environmental impact assessment of packaging systems. This web-based software tool uses environmental indicators, based on the LCA methodology. PIQET functions as a credible, business-ready tool for multi-criteria packaging environmental decision-making and guides materials selection, packaging redesign or packaging performance, and evaluation of environmental requirements (Verghese and Lewis 2005).

**Table 3.3.3** SPA's sustainable packaging indicators

| Sustainable packaging principle | Sustainable packaging indicator |
|---|---|
| 1. Effective | 1.1 Reduces product waste<br>1.2 Improves functionality<br>1.3 Prevents overpackaging<br>1.4 Reduces business costs<br>1.5 Achieves satisfactory return on investment (ROI) |
| 2. Efficient | 2.1 Improves product/packaging ratio<br>2.2 Improves efficiency of logistics<br>2.3 Improves energy efficiency (embodied energy)<br>2.4 Improves materials efficiency (total amount of material used)<br>2.5 Improves water efficiency (embodied water)<br>2.6 Increases recycled content<br>2.7 Reduces waste to landfill |
| 3. Cyclic | 3.1 Returnable<br>3.2 Reusable (alternative purpose)<br>3.3 Recyclable (technically recyclable and system exists for collection and reprocessing)<br>3.4 Biodegradable |
| 4. Safe (clean) | 4.1 Reduces airborne emissions<br>4.2 Reduces waterborne emissions<br>4.3 Reduces greenhouse gas emissions<br>4.4 Reduces toxicity<br>4.5 Reduces litter impacts |

*Source*: Lewis et al. (2007)

One of the applications of the sustainability packaging assessment tool can be found in innovating novel food packaging systems. The tool helped scholars identify optimum sustainable packaging design for food that should balance potential reductions in food loss, the ratio of the environmental impact of the food to the impact of the packaging, the handling of food waste, and the handling of packaging waste (Wikström and Williams 2010). In addition, the evaluation tool surprisingly recognized reusable plastic containers for a variety of fresh produce (Levi et al. 2011; Menesatti et al. 2012; Singh et al. 2006) as a more sustainable option when compared to commonly used corrugated paper boxes (Park et al. 2014).

Inputs and guidance from professionals in different disciplines—such as designers, engineers, technologists, marketers, and environmental managers—would inform a multidisciplinary, collaborative, and holistic approach and benefit the development process of product packaging systems.

The role of packaging technologists in the industry seems to be particularly important for sustainable packaging, as they can provide comprehensive and credible information to others within and external to the organization. This information ranges from packaging material characteristics, to packaging functionality in distribution and use, to processability in manufacturing and filling, and finally to environmental impact (SPC 2011). A significant degree of understanding and skills is needed to appropriately collect and analyze such information and to be able to present the findings to internal company decision-makers (SPC 2011).

Sustainable packaging assessment tools, a wide array of stakeholders, and technologists' information can thus be instrumental in transforming packaging system for sustainability. A closed-loop flow of packaging materials can be economically robust and provide benefits throughout its life cycle, constituting a sustainable packaging system.

In the following section, we discuss the sustainable packaging development process using a case study of Ecovative Design. The company develops an array of environmentally friendly materials that perform like plastics but are made from mushrooms. The mushroom packaging is renewable and biodegradable and can be made with crop waste brought from local farms, showing the four principles of sustainability packaging: effective, efficient, cyclic, and safe.

## Case Study: Ecovative Design

### Company History

Ecovative is a biotech company with the mission of designing the future of sustainable materials using Mycelium Biofabrication Platform. It took its root at Rensselaer Polytechnic Institute (RPI) in Troy, New York, created by Eben Bayer, now CEO, and Gavin McIntyre, now Chief Scientist (Zeller and Zocher 2012). In 2006, the two were classmates in Inventor's Studio, an undergraduate class instructed by RPI Professor Burt Swersey. After a semester of unsuccessful ideas, Bayer pitched the concept of a mushroom-based biopolymer as a replacement for traditional plastic insulation to Swersey. Spurred by the entrepreneurial spirit of their academic backgrounds in product design and engineering, and sharing concern for environmental responsibility, Bayer later approached McIntyre with his idea for a novel mushroom-based material to replace conventional plastics. Though the two had job offers, Swersey provided guidance and funds for the pair to pursue the idea (VentureWell 2014). Instead of following traditional career paths after graduation, the two then founded Ecovative in 2007 (Knapp 2015).

In 2008, Bayer and McIntyre travelled to Amsterdam, Netherlands, to compete in the National Postcode Lottery Green Challenge (NPCLGC) where they won the top prize of $750,000 USD for a technology to mitigate climate change (VentureWell 2014). After winning the NPCLGC, Bayer and

McIntyre transitioned their technology to the packaging industry as a cost-competitive replacement for polypropylene and polystyrene-based foams.

In the years since, Bayer, McIntyre, and their team have evaluated countless fungi species for desired ecological traits and tested their growth in various substrate media, from woodchips Bayer observed at his Vermont farm growing up to agricultural wastes of cotton burr and corn stalks.

During the stage of product development, Ecovative has experimented with shaping the material during growth by applying a mold, akin to the additive process of three-dimensional printing, or through post-growth subtractive processes, such as machining or cutting, to produce or refine bulk growth to a specified shape (Bayer et al. 2011). To augment volume and strength, agricultural waste or wood salvage may be incorporated to create a composite material (Tudryn et al. 2018).

As of 2018, Ecovative has filed for 15 patents and obtained 9 patents with the biofabrication technologies and processes to develop high-performance, sustainable materials, and products. The company's MycoFLEX platform is licensed to other manufacturers making packaging like Dell and Ikea. The platform has been also used for different consumer products that have sustainability challenges, including biofabricated leather that uses the network of mycelial fibers to create the look and texture of a hide from a cow and 3D-print artificial hearts and other body parts in the regenerative medicine industry (Peters 2018). The company employs nearly 50 employees, operating 2 warehouses, Eco-HQ in Troy, New York, at 32,000 square feet, and Eco-East in Green Island, New York, at 20,000 square feet, and generates over $1 million USD in revenue and 1 million pounds of manufactured materials annually (Ecovative Design 2018).

## Ecovative's Product Innovation

The Fungi kingdom represents tremendous diversity at an estimated 1.5 million species (Hawksworth 2001). Among its other superlatives, the kingdom boasts the largest living organism on earth: a specimen of *Armillaria ostoyae* discovered in the Blue Mountains of Oregon is believed to be 2,384 acres in size and between 2,400 and 8,650 years old (Casselman 2007). Abundant fungi serve important ecological roles in the natural environment and are a source of food and medicines such as antibiotics for humans. Fungi have been growing mycelia, their unassuming chitinous root structures, for millennia.

What distinguishes Ecovative's materials is not the mycelia themselves but its leaders' visionary of harnessing fungi's natural, biological growth for niche applications ripe for disruption. As Bayer said to a TED audience in 2010, "the things that these organisms do are far more technologically advanced than anything we can dream of doing today with nanotechnology, with silicon technology, with anything we've gotten, and then by harnessing these innate properties of these organisms, these things that you would be used to seeing in your daily lives, like grass, we can do some incredible things for our planet and some really incredible things for the people living on this planet (Bayer 2011)."

In 2015, Forbes Magazine named Bayer to its eponymous "30 Under 30 List in Manufacturing" (Knapp 2015). When asked about his vision for industrial materials grown from mushrooms, Bayer recounted observing mushrooms' characteristic clumping of wood chips he would shovel for fuel while growing up on a Vermont farm (Schiffman 2013). Yet even as its materials enter the automotive, furniture, and construction markets, Ecovative maintains its original vision as an expanded polystyrene (EPS) replacement, selling its specialized Mushroom® packaging in stock shapes including corner protectors and standard molded shippers. Ecovative also offers manufacture of custom packaging molds above a volume threshold (Ecovative Design 2018).

Under Bayer and McIntyre's leadership, Ecovative leveraged and received numerous government grants and contracts, including US Department of Agriculture's (USDA) Wood Innovation Grant for "Scaled Demonstration of Biological Resin System to Expand the Non-structural Engineered Wood Market," seven awards from US EPA Small Business Innovation Research (SBIR) program, and in June 2017, $9.1 million by Defense Advanced Research Projects Agency's Engineered Living Materials (ELM) program (USDA 2017; USEPA 2017; Ecovative Design 2018). Beyond funding research and development, government assistance provided Ecovative with a test bed to refine and optimize substrate blends to produce material of desired physical specifications, valuable third-party cost and performance data, and exposure to potential stakeholders and niche customers (USDA 2013; Holt et al. 2012). Among them is the National Oceanic and Atmospheric Administration's (NOAA) specialized requirement for single-use readily biodegradable launch vehicles for its tsunami buoys (USDA 2013) which are impractical to recover from the ocean once deployed from ships.

*Furniture.* Ecovative has recently explored processes to layer and press its materials into densities and rigidities suitable for furniture and wood flooring (Knapp 2015) and, in 2016, launched Ecovative Interiors with a limited product line. Offered directly to consumers, MycoBoard is currently used in chair backs by furniture designer Gunlocke and is also available in finished interior acoustic tiles (Ecovative Design 2018). Preliminary evaluations of Ecovative's prototype construction materials—structural insulating panels among them—found them comparable or superior to EPS (USEPA 2012).

*Automotive.* Bayer and McIntyre have also identified the high plastic demand of the automotive industry as a potential market and designed and tested sound-absorbing acoustic panels for automotive bodies and interiors (Pelletier et al. 2013). Results are favorable. In evaluating blends of various agricultural waste substrate, Pelletier et al. (2013) found that even Ecovative's worst-performing composite, utilizing waste cotton bur fiber as a substrate, demonstrated acoustic absorption up to 75% at 1000 Hz. Incentivized by fuel efficiency performance standards, automakers are increasingly turning to lightweight plastic components as alternatives to steel in manufacturing. Plastics contributed to just 6% of vehicle weight in 1970. In 2010, that share was up to 16% and is projected to increase to 18% by 2020 (AT Kearney 2012). Once vehicles reach the end of life, recent EU legislation requires the recycling of 60% of plastic components (AT Kearney 2012). Ecovative's solution is not only recyclable but also fully biodegradable, enabling automakers to meet and exceed increasingly stringent standards.

*Construction.* As one of the Ecovative's first incarnations of a viable construction material, Greensulate™ was marketed as a biodegradable alternative to conventional EPS-based insulating panels (USEPA 2009). As Ecovative scaled up its manufacturing and increased its visibility, it gained the attention of architectural designers and engineers. In 2014, architect David Benjamin installed a 40-foot-tall "Hy-Fi" pavilion at the Museum of Modern Art in New York, constructed from mycelium and corn stalk waste (Peters 2014). The design team was able to consider local sources of agricultural waste and, once the temporary installation was ready for removal, arranged for the bricks to be recycled in the Queens Community Gardens.

Though the "Hy-Fi" pavilion was perhaps more an installation art than a building prototype, it did demonstrate proof of concept and drew attention to construction applications for Ecovative's Mushroom® materials. Perhaps most importantly, Ecovative demonstrated the Hy-Fi's construction feedstock could be sourced from local agricultural operations. By working with communities to refine its supply chains in favor of local sources, Ecovative and its partners could tap into nascent consumer preferences for and pioneer a locally sourced construction materials market, similar to those that popularized now ubiquitous locally grown produce and farm-to-table restaurants.

## Discussion

### Key Driving Forces of Ecovative's Success

Unsustainable practices in the packaging industry are not considered new due to petroleum-based plastic's dominance, but their social and environmental costs have not been fully internalized (Ernst and Young 2013; Hillier et al. 2017). However, the rising volume of packaging plastics along with increasing consumption of paperboard packaging explains why diverse stakeholder groups including consumers have raised serious concerns over the unsustainability of packaging materials through the supply chain (Geyer et al. 2017; Richtel 2016). Some firms in the packaging industry have thus acted to lower social and environmental impacts of packaging, although most responses lead modest changes within the existing industrial practices. Common are projects related to resource efficiency improvement, recycling, or waste-to-energy recovery. Seen in this light, Ecovative's response involving the entrepreneurial procedures of fabricated biomaterials from mycelia is creative and disruptive. It can shape the contour of packaging industry, creating situations from which there is no bridge to those situations that might have emerged in its absence. Ecovative's creative response leaves us with a question of what drives the firm's creative response. This inductive case study pivots the firm's unique capabilities, technical competence for systems thinking, and the ability of engaging the stakeholder matrix. Each element is investigated in detail below.

*Technical competence for systems thinking.* Ecovative has harnessed the power of mushroom to create natural, biodegradable packaging and materials for potential use in multiple industries. Rather than produce, manage, and ideally minimize its own waste stream, Ecovative has focused on the development of technology which is capable of drawing on the waste streams from agricultural processes (Holt et al. 2012). The company's technological innovation is radical and unique in that it can horizontally integrate agricultural organizations, itself, and primary and secondary customers in a novel, innovative way (Larson 2000).

Ecovative's ability to disrupt existing practices employed by incumbents originates from the founding team's profound understanding about natural ecosystem and organisms, competitive imagination, and entrepreneurial leadership. Bayer touts the opportunities of organisms' innate properties and biological processes, many of which cannot be duplicated by technology: "with biology you can tell these organisms to do extra things; to make a compound while you're growing. That's our long-range vision for biofabrication" (Knapp 2015). He also held entrepreneurial leadership, through which he successfully organized a core group of people willing to take risks of failures and to take advantage of a sustainability-driven innovation opportunity that is not quite regarded as appealing.

Because packaging is a low-value good, it is generally not profitable to transport to long distances to primary or secondary customers. To an extent, this characteristic has protected packaging producers in developed countries from lower prices of overseas competitors (Ernst and Young 2013) and insulated established, geographic regions in the United States from innovators like Ecovative, were it to follow a conventional supply chain model.

Ecovative's packaging solution instead upends the traditional manufacturing packaging supply models and connects various nodes into a novel, cross-sector supply chain. Its packaging's primary raw material, agricultural waste, is readily available nationwide. Ecovative's packaging products do not require the capital and infrastructure—not to mention energy-intensive manufacturing and associated waste streams—of traditional cardboard or even bioplastics. Should they be so emboldened, retailers can eliminate the need for a packaging manufacturer, transporters, as well as associated emissions and waste at each node, by producing their own packaging materials in-house and supplanting distant suppliers of paperboard pulp or plastic pellets with a local provider of agricultural waste feedstock (Verghese and Lewis 2007). With little infrastructure investment or utility costs, an OEM could conceivably source its agricultural waste locally within tens of miles (rather than the hundreds of miles characteristic of both paperboard and plastic packaging) and produce its own customized packaging in-house under license from Ecovative. Bayer recognizes supply chain economics are just as important as product performance: "on the raw materials side, we've been able to drive the raw material costing down to be at price parity with the styrene and polyethylene that's used in packaging so we're just finally getting to realize that dream of a triple-threat value proposition" (VentureWell 2014).

*Engaging the stakeholder matrix.* Though Ecovative's applications of fungi mycelium for materials are radical, the fundamental problem of unsustainability in packaging it sought to address was not.

Independent of their lifecycle environmental performance or adoption by industry, high post-consumer content materials and bioplastics likely lowered the acceptance threshold of biomaterials for Ecovative's future customers. With exception of stakeholders already entrenched in the industry, Ecovative's stakeholders included government and industry incumbents, which is very unique to new entrants to the industry (Hall and Martin 2005; USEPA 2009). Bayer is very familiar with the importance of engaging the stakeholder network: "We unite a lot of stakeholders. Commercially, we work with really big companies either on direct customer access or on future projects, and we also work with the government. We've sort of connected to as many stakeholders in our space as we can" (VentureWell 2014).

Ecovative's interactions with government entities crossed both primary (as bona fide or potential customers of Ecovative's bio-based labeled products) and secondary stakeholder (as influencers of regulatory action) domains. Driven by Executive Order 13693, Planning for Federal Sustainability in the Next Decade, the US Department of Agriculture's (USDA) BioPreferred® program sets minimum standards for percent bio-based content among more than 97 product categories (e. g., cleaners, carpet, paint, etc.) and mandates their purchase by federal agencies and contractors (USDA 2015b; Golden et al. 2015). With federal consumption of goods and services valued at $445 billion USD annually (Golden et al. 2015), through USDA's BioPreferred® certification, Ecovative enjoys a competitive advantage to a somewhat captive primary stakeholder customer (USDA 2015a, b). Ecovative's choice to participate in USDA's Agricultural Research Service (ARS) and EPA's Small Business Innovative Research (SBIR) programs engaged these agencies as secondary stakeholders and valuable co-producers, providing capital, lending technical support, and helping to establish objective third-party performance data to assess commercial viability.

Being equally important to collaborating with governmental agencies, paramount to navigating growth is carefully selecting supply chain partners and understanding the requirements of primary and secondary customers (Golden et al. 2015). Ecovative's unique supply chain links together diverse stakeholders in novel relationships. Ecovative entered into an existing packaging industry market by large, established firms. Among them was Sealed Air, a $7 billion company and purveyor of packaging staples like Bubble Wrap®, and a customer base that includes distribution giants US Foods and Kroger Corporation (Sealed Air 2012). An unlikely ally, Sealed Air, has become a manufacturing partner to Ecovative in operations of its Eco-East facility.

## Conclusion

The unsustainability of packaging industry has been under high scrutiny from various stakeholders (Ernst and Young 2013). Being highly visible to consumer, the packaging industry is thus compelled to decarbonize and dematerialize the industry across the entire supply chain, from raw materials to end of life processes for reducing its societal and environmental impacts (Hillier et al. 2017).

Identifying the need to modify their production practices and processes, some firms in the packaging industry have attempted to seize a market opportunity for environmentally friendly packages and bio-based materials that can replace petroleum-based ones.

More than a decade ago, Ecovative Design, a biomaterials company growing packaging products with mycelium, envisioned the need of responsible product designs in packaging. Rather than incrementally changing the status quo of conventional packaging products, the company has brought an entirely new material solution to market by harnessing the natural mycelia root structures of fungi. Ecovative is then able to produce materials comparable in cost and performance to EPS and engineered cardboard securely bound by pressure physically and enzymatically by a completely natural, chitinous biopolymer (Haneef et al. 2017). The company enters the automotive, furniture, and construction markets, illustrating boundless product application options that have not been yet investigated or claimed (Ecovative Design 2018). Companies partnering with Ecovative for sustainable packaging alternatives include large retailers like Dell and Ikea. Innovative firms seeking bio-based materials (e.g., biofabricated leather) and growing meat without livestock are collaborating with Ecovative to find out the optimal applications of the Ecovative's innovative MycoFLEX platform. The medical start-ups focusing on regenerative medicines also plan to use the Ecovative's approach in an attempt to develop 3D-print artificial hearts and other body parts (Peters 2018).

Relying on the inductive case study approach, this study finds that Ecovative's creative innovation would be attributed to technical competence for systems thinking and the firm's capacity of engaging the stakeholder matrix. The two elements facilitate getting closed-loop thinking be transformed into the technological process of growing trays of mycelia within controlled temperature, humidity, airflow, and other factors and by which the shape and density of mycelia can be fully controlled. Utilizing the Ecovative's approach for biofabrication technologies presents an immense market prospect, because biofabrication has been emerged as a twenty-first-century manufacturing paradigm, but its development has been in its infancy (Mironov et al. 2009). A huge innovation opportunity for sustainability thus relates to sustained firm value that is not achievable solely through continuous, incremental improvement (Hart 2005).

In sum, the Ecovative's approach pivots on the significance of entrepreneurial firms' innovative initiatives based on their eco-innovation capabilities, technical competence for systems thinking, and ability of engaging with diverse stakeholders. The approach has proven enough to disrupt the ruts of existing practices in packaging industry. Extending this approach and encouraging firms' creative response for discontinuity, society can advance its sustainability and radically lower social and environmental impacts from today's old, existing unsustainable practices.

## Exercises in Practice

- Identify a sustainability challenge in an industry that requires a systems-thinking approach to innovate the entire industry's unsustainable practices. Discover which kind of technical competence is needed to stymie the traditional production patterns across the unsustainable supply chain.
- Explore available opportunities to engage with stakeholders that may provide essential financial support and technical advice during the process of ecological modernization and creative disruption for sustainability.

## Key Lesson for Engaged Sustainability

This case study illustrates the potential of technical competence along with a systems-thinking skill could upend the highly mature industrial supply chain. Engaging with a diverse set of stakeholders would also be another element to break through the unsustainable pattern of industry practices.

## Reflection Questions

- How can new market entrants seize the opportunity to innovate a highly mature industry that could be rigid in bringing new innovative changes and ecological modernization?
- How can an innovative firm balance direct stakeholder engagement while protecting its intellectual property?
- What other industries could follow Ecovative's licensing model to get their sustainability ideas to market?
- What challenges may be presented if new market entrants target an incumbent solution and its associated supply chain?
- How can regulators not only incentivize firms with technical competence but also promote the scalability of the sustainability solutions to enhance industry-wide transformation for sustainability?
- Are there any examples that are synonymous with Ecovative in other industries? If then, what are the features that would make Ecovative distinct from those illustrations?

[...]

## References

AT Kearney. (2012). Plastics. The future for automakers and chemical companies. https://www.atkearney.com/documents/10192/244963/Plastics-The_Future_for_Automakers_and_Chemical_Companies.pdf/28dcce52-affb-4c0b-9713-a2a57b9d753e

Bayer, E. (2011). Eben Bayer: Drinking trees [Video file]. Retrieved from https://www.youtube.com/watch?v=VTsH8qgIb80

Boons, F., Montalvo, C., Quist, J., & Wagner, M. (2013). Sustainable innovation, business models and economic performance: An overview. *Journal of Cleaner Production, 45*, 1–8.

Braungart, M., & McDonough, W. (2002). *Cradle to cradle. Remaking the way we make things.* New York: North Point Press.

BusinessWire (2018). The global market for plastic packaging (2017–2026) to grow at 5.4% CAGR-environmental concern is hampering growth. https://www.businesswire.com/news/home/20180828005731/en/Global-Market-Plastic-Packaging-2017-2026-Grow-5.4

Casselman, A. (2007, October 4). Strange but true: The largest organism on earth is a fungus. *Scientific American.* https://www.scientificamerican.com/article/strange-but-true-largest-organism-is-fungus/

Christensen, C. (1997). *The innovator's dilemma.* Boston: Harvard Business School Press.

De los Rios, I. C., & Charnley, F. J. S. (2017). Skills and capabilities for a sustainable and circular economy: The changing role of design. *Journal of Cleaner Production, 160*, 109–122.

De Soto, H. (2000). *The mystery of capital.* New York: Basic Books.

Department of Energy & Environment (DOEE). (2014). Sustainable DC omnibus amendment act of 2014. https://doee.dc.gov/foodserviceware

Department of Sanitation, New York City (DSNY). (2017). Determination on the recyclability of food-service foam pursuant to local law 142 of 2013. https://www1.nyc.gov/assets/dsny/docs/2017-05-12FoamDetermination_FINAL.pdf

Dove, L. (2017). Has online shopping changed how much cardboard we use? https://science.howstuffworks.com/environmental/green-science/online-shopping-cardboard-consumption-industry-amazon.htm

Ecovative Design. (2018). How it works. https://ecovativedesign.com/how-it-works

Ernst & Young. (2013). Unwrapping the packaging industry: Seven factors for success. http://www.ey.com/Publication/vwLUAssets/Unwrapping_the_packaging_industry_%E2%80%93_seven_factors_for_success/$FILE/EY_Unwrapping_the_packaging_industry_-_seven_success_factors.pdf

Feiner, L. (2017, August 12). Why online shopping may not save the cardboard box. *Boston Globe.* https://www.bostonglobe.com/business/2017/08/11/why-online-shopping-may-not-save-cardboard-box/s2euhXKXpRhDWoOzmu2CNO/story.html

Foerstl, K., Azadegan, A., Leppelt, T. L., & Hartman, E. (2015). Drivers of supplier sustainability: Moving beyond compliance to commitment. *Journal of Supply Chain Management, 51*(1), 67–92.

Geyer, R., Jambeck, J. R., & Law, K. L. (2017). Production, use, and fate of all plastics ever made. *Science Advances, 3*(7), 1–5.

Golden, J. S., Handfield, R. B., Daystar, J., & McConnell, T. E. (2015). An economic impact analysis of the US biobased products industry: A report to the Congress of the United States of America. *Industrial Biotechnology, 11*(4), 201–209.

Gopaldas, A. (2015). Creating firm, customer, and societal value: Toward a theory of positive marketing. *Journal of Business Research, 68*, 2446–2451.

Green, D. (2017). Amazon fixed the most annoying thing about receiving online orders. *Business Insider.* http://www.businessinsider.com/amazon-fixes-packaging-to-be-more-efficient-2017-12

Hajer, M. A. (1995). *The politics of environmental discourse: Ecological modernization and the policy process.* Oxford, UK: Oxford University Press. ISBN 0-19-82769-8.

Hall, J. K., & Martin, M. J. C. (2005). Disruptive technologies, stakeholders, and the innovation value-added chain: A framework for evaluating radical technology development. *Research & Development Management, 35*(3), 273–284.

Haneef, M., Cesuracciu, L., Cahale, C., Bayer, I. S., Heredia-Guerroro, J. A., & Athanassiou, A. (2017). Advanced materials from fungal mycelium: Fabrication and tuning of physical properties. *Nature, 7*, 41292. https://doi.org/10.1038/srep41292.

Hart, S. L. (2005). Innovation, creative destruction and sustainability. *Research-Technology Management, 48*(5), 21.

Hawksworth, D. L. (2001). The magnitude of fungal diversity: The 1.5 species estimate revisited. *Mycological Research, 105*(12), 1422–1432.

Hillier, D., Comfort, D., & Jones, P. (2017). The packaging industry and sustainability. *Athens Journal of Business and Economics, 3*(4), 405–426. ISSN 2241-794X.

Holt, G. A., Mcintyre, G., Flagg, D., Bayer, E., Wanjura, J. D., & Pelletier, M. G. (2012). Fungal mycelium and cotton plant materials in the manufacture of biodegradable molded packaging material: Evaluation study of select blends of cotton byproducts. *Journal of Biobased Materials and Bioenergy, 6*(4), 431–439.

Hopewell, J., Dvorak, R., & Kosior, E. (2009). Plastics recycling: Challenges and opportunities. *Philosophical Transactions of the Royal Society of London. Series B, Biological Sciences, 364*(1526), 2115–2126.

Howland, D. (2017). Amazon is scrambling to minimize packaging. *Retail Dive.* https://www.retaildive.com/news/amazon-is-scrambling-to-minimize-packaging/513634/

Iles, A., & Martin, A. N. (2013). Expanding bioplastics production: Sustainable business innovation in the chemical industry. *Journal of Cleaner Production, 45*, 38–49.

James, K., Fitzpatrick, L., Lewis, H., & Sonneveld, K. (2005). Sustainable packaging system development. In W. Leal Filho (Ed.), *Handbook of sustainability research.* Frankfurt: Peter Lang Scientific Publishing.

Janicke, M. (2008). Ecological modernization: New perspectives. *Journal of Cleaner Production, 16*(5), 557–565.

Jay, J., & Gerand, M. (2015). Accelerating the theory and practice of sustainability-oriented innovation. MIT Sloan School working paper 5148-15.

Kates, R., Parris, T. M., & Leiserowitz, A. A. (2005). What is sustainable development?: Goals, indicators, values, and practice. *Environment, 47*(3), 9–21.

Kim, Y., & Darnall, N. (2016). Business as a collaborative partner: Understanding firms' sociopolitical support for policy formation. *Public Administration Review, 76*(2), 326–337.

Knapp, A. (2015, May 6). This entrepreneur is literally growing the future of manufacturing. *Forbes.* https://www.forbes.com/sites/alexknapp/2015/05/06/this-entrepreneur-is-literally-growing-the-future-of-manufacturing/#2abbc7f9210b

Lackey, R. (2007). Science, scientists, and policy advocacy. *Conservation Biology, 21*(1), 12–17.

Larson, A. L. (2000). Sustainable innovation through an entrepreneurship lens. *Business Strategy and the Environment, 9*, 304–317.

Levi, M., Cortesi, S., Vezzoli, C., & Salvia, G. (2011). A comparative life cycle assessment of disposable and reusable packaging for the distribution of Italian fruit and vegetables. *Packaging Technology and Science, 24*, 387–400.

Lewis, H., Fitzpatrick, L., Verghese, K., Sonneveld, K., & Jordon, R. (2007). Sustainable packaging redefined. http://nbis.org/nbisresources/packaging/sustainable_packaging_guidelines.pdf

Mason, M. (2011). The sustainability challenge. In J. Brady, A. Ebbage, & R. Lunn (Eds.), *Environmental management in organizations* (pp. 525–532). London: Earthscan.

Menesatti, P., Canali, E., Sperandio, G., Burchi, G., Devlin, G., & Costa, C. (2012). Cost and waste comparison of reusable and disposable shipping containers for cut flowers. *Packaging Technology and Science, 25*, 203–215.

Mironov, V., Trusk, T., Kasyanov, V., Little, S., Swaja, R., & Markwald, R. (2009). Biofabrication: A 21st century manufacturing paradigm. *Biofabrication, 1*(2), 1–16. https://doi.org/10.1088/1758-5082/1/2/022001.

Mol, A. P. J. (1995). *The refinement of production: Ecological modernization theory and the chemical industry.* Utrecht: Van Arkel.

Niero, M., Hauschild, M. Z., Hoffmeyer, S. B., & Olsen, S. I. (2017). Combining eco-efficiency and eco-effectiveness for continuous loop beverage systems. *Journal of Industrial Ecology, 21*(3), 742–753.

Park, S., Lee D. S., & Han J. H. (2014). Eco-design for food packaging innovations. In J. H. Han (Ed.), *Innovation in food packaging* (pp. 537–547). Academic. https://doi.org/10.1016/C2011-0-06876-X.

Pelletier, M. G., Holt, G. A., Wanjura, J. D., Bayer, E., & McIntyre, G. (2013). An evaluation study of mycelium based acoustic absorbers grown in agricultural by-product substrates. *Industrial Crops and Products, 51*, 480–485.

Peters, T. (2014). Sustaining the local: An alternative approach to sustainable design. *Architectural Design, 85*, 136–141.

Peters, A. (2018). Can mushrooms be the platform we build the future on? *FastCompany.* https://www.fastcompany.com/90246740/can-mushrooms-be-the-platform-we-build-the-future-on

Pielke, R. J. (2002). Better safe than sorry. *Nature, 419*(6906), 433–434.

Pierce, L. M. (2017). Amazon on creating commerce packaging that's great for all: Customers, companies and the environment. *Packaging Digest.* http://www.packagingdigest.com/optimization/amazon-on-creating-ecommerce-packaging-thats-great-for-customers-companies-and-envi ronment-2017-04-14

Prahalad, C. K., & Hart, S. L. (2002). The fortune at the bottom of the pyramid. *Strategy+Business, 26*, 54–67.

PricewaterhouseCoopers. (2010). Sustainable packaging: Threat or opportunity? https://www.pwc.com/gx/en/forest-paper-packaging/pdf/sustainable-packaging-threat-opportunity.pdf

Raffensperger, C., & Tickner, J. (1999). *Protecting public health and the environment: Implementing the precautionary principle.* Washington, DC: Island Press.

Richtel, M. (2016, February 16). E-Commerce: Convenience built on a mountain of cardboard. *The New York Times.* https://www.nytimes.com/2016/02/16/science/recycling-cardboard-onlineshopping-environment.html

Rigamonti, L., Grosso, M., Moller, J., Sanchez, V. M., Magnani, S., & Christensen, T. H. (2014). Environmental evaluation of plastic waste management scenarios. *Resources, Conservation and Recycling, 85*, 42–53.

Schiffman, R. (2013). One minute with ... Eben Bayer. *New Scientist, 218*(2921), 29.

Schumpeter, J. A. (1947). The creative response in economic history. *Journal of Economic History, 7*(2), 149–159.

Sealed Air. (2012). Sealed air and Ecovative complete agreement to accelerate commercialization of new sustainable packaging material. http://ir.sealedair.com/phoenix.zhtml?c=104693&p=irolnewsArticle_Print&ID=1706817

Singh, S. P., Chonhenchob, V., & Singh, J. (2006). Life cycle inventory and analysis of reusable plastic containers and display-ready corrugated containers used for packaging fresh fruits and vegetables. *Packaging Technology and Science, 19*, 279–293.

Starik, M., & Kanashiro, P. (2013). Toward a theory of sustainability management: Uncovering and integrating the nearly obvious. *Organization and Environment, 26*(1), 7–30.

Sustainable Packing Coalition. (2011). Definition of sustainable packaging. https://sustainablepackaging.org/wp-content/uploads/2017/09/Definition-of-Sustainable-Packaging.pdf

Tudryn, G. J., Smith, L., Freitag, J., Bucinell, R., & Schadler, L. (2018). Processing and morphology impacts on mechanical properties of fungal-based biopolymer composites. *Journal of Polymers and the Environment, 26*(4), 1473–1483.

United Nations. (1992). *Rio declaration on environment and development.* Rio de Janeiro: United Nations. http://www.unep.org/Documents.Multilingual/Default.asp?DocumentID=78&ArticleID=1163

United Parcel Service (UPS). (2017). Packaging guidelines: Billable weight. https://www.ups.com/us/en/help-center/packaging-and-supplies/determine-billable-weight.page

United States Department of Agriculture (USDA). (2013). Biodegradable packaging from cotton waste. *Agricultural Research, 61*(10), 16–18.

United States Environmental Protection Agency (USEPA). (2009). *Ecovative design: Growing America's green economy with research and innovation.* Office of Research and Development. https://archive.epa.gov/ncer/publications/web/pdf/ncse-greensulate.pdf

United States Environmental Protection Agency (USEPA). (2012). Development and demonstration of a low embodied energy, construction material that replaces expanded polystyrene and other synthetic materials. EPA contract number EPD10058.

United States Environmental Protection Agency (USEPA). (2017). *Ecovative design: Greensulate| growing America's green economy with research and innovation.* Office of Research and Development. https://archive.epa.gov/ncer/publications/web/pdf/ncse-greensulate.pdf

USDA. (2015a). Driving the bioeconomy: Economic impact of the biobased products industry. Presentation by Marie Wheat, Industry Economist, USDA BioPreferred Program, to the BIO World Congress on Industrial Biotechnology. 22 July 2015.

USDA. (2015b). *Development of scaled manufacturing for mycological soilless growth media.* National Institute of Food and Agriculture. Grant number 2015-33610-23814.

USDA. (2017). U.S. Forest Service awards grants to expand and accelerate wood energy and wood products markets in 19 States. U.S. Forest Service Press Release. 24 May 2017.

USEPA. (2014). Advancing sustainable materials management: Facts and figures. https://www.epa.gov/smm/advancing-sustainable-materials-management-facts-and-figures

USEPA. (2015). Documentation for Greenhouse Gas Emission and Energy Factors Used in the Waste Reduction Model (WARM). Office of Resource Conservation and Recovery. https://archive.epa.gov/epawaste/conserve/tools/warm/pdfs/WARM_Documentation.pdf

USEPA. (2016a). Documentation for greenhouse gas emission and energy factors used in the waste reduction model (WARM). Office of Resource Conservation and Recovery. https://19january2017snapshot.epa.gov/sites/production/files/2016-03/documents/warm_v14_containers_packaging_non-durable_goods_materials.pdf

USEPA. (2016b). Advancing sustainable materials management: 2016 Recycling Economic Information (REI) report. October 2016. EPA530-R-17-002.

Van Haaren, R., Themelis, N., & Goldstein, N. (2010). The state of garbage in America. *Biocycle, 51*(10), 16–21.

VentureWell. (2014). VentureWell idea to impact, *Ecovative*. https://www.youtube.com/watch?v=HqmCSml15jU

Verghese, K., & Lewis, H. (2005). Sustainable packaging: How do we define and measure it. Presented at the 22nd International Association of Packaging Research Institutes Symposium.

Verghese, K., & Lewis, H. (2007). Environmental innovation in industrial packaging: A supply chain approach. *International Journal of Production Research, 45*(18–19), 4381–4401.

Wikström, F., & Williams, H. (2010). Potential environmental gains from reducing food losses through development of new packaging—A life-cycle model. *Packaging Technology and Science, 23*, 403–411.

World Economic Forum, Ellen MacArthur Foundation and McKinsey & Company. (2016). The new plastics economy: Rethinking the future of plastics. http://www.ellenmacarthurfoundation.org/publications

York, R., & Rosa, E. A. (2003). Key challenges to ecological modernization theory. *Organization and Environment, 16*(3), 273–288.

Zeller, P., & Zocher, D. (2012). Ecovative's breakthrough materials. *Fungi, 5*(1), 51–56.

## DISCUSSION QUESTIONS

1. Packaging industry faces sustainability challenges. What are the elements of unsustainability in plastics and paperboard?
2. What are the regulatory contexts of the packaging industry in the United States and in the EU? How do they present eco-innovation opportunities to the packaging industry?
3. Ecovative Design's mushroom-based packages present a possibility for improving total sustainability in the packaging industry. Using the four sustainable packaging criteria (effective, efficient, cyclic, safe, in Table 1), explain the extent to which the Evocative Design products are sustainable.
4. Creative destruction framework has been useful in understanding the disjointed, dynamic social and economic changes. Beyond the packaging industry, where are other instances where you see creative destruction phenomena bringing sustainability innovation?

READING 3.4

# The Inclusive City

## Urban Planning for Diversity and Social Cohesion

By Franziska Schreiber and Alexander Carius

Every week, about 3 million people move to cities worldwide. Over the coming decades, such migration will contribute to an increase in the urban share of the global population from 54 percent in 2014 to 66 percent in 2050. Although migration is not a new phenomenon, the current pace of rural-urban migration, both within and between countries, is unprecedented. In developing and emerging economies, this has led to the mushrooming of megacities such as Cairo, Jakarta, Lagos, Manila, and Mumbai. However, cities are not only growing in population, but also becoming increasingly diverse and ethnically heterogeneous. This twofold process poses great challenges, as cities have to manage the multi-faceted integration of their arriving newcomers into society and urban life, as well as ensure continued social cohesion.[1]

Strong integration policies are needed that support urban migrants in finding jobs, living in socially mixed neighborhoods, learning the language, and enabling their children to go to school. In addition to policies related to education, health care, the job market, housing, and finance, the ways that cities are designed and constructed are important elements of integration policy. For example, well-designed urban patterns and functioning public spaces that serve as meeting places for urban dwellers can aid in facilitating interaction, connectivity, and social mixing—all important aspects of cohesive cities.

Various urban planning and design measures can be used to strengthen the relationship between space and social integration, helping to address the challenges that cities face with respect to migration, segregation, and socioeconomic polarization. At the national level, programs and frameworks can enable actions in cities and neighborhoods to improve the social and economic conditions of residents, as examples from Germany, Denmark, India, and South Africa illustrate. At the local level, city-wide and neighborhood planning can develop compact, well-connected and integrated urban patterns that facilitate social interaction and integration, as illustrated by case studies from Berlin, Germany; Guangzhou, China; Medellín, Colombia; and Oslo, Norway. Planning and design approaches that support "inclusive cities" and greater social cohesion include land-use planning, integrated land-use and transport planning, upgrading street networks, and public-space design.

## Tackling Growing Urban Challenges

In our increasingly urbanized world, cities function as a melting pot for people with differing cultural backgrounds, religions, interests, and social status. In this context, cities and municipalities face the twin challenges of not only absorbing the influx of people from diverse social and ethnic backgrounds, but also counteracting the trend of rising socioeconomic polarization and the segregation of cities into privileged and disadvantaged neighborhoods.

These two challenges are often intertwined and need to be approached holistically. Although research indicates that "no intrinsic link between deprivation and ethnic heterogeneity" exists, there is ample evidence that poorly managed urban migration results in the marginalization and segregation of people with different backgrounds. Questions related to the impact of immigration and ethnic diversity on the social fabric in cities are being debated in countries across the globe. Such discussions have been particularly prominent in the context of the refugee crisis in the European Union, where hundreds of thousands of refugees from conflict-torn and fragile regions, such as Afghanistan, Eritrea, Iran, Iraq, Syria, and the Western Balkans, are seeking asylum.[2]

Although many cities and municipalities are demonstrating courage, flexibility, and creativity in organizing ad hoc accommodation, care, and food for new migrants, the long-term challenge will be to ensure their full integration into society and to create acceptance among the local population. The latter is related to the rise of xenophobia and to fears about the consequences of uncontrolled, overwhelming migration, such as added competition in the labor market or a decline of social cohesion. Such fears have arisen in many European countries in response to the influx of refugees, and local governments need to take these concerns seriously in order to counteract the prevailing perception of migration as a "problem."

In addition to managing the integration of immigrants, cities and municipalities must provide sufficient infrastructure to accommodate their growing and diversifying populations and to avoid the emergence of new inequalities in urban areas while fostering social cohesion. For example, local governments must meet the increasing demand for housing and provide sufficient infrastructure and basic services, such as electricity, water, sanitation, health care, and education. Cities in developing and emerging countries, in particular, often lack the capacity to meet these needs and are confronted with the sprawl of informal settlements and slums (and thus an intensification of social and spatial segregation). Between 1990 and 2012, the share of the urban population living in slum areas in developing regions increased from 35 percent to 46 percent.[3]

The huge demand for housing is a challenge in developed countries as well, where rental prices are rising rapidly and the amount of social housing is declining, with adverse impacts on the social structure in neighborhoods. According to a government-conducted housing survey, the social housing stock in the United Kingdom has declined from 5.5 million homes in 1980/81 to 3.8 million homes in 2010/11, suggesting that people increasingly face difficulties in accessing adequate, affordable, and secure housing. Although the United Kingdom was once a forerunner in providing public housing, this achievement has been undermined by recent polices, such as the "Right to Buy," under which millions of social-housing units were sold. As waiting lists for social housing lengthen due to the slow construction of new houses, not even half of the demand for this housing is being met, and the degree of spatial segregation between the rich and poor in U.K. cities is increasing.[4]

Policies are needed at the national and local levels to support integration and to counteract segregation through infrastructure measures. However, the work of urban planners and designers also can contribute greatly to social cohesion. Even though the reorganization of space to create more-integrated urban patterns (for example, socially and functionally mixed areas that are well connected and easily accessible) and physical interventions (such as urban design measures in public spaces) cannot solve the roots of social and economic problems, they can aid in creating more-inclusive cities. Karin Peters and her colleagues at Wageningen University in the Netherlands argue that "interactions in daily life between people across ethnic divides are one way of creating social cohesion, because they provide the basis for bonds between individuals." It therefore is important to consider what (and how) planning and design measures at different scales, including the national, city, and neighborhood levels, can foster social interaction and integration in social networks.[5]

Some cities and countries have successfully implemented inclusive national and local plans, policies, and measures that provided a "spatial fix" to social problems and initiated positive locational dynamics. In Colombia, the city of Medellín implemented an innovative public transport system to connect poor and formerly inaccessible districts with the rest of the city, helping to enhance quality of life, attract tourists, and reduce the level of crime in these areas; however, this move did not solve the fundamental roots of poverty of many residents. The International Organization for Migration notes that, to achieve the greatest impact, "effective national and international instruments and institutions also need to be put in place." Planning and design measures should be embedded into a broader urban-cohesion policy, which involves a range of policy approaches in the areas of education, health care, employment, housing, and finance.[6]

## From Exclusion to Interaction to Cohesion

There is a common perception that the quality of public and civic life is in alarming decline worldwide. Since the 1970s, economic inequality has grown, resulting in socioeconomic polarization and spatial segregation, especially in urban areas. More than two-thirds of the urban population lives in cities where the income gap has widened sharply in the past three decades. The level of income inequality in these cities often surpasses the United Nations alert line of 0.4, based on the so-called Gini coefficient, which ranges from 0 (everyone has the same income) to 1.0 (maximum inequality of income). (See Figure 3.4.1.)[7]

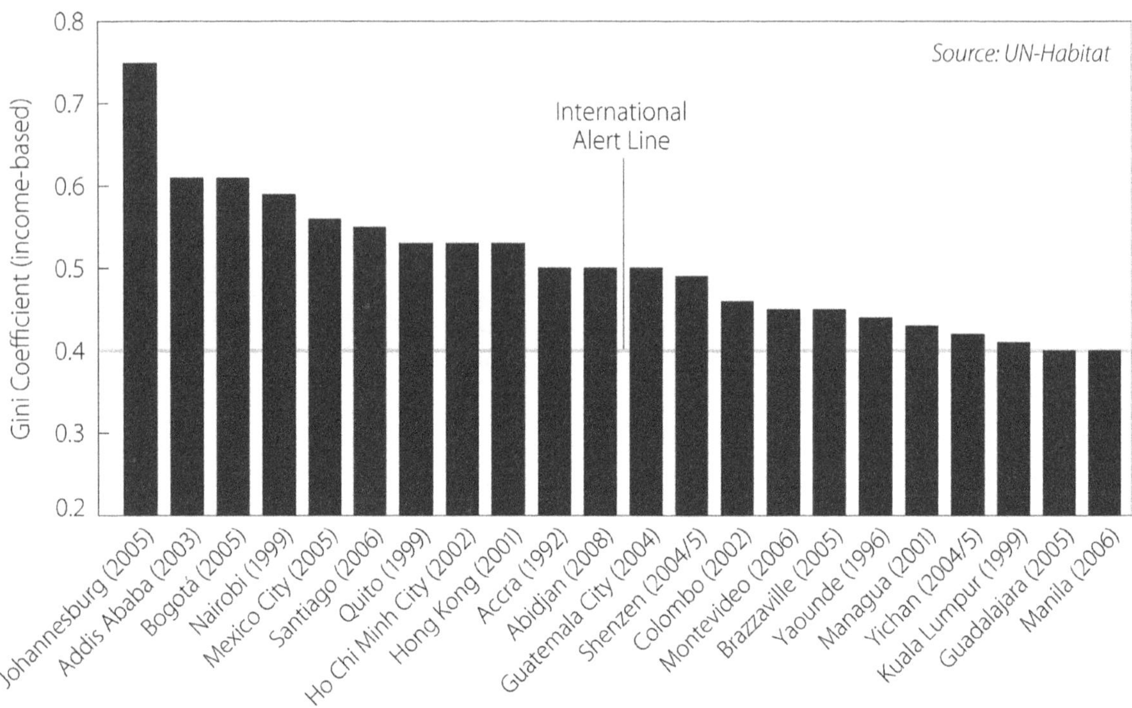


**Figure 3.4.1** Most Unequal Cities by Income, Selected Cities in the Developing World, 1992–2008

In cities of developing and emerging countries, informal and illegal settlements accommodate up to 80 percent of the urban population, and the urban divide is often reflected in the spatial configuration of the city. But rising income inequality is also a challenge in developed countries. According to recent studies, the degree of segregation by income has risen in 11 of 13 major European cities, including Madrid and Vienna, as well as in 27 of the 30 largest major metropolitan areas in the United States, such as Houston and Los Angeles.[8]

Although the reasons for this trend are manifold, several key processes can be identified. In developed countries, the main factors driving segregation in cities are globalization, the withdrawal of government support, economic restructuring, and the lack of investment in social housing. The transition from a manufacturing to a service-based economy has led to a dramatic change in the job market. Fewer employment contracts are unlimited, many people work under precarious conditions and need more than one job to survive, and the service sector is not able to accommodate all the workers that lost their jobs in the context of de-industrialization.[9]

Moreover, cities and municipalities are cutting down on social expenditures and public services, while reducing or stopping investments in social and affordable housing, with the result being a rapidly decreasing low-income housing stock. This comes mostly at the expense of already disadvantaged population groups and exacerbates the separation of low- and high-income groups in urban areas.

Those residents who have the resources move to neighborhoods with better schools, while others who cannot afford the rising rents are displaced to the edge of the city. Consequently, global and local restructuring processes are closely intertwined and result in spatial patterns that reflect and accelerate inequality and exclusion in cities. (See Chapter 7.)[10]

The reasons for segregation in cities of developing and emerging countries relate mainly to the rise of the middle class, racial discrimination, provision of secure tenure, and economic liberalization, as well as to world-class city aspirations that often result in massive infrastructure and urban renewal projects with large-scale displacement of low-income or illegal groups. This prevailing trend of socioeconomic exclusion and spatial fragmentation has adverse consequences for the urban realm. As UN-Habitat explains: "[It] is impacting negatively on social cohesion and reduces the economic vibrancy and the overall prosperity of the city, including the quality of life of the citizens. Informal settlements and disconnected peripheries, dysfunctional public space and increasing insecurity are often the apparent results."[11]

Recognition of the negative impacts of exclusion and segregation calls for measures that "foster the development of a harmonious society in which all groups have a sense of belonging, participation, inclusion, recognition and legitimacy," according to researchers Gerard Boucher and Yunas Samad. Urban planners and designers can play an important role in this context, helping to support "inclusive cities" that value all people and their needs equally. The concept of inclusive cities often is approached through the lens of a particular marginalized group, such as the elderly, children, slum dwellers, migrants, the unemployed, or disabled people. Social cohesion is an important component of the inclusive city and is based on the notion of community building, cooperation, and social relations among persons of different socioeconomic and ethnic backgrounds. Urban planning and design measures at different scales can contribute to forming social ties and interaction—a prerequisite for social cohesion and help to create a feeling of belonging in increasingly diverse and fragmented cities.[12]

## National Urban Planning Programs and Frameworks

Socioeconomically deprived neighborhoods and city districts, which often are characterized by a high concentration of migrants and their descendants, cannot be understood in isolation. Their roots lie far beyond the local context. National and regional programs are needed to provide a framework for jump-starting local initiatives and to allocate financial means for these initiatives to work. As UN-Habitat has observed, "[r]ecent experiences have clearly shown that social integration, inclusion and cohesion can be promoted through interventions at different scales."[13]

National programs are only effective, however, if they are well-designed and are supported by institutional and governance structures. A review of four national planning programs implemented in Germany, Denmark, India, and South Africa demonstrates that numerous factors determine their success on the ground. (see Box 3.4.1.) These factors include: the selection process for deprived

## Box 3.4.1 A Review of Four National Urban Planning Programs

### *Social City Program*

Germany's Social City Program was established in 1999 with the objective of stabilizing and upgrading socially and economically deprived urban areas. It seeks to achieve social cohesion in often ethnically heterogeneous neighborhoods through an integrated approach that combines physical and social interventions in the target areas. As an important element of the federal urban development policy, the program was equipped with €150 million ($160 million) in 2015 (a significant increase from previous years) and had funded 659 actions in 390 cities as of the end of 2014.

### *National Urban Renewal Program*

Based on the observation that poverty is increasingly urbanizing, South Africa's National Urban Renewal Program was established in 2001 as a 10-year initiative to promote socio-political, economic, and spatial integration of selected urban areas. The program focused primarily on exclusion areas (socially, economically, and racially) and supported eight urban districts in six cities, which were characterized by high levels of crime, poor connectivity to surrounding neighborhoods, high unemployment rates and inequality, and shortage of formal housing stock. Measures implemented under the program ranged from enhancing employment opportunities to enhancing access to the areas through better transportation services and improving education, local economies, and social capital.

### *Kvarterløft Program*

Denmark's national urban regeneration program, Kvarterløft, ran from 1997 to 2007 and was later followed by the financially reduced Omradefornyelse. The area-based program was set up with the aim of addressing increasing social problems and the spatial concentration of immigrants and refugees. The program combined measures targeting both people and places and fostered coordinated and integrated approaches among different public sectors and by involving the local community.

### *Jawaharlal Nehru National Urban Renewal Mission*

In contrast to the national programs mentioned above, India's Jawaharlal Nehru National Urban Renewal Mission did not apply an area-based approach but was launched in 2005 (and ran until 2015) with the goal of redeveloping entire cities and towns (65 in total) by making them more equitable, livable, and economically productive. With an investment of $20 billion, the program focused on upgrading infrastructure services and providing basic services to the urban poor. Its implementation faced numerous challenges, however, due to a lack of planners trained to realize integrated approaches, a shortfall in strengthening local governance, and a delay in financial flows from the national to the state governments.

*Source*: See endnote 14.

areas, the need for an integrated approach that combines physical and social measures, building local capacity, providing adequate financial resources, and conducting monitoring and evaluation.[14]

First, the selection process of targeted areas is critical to the success of interventions carried out at the local level. Yet the decision to declare a neighborhood "deprived" is often in different hands. In the case of South Africa and India, the national programs were centrally driven, which meant that the target areas were chosen top-down by either the national or state governments, without any consultation of local actors. Yet involving the local level and applying a bottom-up selection process—for example, by asking municipalities or communities to submit an expression of interest for participating in the program—are crucial for creating ownership. A proposal submitted by neighborhoods or cities simultaneously indicates awareness and their openness to change, thus increasing the chances of success in the long run. Both the German and Danish programs set up such an application process, which also helped them gain greater visibility and impact.

Second, the goal of social cohesion and interaction cannot be achieved solely through physical interventions, such as renovating residential buildings, improving lighting in public spaces, and reducing the number of housing units to combat vacancy. Rather, physical measures need to be combined with social measures aimed at improving living conditions in districts, such as creating new employment opportunities, providing better social and cultural facilities, and designing attractive public spaces that invite residents to stay and interact. The German program seeks to achieve exactly this: to upgrade the built environment while enhancing the situation of the local residents. Activities funded through the program range from modernization of buildings and the living environment; to supporting business start-ups, training, and education initiatives; to promoting language learning and fostering ethnic entrepreneurship and self-employment of immigrants and their descendants.[15]

Other programs, such as the Danish and South African ones, also highlight the need for combined social and physical efforts and place particular emphasis on the participation of local residents. On paper, such programs stress the need for combining physical and social interventions; however, their practical implementation remains controversial and widely criticized. Financially, infrastructure measures and physical upgrading have been the predominant focus of these programs, whereas social

**Figure 3.4.2** Part of the Jawaharlal Nehru National Urban Renewal Mission (JNNURM) was funding for thousands of transit buses, including this one in Pune
*Source*: Rowan Vaz

initiatives and civic participation remain underrepresented. Denmark's Kvarterløft program, for example, claimed to focus on social initiatives and participation, yet more than 90 percent of the financial resources have been spent on physical improvements.[16]

Third, cities and municipalities often lack sufficient financial and personnel capacities and face weak coordination among different planning departments. The latter, in particular, poses a huge obstacle to the goal of simultaneously implementing social and physical measures, which can create fruitful synergies. For example, when designing a new public space, it would be advantageous to also consider how this could be coupled with providing space for local shops and a new community center, to create a vibrant place of interaction. However, coordination and communication is often insufficient, not only within the city administration, but also between different levels of administration. This can lead to different levels of administration having different understandings of the objectives to be achieved through the program, resulting in incoherence during implementation. The Indian and South African cases demonstrate that well-trained personnel, as well as structures and reforms at the local level, are needed to ensure that national objectives can be translated into local action.[17]

Fourth, because financial constraints often are major barriers to the implementation of concrete actions in cities, a national scheme that provides financial support for personnel and capacity building resources in cities can help in realizing concrete projects at the local level. Moreover, such a scheme can help finance the creation of the new institutions and agencies that may be necessary to manage and coordinate national programs on the ground. As part of the Social City program in Berlin, neighborhood management offices were gradually introduced in the target areas after 2005, with the overall goal of empowering local residents and involving them in decision-making processes and the development of their area. Neighborhood councils, consisting of and elected by local actors, decide how and for what projects the funds from the program can be used, and they also maintain the dialogue with the neighborhood management teams and the governmental administration. The neighborhood management offices facilitate networking and communication among existing nongovernmental organizations, businesses, and other social and cultural initiatives in the area to bundle and mobilize local resources.[18]

Fifth, monitoring and evaluation are key to tracking progress on the implementation of a program, identifying gaps, making adjustments where needed, and reviewing progress. However, systematic monitoring and evaluation often are not mandatory, and a lack of reliable data makes such initiatives difficult. Lessons learned from Denmark demonstrate the need to develop realistic indicators for measuring a program's progress and success, especially for aspects such as participation and empowerment, as well as establishing a continuous monitoring system.[19]

In sum, national programs can provide an important framework for local initiatives to work on the ground, yet respective mechanisms and structures must be in place to ensure greater impact. Although the four national programs discussed above were able to achieve positive change in the target areas, these were related mainly to upgrading the built environment, such as by renovating buildings and improving public plazas and other spaces. Social needs were often overlooked, and measures targeting the socioeconomic status of residents (for example, access to jobs, education, mobility, culture) were too limited. Many of the initiatives also had too short a time frame to create long term change. It is crucial that national programs have a long-term scope and be based on continued political commitment. Interventions at the local level also need a scope that goes beyond the target areas in order to avoid stigmatizing them without ultimately remedying the situation.[20]

## City-wide and Neighborhood Planning

National urban planning frameworks can—if designed properly—serve as a catalyst for local action to upgrade socioeconomically deprived urban areas. While national programs deliver pivotal framework conditions, their ultimate success rests on initiatives at the city and neighborhood levels. Key to designing sustainable and inclusive neighborhoods and cities is the ability to read and understand their language. Urban planners and designers need to carefully observe and analyze people's behavior in the urban realm and to design streets, public spaces, and entire neighborhoods accordingly. As author Jan Gehl puts it, to create "cities for people" or "people-friendly" cities, urban planning has to apply the human dimension that is focused on creating city spaces as *meeting places* for urban dwellers.[21]

A variety of planning and design measures allow for compact, well-connected, and integrated urban patterns that promote social cohesion in cities and provide spaces of encounter and social interaction. Among these are: land-use planning, the promotion of mixed-use areas with good access to public transport (via transit-oriented development), the rearrangement of street patterns, and public space design.

## Land-use Planning for Balanced Urban Development

Land-use planning provides an important tool to guide and influence the development of cities. The consideration of not only economic aspects, but also environmental and social values, in land-use planning is necessary to allow for balanced and sustainable urban development. For example, community gardens fulfill important sociocultural functions and contribute greatly to social cohesion and food security. (See Box 3.4.2.) Yet in times of neoliberal city practices and enduring privatization of public land and properties in cities around the globe, such grassroots initiatives usually lack sufficient financial resources to continue.[22]

The recent wave of privatization has profound impacts on the urban realm and fails to acknowledge the increasing sociocultural complexity characterizing contemporary cities. It gradually diminishes the availability of spaces where new forms of social relations potentially could be formed. The selling of public assets, such as former school buildings, is often a shortsighted strategy that could cause unforeseen problems, as shown by the experience of Berlin. To consolidate the city's financial situation, the Berlin government established a property fund in 2001 to generate revenues through sales of city-owned land and properties in an auctioning process, without consideration of other aspects, such as the social value of initiatives. Some 400–500 public assets were sold annually, greatly reducing the number of city-owned properties. Yet when the unprecedented influx of refugees prompted a need for large-scale accommodations, the city government was forced to buy back buildings at much higher prices. Taking a more holistic and balanced approach in handling city-owned land and properties is key to preserving non-commodified spaces in cities and to retaining an adequate capacity to react in times of crisis. (See Chapter 16.)[23]

### Box 3.4.2 Pro Huerta: Urban Agriculture and Food Security in a Changing World

As urban populations swell, many cities are struggling to ensure food security and adequate nutrition in the face of challenges such as climate change, economic and natural disasters, farmland degradation, and the immense barriers that the urban poor face to accessing fresh, nutritious food. Experiences with the Pro Huerta ("Pro Garden") program in Argentina and Haiti suggest that there are effective ways not only to improve nutrition, but also to shore up social resilience among vulnerable populations.

### ***Buenos Aires and Rosario, Argentina***

Argentina's National Institute of Agricultural Technology approved the Pro Huerta program in 1990 as a means to address the serious economic and food security challenges affecting the country, including a dramatic jump in food prices in Buenos Aires. Pro Huerta was formally adopted under the National Food Security Plan in 2003, and, in 2011, the government pledged more than $10 million to expand the program.

Pro Huerta helps Buenos Aires's poorest populations diversify their diets, access fresh food, lower their food budgets, and increase their incomes. The program is designed to boost self-sufficiency by providing the tools necessary to build food gardens, including seed kits, chickens and rabbits, and training in pest control, animal husbandry, and organic gardening methods. By late 2015, the program had helped set up more than 56,000 family gardens—supplementing the diets of some 350,000 people, or nearly 11.5 percent of the city's population—as well as more than 900 school gardens and 500 community gardens. A family garden can produce 200 kilograms of vegetables annually, enough for a five-person family.

Pro Huerta launched in Argentina's third largest city, Rosario, in February 2002. At that time, roughly 60 percent of the city's population was living below the poverty line, and food staples had quadrupled in cost, leading to theft and rioting. The Rosario government's Urban Agriculture Program and a local group, CEPAR, partnered to pilot the Pro Huerta model, offering tools and seeds to 20 gardening groups. By 2004, 800 community gardens were growing food for 40,000 residents.

The Pro Huerta program was successful in repurposing vacant land—comprising more than one-third of Rosario's land area—for gardens. The city has since updated its land-use laws to include urban farming and is building a green belt of parks and multi-scale gardens. Pro Huerta also has created venues for direct marketing to the public and has set up cooperatives that prepare and sell produce, soups, jams, and natural cosmetics. By 2004, 10,000 low-income households in Rosario were selling enough produce to lift themselves above the poverty line. An estimated two-thirds of participants were women.

In 2013, as the city's economy improved, participation dropped to some 1,800 residents, almost 14 percent of them full-time producers. The Pro Huerta program has been replicated in 88 percent of Argentina's municipalities, with more than 630,000 gardens and 130,000 farms providing food for over 3.5 million people nationally. A network of 20,000 promoters manages the program, participating in agro-ecological fairs and working with thousands of institutions and organizations across Argentina.

### ***Haiti***

The Pro Huerta program also has spread to Brazil, Colombia, Guatemala, Venezuela, and Haiti, a country that suffers from widespread poverty, inadequate nutrition, and high dependence on food imports. Haiti launched Pro Huerta in 2005 with support from the Argentine Fund for Horizontal Cooperation, adapting the program to the local context and using local leadership to manage it. Argentinian experts trained a team of Haitian agricultural engineers, who then taught a network of volunteer promoters—mostly women—how to provide trainings within their communities. Between 2005 and 2008, these efforts helped establish 16,086 family gardens, 2,700 school gardens, and 1,900 community gardens.

In addition to producing food, Pro Huerta has resulted in the creation of resilient social networks that have helped communities respond to disruptions. In 2008, after Hurricanes Gustav and Ike destroyed thousands of gardens across Haiti, the program bounced back thanks to robust community cohesion. By the end of 2009, 1,843 promoters, 11,465 gardens, and more than 80,000 participants were active in the program. Following the 2010 Haiti earthquake, Pro Huerta was instrumental in fighting the cholera outbreak, providing more-nutritious diets for susceptible populations, offering expertise on food handling, and building special water storage facilities and sand filters to avoid disease transmission.

According to a Pro Huerta survey, 93 percent of program participants in Haiti improved their food situation, 86 percent of households were able to access a greater variety and quantity of food, and household spending was halved to just 33 percent of monthly income. In 2014, the Union of South American Nations pledged $3 million to extend Pro Huerta to 2016, with the goal of nearly doubling participation to 220,000. Haiti hopes to extend the program to 1 million participants by 2019.

***Lessons Learned***

In Argentina, the Pro Huerta program was predominantly a response to short-term economic disturbance; however, the model also performs strongly in countries, such as Haiti, that face continuous threats to food security. In a world where food supply and access are increasingly affected by variations in climate, environmental conditions, equity, and natural and economic disasters, urban agriculture programs such as Pro Huerta can be used to empower underserved communities, providing them with the tools to build a healthier life and to help them cope with future turmoil and change.

Kristina Solheim, Program Manager, goNewHavengo

*Source*: See endnote 22.

## Integrating Land-use and Transport Planning to Foster Social Cohesion: The Example of Transit-oriented Development (TOD)

At the neighborhood level, integrated land-use and transport planning—coupled with the creation of high-density mixed-use areas—facilitates demographic, socioeconomic, and cultural diversity. In particular, transit-oriented development (TOD) has become a popular planning approach to create inclusive, connected communities through spatial planning. Regulatory and incentive mechanisms, such as local planning schemes, educational campaigns, and incentives for developers and communities, are crucial for successful implementation. TOD is based on the principle of designing high-quality mixed-use areas around transit stations to enhance access to public transport and pedestrian- and cyclist-friendly environments while reducing dependence on private cars. Areas that prioritize walking and cycling typically are characterized by higher levels of social interaction and help residents who are unable to afford a car to overcome transport poverty. (See Chapter 11.)[24]

The design of mixed-use areas follows the idea of creating "urban villages" where residents are provided with housing, transportation, community and recreational facilities and services, public spaces, and retail within a short distance. To facilitate community diversity and social cohesion, these services and facilities should cater to the needs of different social groups with varying interests and demands. TOD therefore should be designed and managed in a way that allows for diversity in housing (for example, in design, form, tenure, and affordability), land-use, employment, and retail, and that provides multiple public and open spaces as focal points for the community. Safeguarding community diversity over the long run requires long-term investments in social housing and community infrastructure. Further, developing a TOD precinct requires a continuous participatory planning process that targets a diversity of groups to build ownership and a shared sense of identity.[25]

Well-designed TOD offers numerous environmental benefits. The continued rise in transport volumes not only leads to increasing traffic congestion, but also contributes to environmental and health challenges such as rising air pollution and greenhouse gas emissions. Designing neighborhoods based on the principle of walkability and cycling as well as good access to public transport is urgent. TOD holds tremendous potential in countries like China. (See Chapter 7.) The country's third largest city, Guangzhou, has invested massively in a highly efficient bus rapid transit (BRT) system and is building new promenades and bicycle lanes to encourage walking and cycling.

Guangzhou's BRT system, which is the first worldwide that is fully integrated with a metro system, carries more than 800,000 passengers daily and has significantly reduced traffic jams and vehicle kilometers traveled. Thanks to multiple sub-stops and passing lanes at each station, average bus speeds increased from about 15 kilometers per hour to about 22 kilometers per hour—an attractive and speedy alternative to individual motorized transport. The network of small, walking-oriented streets surrounding the city's Shipaiqiao station is being complemented by new high-density commercial

**Figure 3.4.3** Dedicated BRT lanes on Tianhe Road, Guangzhou
*Source*: David290

and residential developments, helping to revitalize the entire area. Shipaiqiao station and its surrounding area are now easily accessible by public transport and have become a prime location for shopping, working, living, and strolling.[26]

## Upgrading Street Networks to Reintegrate Neighborhoods

Streets can have a great impact on the vitality and integration of a given area. They are not only a means of transportation, but also a fundamental shared public space that facilitates numerous social, cultural, and economic activities and allows people to interact. Well-designed street patterns that facilitate connectivity and mobility can counteract socio-spatial segregation and help to re-integrate areas into city structures.

UN-Habitat promotes a street-led approach to the citywide transformation and regeneration of slum areas in many developing and emerging countries. The absence of streets and open spaces segregates and disconnects slums from the rest of the city. Done right, the upgrading of street networks in slums can bring advantages including security of land tenure, future consolidation of settlements, optimization of land use, poverty reduction, and increased social interactions among residents. However, upgrading of street networks also requires political will and needs to be based on a strong participatory planning process. The latter is a necessary precondition not only to create ownership, but also to conduct a reliable inventory of the physical configuration and socio-spatial structure of a settlement. Participatory planning also helps to inform the design of area-based plans and street patterns that capture the "multiple functions of streets based on nuances of everyday practices of street life and people's aspirations."[27]

The Integrated Program for the Improvement of Squatter Areas (PRIMED) in Medellín, Colombia, provides a good example of the benefits of well-designed street networks. Based on strong political will and the desire to counteract spatial exclusion and promote social development in deprived areas, the program facilitated the application of an innovative public transport system based on cable cars connecting the target areas with the rest of the city. (See Chapter 4.) The first cable car line was implemented in the poor and densely populated northeastern district, which was characterized by minimal road infrastructure and thus a lack of accessibility. The program was not limited to the implementation of the transport system, however, but also combined urban upgrading measures, including interventions in public spaces, social housing, and other social infrastructure, which were realized in a participatory manner.[28]

Impact studies reveal that these combined interventions helped to upgrade Medellín's densely populated and low-income neighborhoods and integrate them into the city's fabric. They also boosted the quality of life of the urban poor by enhancing accessibility for local residents and outsiders alike, improving air quality, counteracting stigmatization of these areas, and providing local residents with a sense of social and political inclusion. Levels of violence and crime in the neighborhoods surrounding the cable car lines dropped significantly, which helped to revitalize public life. In addition to social and mobility aspects, the PRIMED program considered environmental outcomes. The Metro Company, which evaluates the environmental performance of the cable car system and monitors the reduction in greenhouse gas emissions, concludes that the hydroelectric aerial cable cars could help to reduce up to 121,029 tons of carbon dioxide between 2010 and 2016, compared to the fossil fuel-operating vehicles that the system replaces.[29]

Although the upgrading of street networks can support development, foster integration, and bring environmental benefits, it often requires demolition and relocation to make space for the construction of new streets or an aerial cable car public transport system. This tradeoff was evident in the case of Medellín and had to be negotiated within the community. Overall, however, improved street networks have great potential to integrate entire neighborhoods into city systems and to improve the quality of life of local residents.

## Public Space Design

Public spaces allow people to meet and interact on ostensibly neutral ground. They provide a democratic space for different social groups to participate in civic activities. Especially in developing and emerging countries, where urban inhabitants often live in densely populated housing areas with few economic resources, public spaces form a fundamental part of community life. Urban parks, in

**Figure 3.4.4** A sunny July day on the waterfront promenade at Aker Brygge in Oslo
*Source*: Jean-Pierre Dalbéra

particular, serve as a vital public space where everyday experiences are shared and negotiated among different social and ethnic groups, and where numerous opportunities for intercultural interaction exist.

Extensive city improvements, such as upgrading street networks, are costly and time-consuming. However, small interventions in public spaces—such as improvements to bench seating, providing movable chairs, closing streets to car use, and laying new pavement to encourage pedestrian traffic—can make a huge difference and help reinforce daily life in a fast and cost-efficient manner. For example, the location of street furniture has a compelling effect on how public space is used and accepted and how long people tend to stay and interact with strangers.[30]

The post-industrial waterfront promenade at Aker Brygge in Oslo is a good example of how urban design can influence social interaction. As part of a broader neighborhood renovation project in the 1990s, old benches on the promenade were replaced with Parisian-style double park benches, and the overall seating capacity was increased. Consequently, the number of people sitting in the area more than doubled, and social interactions among strangers multiplied. Some two decades later, the same architects were tasked with adapting and renewing the area, again with an emphasis on encouraging social interaction and diversity. They developed a "site-specific concept for street furniture and 'staying,'" which aided in creating numerous opportunities to sit, lie, eat, read, or chat with acquaintances or strangers. The pedestrian and bicycle path was reorganized to create wider, more generous public spaces, and sun loungers and comfortable benches were installed, inviting people to sunbathe and lie down. Although the provision of sufficient seating opportunities within cities and neighborhoods is crucial, other factors—such as views and orientation toward street activities, as well as movability of seating options—determine the vitality of a place.[31]

## Conclusion

Socioeconomic polarization and spatial segregation have become prevailing trends in cities worldwide, with adverse impacts on quality of life and social cohesion. As cities become increasingly diverse, these trends often have an ethnic component as well. Many socioeconomically deprived areas are characterized by a high concentration of migrants, making their multi-faceted integration into city life more challenging. Consequently, finding solutions to counteract disparities and inequalities while strengthening relations and interactions among socially and ethnically diverse groups has become an urgent matter.

Although urban planners and designers cannot solve the roots of exclusion and inequality per se, they can aid in increasing the accessibility and integration of deprived areas and provide spaces that increase the chances of interaction and the forming of social relations among people from differing ethnic backgrounds. National urban planning programs offer a useful framework for local initiatives to kick off and work on the ground. Applying an integrated approach that effectively combines social and physical measures, coupled with a bottom-up selection process, capacity building, the establishment of governance structures, the provision of financial resources, and monitoring and evaluation is key for the success of national programs.

At the city and neighborhood levels, numerous approaches and measures have been tested globally to overcome socio-spatial segregation and exclusion. In particular, the creation of mixed-use and socially mixed areas—coupled with good access to public transport, housing diversity, and sufficient provision of vibrant public spaces that facilitate inter-ethnic encounters—are promising ways to enhance social cohesion. Approaches and planning principles, such as socioeconomically balanced land-use planning, transit-oriented development, and upgrading street patterns, have been successful in building well-connected, compact, and integrated urban patterns that allow for sustainable urban development. Well-designed public spaces also can serve as a key locus where new forms of sociability can emerge. Urban planners and designers have the tools and instruments at hand to contribute greatly to social cohesion in cities, yet political will and the participation of a broad array of stakeholders, including local residents, is a fundamental precondition to the success of any measure.[32]

## Endnotes

1. UN-Habitat, *State of the World's Cities 2008/2009: Harmonious Cities* (Nairobi: 2009); United Nations Department of Economic and Social Affairs (DESA), Population Division, *World Urbanization Prospects: The 2014 Revision, Highlights* (New York: 2014); International Organization for Migration (IOM), *World Migration Report 2015. Migrants and Cities: New Partnerships to Manage Mobility* (Geneva: 2015).

2. Mary J. Hickman and Nicola Mai, "Migration and Social Cohesion. Appraising the Resilience of Place in London," *Population, Space and Place* 21, no. 5 (2015): 431.

3. UN-Habitat, *State of the World's Cities 2012/2013: Prosperity of Cities* (London: Routledge, 2013), 150.

4. U.K. Department for Communities and Local Government, *English Housing Survey 2010 to 2011: Headline Report* (London: 2012); Patrick Butler, "'Inadequate, Unaffordable, Insecure': UK Housing's Decline and Fall," *The Guardian* (U.K.), September 11, 2013.

5. Karin Peters, Birgit Elands, and Arjen Buijs, "Social Interactions in Urban Parks. Stimulating Social Cohesion?" *Urban Forestry & Urban Greening* 9, no. 2 (2010): 93–100.

6. UN-Habitat, *Urban Planning and Design for Social Cohesion. Concept Note World Urban Forum* (Medellín, Colombia: April 2014), 2; IOM, *World Migration Report 2015*, 4.

7. Gerard Boucher and Yunas Samad, "Introduction. Social Cohesion and Social Change in Europe," *Pattern of Prejudice* 47, no. 3 (2013): 197; UN DESA, United Nations Development Programme (UNDP), and Office of the United Nations High Commissioner for Human Rights (OHCHR), *Habitat III Issue Papers—1 Inclusive Cities* (New York: 2015). Figure 3.4.1 from UN-Habitat, *State of the World's Cities 2010/2011: Cities for All—Bridging the Urban Divide* (New York: 2011), 73.

8. UN DESA, UNDP, and OHCHR, *Habitat III Issue Papers*; Tiit Tammaru et al., eds., *Socio-Economic Segregation in European Capital Cities. East Meets West* (London: Routledge, 2015); Richard Fry and Paul Taylor, *The Rise of Residential Segregation by Income* (Washington, DC: Pew Research Center, August 1, 2012).

9. Tammaru et al., eds., *Socio-Economic Segregation in European Capital Cities.*

10. Hartmut Häussermann, "Wohnen und Quartier: Ursachen sozialräumlicher Segregation," in Ernst-Ulrich Huster, Jürgen Boeckh, and Hildegard Mogge-Grothjahn, *Handbuch Armut und soziale Ausgrenzung* (Wiesbaden: VS, 2008), 335–49.

11. Jane Parry, *Issue Paper on Secure Tenure for Urban Slums. From Slums to Sustainable Communities: The Trans-formative Power of Secure Tenure* (Atlanta and Brussels: Habitat for Humanity and Cities Alliance, 2015); UN-Habitat, *Urban Planning and Design for Social Cohesion*, 2.

12. Boucher and Samad, "Introduction. Social Cohesion and Social Change in Europe"; Peters, Elands, and Buijs, "Social Interactions in Urban Parks"; Talja Blokland, Carlotta Giustozzi, and Franziska Schreiber,

"The Social Dimensions of Urban Transformation: Contemporary Diversity in Global North Cities and the Challenges for Urban Cohesion," in Harald A. Mieg and Klaus Töpfer, *Institutional and Social Innovation for Sustainable Urban Development* (Oxon and New York: Routledge, 2013), 125.

13. UN-Habitat, *Urban Planning and Design for Social Cohesion*, 1.

14. Box 3.4.1 from the following sources: German Federal Ministry for the Environment, Nature Conservation, Building and Nuclear Safety, *Social City Program* (Berlin: 2015); Alexandra Galeshewe et al., *National Urban Renewal Programme. Implementation Framework* (Pretoria: Department of Provincial and Local Government, Republic of South Africa, undated); Michael E. Leary and John McCarthy, *The Routledge Companion to Urban Regeneration* (London and New York: Routledge, 2013), 402; Hans Skifter Andersen and Louise Kielgast, *Area-based Initiatives in Denmark—"Kvarterløft": Addressing Increasing Social Problems and Concentration of Immigrants and Refugees in Seven Neighborhoods* (Copenhagen: Danish Building Research Institute, June 2003).

15. German Institute of Urban Affairs, *Status Report. The Programme "Social City" (Soziale Stadt)—Summary* (Berlin: Federal Ministry of Transport, Building and Urban Affairs, 2008).

16. Galeshewe et al., *National Urban Renewal Programme*; Thomas Franke and Wolf-Christian Strauss, *Management gebietsbezogener integrativer Stadtteilentwicklung. Ansätze in Kopenhagen und Wien im Vergleich zur Programmumsetzung "Soziale Stadt" in deutschen Städten* (Berlin: German Institute of Urban Affairs, 2005).

17. Franke and Strauss, *Management gebietsbezogener integrativer Stadtteilentwicklung*; Ivan Turok, *The Evolution of National Urban Policies: A Global Overview* (Nairobi: UN-Habitat and Cities Alliance, 2014).

18. Senatsverwaltung für Stadtentwicklung, "The Neighborhood Council Within the Neighborhood Management Process," handout at the 3rd Congress of Berlin's Neighborhood Councils (Berlin: March 20, 2010).

19. Franke and Strauss, *Management gebietsbezogener integrativer Stadtteilentwicklung.*

20. Ellen Højgaard Jensen and Asger Munk, *Kvaterløft. 10 Years of Urban Regeneration. Ministry of Refugees, Immigration and Integration Affairs* (Copenhagen: 2007).

21. Jan Gehl, *Cities for People* (Washington, DC: Island Press, 2010).

22. Chris Firth, Damian Maye, and David Pearson, "Developing 'Community' in Community Gardens," *Local Environment: The International Journal of Justice and Sustainability* 16, no. 6 (2011): 555–68. Box 18–2 based on the following sources: International Network for Economic, Social & Cultural Rights, "Report and Recommendation on Request for Inspection, Re: Argentina—Special Structural Adjustment Loan 4405-AR (Pro-Huerta Case)," 2012, https://www.escr-net.org/node/364789; Ana Bell, "Community Gardens Boost Self-sufficiency in Argentina," Panos London, August 31, 2012; Ministry of Foreign Affairs and Worship of Argentina, "Desarrollo sustentable: Haiti—autoproduccíon de alimentos frescos Pro Huerta," http://cooperacionarg.gob.ar/en/haiti/autoproduccion-de-alimentos-frescos-pro-huerta;

Instituto Nacional de Tecnología Agropecuaria (INTA), "Pro Huerta," http://prohuerta.inta.gov.ar/; Walter Alberto Pengue, "Aún nos quedan las manos y la tierra," *El Diplo* 38 (August 2002); Municipality of Rosario, "Indicadores Demograficos," November 23, 2015, www.rosario.gov.ar/sitio/caracteristicas/indicadores.jsp; United Nations Food and Agriculture Organization, "Rosario," in *Growing Greener Cities in Latin America and the Caribbean* (Rome: 2013); Ferne Edwards, "Sustainable City & Model—Urban Agriculture in Argentina," Sustainable Cities Network, July 13, 2007, www.sustainablecitiesnet.com/models/model-urban-agriculture-in-rosario-argentina/; Ministry of Social Development of Argentina, "Pro Huerta," 2013, www.desarrollosocial.gob.ar/wp-content/uploads/2015/08/1.-M--s-sobre-PRO-HUERTA.pdf; Canadian International Development Agency and Inter-American Institute for Cooperation on Agriculture (IICA), "Argentina, Canada and Haiti Join Efforts to Improve Food Security. Project for Self-sufficiency in the Production of Fresh Foods in Haiti Is Expanded," press release (Haiti: June 2008); IICA, "Program for Fresh Food Self-sufficiency in Haiti: Pro-Huerta 2005-2008," *Comuniica*, January–April 2008; Pan-American Health Organization and Ministerio de Relaciones Exteriores, Comercio Internacional y Culto de la República Argentina, *South-South Cooperation: Triangular Cooperation Experience Between the Government of the Argentine Republic and the Pan-American Health Organization/World Health Organization* (Buenos Aires: October 2009); "Lessons Learned in Argentina Helping Haiti Cope with Cholera," *New Agriculturalist*, December 2010; "Haiti Agriculture: True Success of Pro Huerta Program in Haiti," *Haiti Libre*, March 23, 2015; "Haiti—Agriculture: The Argentinean Program Pro Huerta Extended Until 2016," *Haiti Libre*, January 17, 2014.

23. Jacqueline Groth and Eric Corjin, "Reclaiming Urbanity: Intermediate Spaces, Informal Actors and Urban Agenda Setting," *Urban Studies* 42, no. 3 (2005): 503–26; David Harvey, *Rebel Cities: From the Right to the City to the Urban Revolution* (London and New York: Verso, 2012); Franziska Schreiber, "Viele viele Frei(t)räume: The Prinzessinnengarten and Contemporary Land Use Conflicts in Berlin," anstiftung.de/downloads/send/15-forschungsarbeiten-urbane-gaerten/173-the-prinzessinnengarten-and-contemporary-land-use-conflicts-in-berlin.

24. The Queensland Government, *Transit Oriented Development: Guide to Community Diversity* (Brisbane: Queensland Department of Infrastructure and Planning, 2010); Gehl, *Cities for People*; Xuemei Zhu et al., "A Retrospective Study on Changes in Residents' Physical Activities, Social Interactions, and Neighborhood Cohesion After Moving to a Walkable Community," *Preventive Medicine* 69, no. 1 (2014): 93–97.

25. Gehl, *Cities for People*, 7.

26. Institute for Transportation and Development Policy—China, *Best Practices in Urban Development in the Pearl River Delta* (Guangzhou: December 2012), 81–88.

27. UN-Habitat, *Streets as Tools for Urban Transformation in Slums. A Street-led Approach to Citywide Slum Upgrading* (Nairobi: 2012), 15.

28. Julio D. Dávila and Diana Daste, "Aerial Cable-Cars in Medellín, Colombia: Social Inclusion and Reduced Emissions," in Mark Swilling et al., *City-Level Decoupling: Urban Resource Flows and the Governance of*

*Infrastructure Transitions. Case Studies from Selected Cities.* A Report of the Working Group on Cities of the International Resource Panel (Paris: United Nations Environment Programme, 2013), 47–48.

**29.** Ibid.

**30.** Gehl, *Cities for People*, xii.

**31.** Link Arkitektur, "Stranden—Aker Brygge," http://linkarkitektur.com/en/Projects/Stranden-Aker-Brygge.

**32.** Justus Uitermark, "'Social Mixing' and the Management of Disadvantaged Neighbourhoods: The Dutch Policy of Urban Restructuring Revisited, *Urban Studies* 40, no. 3 (2003): 531–49.

## DISCUSSION QUESTIONS

1. What are the most significant environmental challenges in cities these days? Are the problems the same in the developed world and developing world?
2. What is the notion of social cohesion? How has the concept experimented with? Explain the approach to enhancing social cohesion in national urban planning programs.
3. Do you believe the design of mixed-use areas could facilitate community diversity and social cohesion? What are the practical mechanisms to realize mixed-use areas to promote community diversity and social cohesion?
4. Transit-oriented development (TOD) has become a popular planning approach to create inclusive, connected communities through spatial planning. It is considered beneficial since it can not only enhance social cohesion but also offer environmental benefits. What are the environmental benefits? Do you think the TOD could also generate unintended adversarial environmental impacts?

READING 3.5

# Renewable Energy Delivery and Expansion with Public and Private Partnerships for the Global South

By Kyoo-Won Oh and Younsung Kim

## Introduction

Energy is necessary for individuals' daily lives, a foundation of the shared activities in a society, and an important source of economic growth in a country in this increasingly modernized world. The provision of stable energy in a country is thus one of the top priorities for policymakers as an independent energy policy and an important cross-cutting policy that affects the entire economy and its different industrial sectors (Chaurey et al., 2012).

In pursuing energy policy, the energy supply issue has been confounded by climate change concerns these days. With the increasing scientific evidence for climate change (IPCC, 2018), the international policy community has agreed to limit global mean temperature increase below 1.5°C at the Paris climate conference (UNFCCC, 2016). Before and during the conference, both developing and developed countries submitted comprehensive national climate action plans, and the plans included renewable-based energy supply as a climate mitigate action. Evidently, renewable-based energy system transition and expansion can be an ideal way to address a twofold energy provision challenge, meeting increased energy access needs, particularly in the Global South, and transitioning to a clean energy system to address climate change.

Among various policy support mechanisms, well-designed public–private partnerships (PPPs) could be one of the potentially viable options for providing renewable-based energy services in developing countries (Kruckenberg, 2015; Martins et al., 2011). In the face of insufficient government investments due to the limited public budgets, PPPs would overcome the budgetary constraints of capital-intensive renewable energy projects demanding high up-front costs and inducing high efficiencies in the operation and maintenance of renewable energy. PPPs would also enable public entities to gain access to private sectors' cutting-edge technical expertise, innovative financing solutions, and efficient delivery of public goods in a timely manner, essential in the stages of project development, operations, and maintenance. However, most energy projects in developing countries had traditionally relied on single-handedly public efforts. The government-initiated projects often led to project delays or failures when they are less capable of ensuring affordable service fees for the poor, drawing community engagement and establishing well-functioning institutional management systems (Komendantova et al., 2012; Martins et al., 2011; UNDP 2011). In this light, PPPs can be a handy tool for public managers or policymakers in developing countries to achieve energy access goals with renewable energy.

The current literature on PPP has rarely discussed the significance of PPPs for increased energy access in the context of developing countries. Some prior studies examined the application of PPP arrangements in the energy sector, but they are limited in that their focus is mainly on developed nations (Dinica, 2008; Martins et al., 2011) or large-scale projects in urban areas (Komendantova et al., 2012). In this article, we first discuss the overall benefits and drawbacks of renewable energy development. Furthermore, details of PPP arrangements and risk allocations for renewable energy development are also examined. We then explore a case of a 5 megawatts (MW) mini-size rooftop solar project in Gujarat, India, and discuss what makes this case proven to be successful. In doing so, our study indicates that if a PPP is well-designed, it can be an efficient, effectively affordable mode of small-scale electrification for sustainable energy supply in developing and emerging economies.

## Benefits and Drawbacks of Renewable Energy Development

Renewable energy is defined as an energy source "derived from natural processes that are replenished constantly" (IEA, 2002). Its various forms include electricity and heat generated from solar, wind, ocean, hydropower, biomass, geothermal resources, and biofuels, and hydrogen drawn from renewable resources. Given the non-depletion of resources and less harmful environmental impacts, renewable energy has received broad support internationally compared to fossil fuels or nuclear energy. However, promoting renewable energy development in a country would eventually depend on various factors. For instance, a country's concerns over fossil fuel reserves, imported fossil fuels price fluctuations, cost-ineffectiveness in existing power infrastructure, and high climate risks would create a favorable policy environment, resulting in a strategic direction toward renewable energy production (Dinica, 2008). Political stability and policy support would also bring more renewable projects in developing and emerging countries (Komendantova et al., 2012).

Renewable energy development provides various benefits. First, it strengthens energy security and independence through a diversified energy mix with locally produce energy, therefore enabling a stable power supply to various economic activities in a country. Second, renewable energy allows a country to contribute to slowing down the threat of climate change by lowering greenhouse gas emissions during electricity generation and avoiding some of the related economic losses caused by climate change. Third, new business and job opportunities in various sectors would be created during the deployment of new renewable-based technologies, which would positively shape national competitiveness and economic growth.

However, there are several drawbacks to renewable energy development. First, while renewable technologies have made great leaps, their power generation efficiencies remain still lower than those of conventional fossil fuel–fired power generation. As such, in order to promote renewable project development, governments have adopted diverse forms of financial support mechanisms such as fiscal incentives, direct and indirect subsidies, tax exemptions, and soft loans. In particular, feed-in tariffs (FITs) have been well-favored by many developed countries, including Germany. The FIT scheme provides legal guarantees for long-term purchase contracts with utility companies at a fixed attractive price (Dinica, 2008), leading private investors to a high level of assurance on the financial projection of renewable energy projects and thus facilitating renewable energy market generation (Komendantova et al., 2012).

Second, renewable energy projects pose a capital-intensive cost structure where high up-front costs are required at the stages of project development and construction (Sovacool, 2011). High capital costs incur as renewable energy projects include a supply-chain bottleneck where there are still fewer companies with required renewable technologies than the existing demands. Moreover, additional costs are required to connect to the electricity grid, when in most cases, renewable energy plants are located remotely and distant from end-users. Renewable energy intermittency, for example, daytime for solar energy, the wind blowing for wind energy, and rainy season for hydro energy, is also translated into high costs (Komor, 2004). Therefore, it is widely perceived that renewable energy is not cost-competitive as compared to fossil fuels. However, the true costs of fossil fuel–fired power generation should be higher than the currently projected ones when environmental and social costs concerning negative externalities (e.g., industrial pollution and natural resource depletion) are captured. Fossil fuel subsidies also distort the true costs of fossil fuel–based power generation, lowering actual renewable-based electricity generation costs (Bridle & Kitson, 2014).

## Renewable Energy Projects in Developing Countries

In many parts of the world, around 1.4 billion people still do not have access to electricity. More than 2.6 billion people in developing countries rely on traditional biomass for cooking and heating (World Bank, 2014). This lack of access to modern energy services continues to impede sustainable development. It also reflects an imminent need for installing modern energy service systems in developing countries, especially in South Asia and Sub-Saharan Africa (REN 21, 2016). If it is developed in a way to ensure financial affordability and technical sustainability, renewable energy has a huge potential for meeting these countries' energy needs, especially when combined with the use of mini-grids in un-electrified peri-urban and rural areas. Thus, facilitating energy access through renewables has become an influential policy agenda in developing countries (Chaurey et al., 2012, REN 21, 2016; UNDP, 2009).

Against this backdrop, the renewable energy market has grown exponentially in the last decade and continues to build its global electricity market share. Renewables such as modern biomass, solar, geothermal, wind, tidal, and wave, but excluding large hydro projects, accounted for 7.1% of the total world electricity generation in 2013 (REN 21, 2016), as compared to 2% in 2004 (REN 21, 2005). With the total investment of $241.6 billion from public and private entities, renewable energy accounts for 55% of the new generating capacity installed worldwide in 2013 (UNEP, 2017). Renewable energy investment in developing countries has also shown a drastic increase from $8 billion in 2004 to $116.6 billion in 2016, mostly in Latin America and the Caribbean and some developing Asia.

From the analysis of around 1,700 renewable energy projects from 1990 to 2012 on Private Participation in Renewable Energy (PPRE) Database of World Bank (2014), we identified several trends as follows. First, the wind has been the most active technology deployed since 1990. In 2012, there were 25,954 MW of wind energy projects with private participation that reached financial closure in developing countries, and total project costs were about $46 billion. Many of the wind energy projects have been developed in Latin America and the Caribbean. At the same time, East Pacific Asia showed the least total electrification capacity in both financed and pipeline wind power projects. Solar technology ranks second, and its rapid growth in complete pipeline projects was recently made for the past five years. In 2012 alone, 1,798 MW of PPP solar projects reached financial closure in developing countries, and their total project costs were estimated at $7.5 billion. The Sub-Saharan region has been very active in attracting foreign private investments in renewable energy projects, and South Africa has been the most active in the region. Chile has also shown the highest commitment to creating favorable energy, as solar projects with nearly 1,739 MW of total solar capacity were installed. In doing so, Chile almost doubled South African's installments' full capacity in 2012.

However, geothermal and other renewables (wave and tidal) have not been actively tapped, resulting in a small number of pipeline and financed projects. Geothermal projects were proposed in a few countries such as Indonesia, Bangladesh, and Malaysia, with their total capacity being 840 MW since 1990. In 2011, there was only one wave energy project proposed off the Kenyan coast with a capacity of 100 MW concerning other technologies. The development of biomass energy has also been slow, and its contribution is still a marginal component of the total renewable energy supply. Only 3% of the total financed renewable projects were based on biomass energy, and 582 MW of projects with private participation reached financial closure in developing countries. Most biomass energy projects proposed and implemented were limited in five countries, China, Brazil, Romania, India, and Uganda.

Regional disparity is one of the critical features in renewable energy development of the developing world. Latin America and the Caribbean, and East Asia and Pacific are the most active regions in renewable energy supply, while the African region with the lowest electrification rate still suffers from the fewer pipeline and financially closed renewable energy projects. This uneven regional distribution would be in part attributed to the availability of subsidy-based incentives offered to project developers, along with relatively low political risks to private investors and a higher level of bankability in large middle-income countries, including China, India, and Brazil.

Our analysis of PPRE also indicates that most PPP projects in developing countries were promoted by federal governments' initiatives, reflecting the centralized governance system for energy development and planning in developing countries. Noticeably, around 80% of renewable projects were contracted by federal governments. In comparison, state and local governments made only 5% of PPP arrangements, mainly in India, Thailand, China, Malaysia, and Mexico. In contrast, PPP-based renewable energy development in developed countries tends to constitute a meta-governance system by involving federal, state, local governments, and sometimes independent legal bodies incorporated in a country (Koch & Buser, 2006).

## Public–Private Partnership Arrangement in Renewable Energy Development

PPP is a procurement method where private and public sectors jointly undertake a project to provide public goods or facilities, which otherwise would have been undertaken only by the public sector (Martins et al., 2011). The public partner can take different forms, such as the central and local government, or even independent legal bodies incorporated in the state or regional and local administration (Koch & Buser, 2006). In traditional government procurement, the private sector delivers only certain limited tasks required for a larger project, while the government's responsibility is to monitor and consolidate the various works undertaken by different private sector companies for larger system delivery. Under a PPP structure, the private sector resumes a broader range of responsibilities depending on how project risks are allocated between the public and the private sector (Komendantova et al., 2012).

### Roles of the Private Sector in Renewable Energy PPP

In many developing countries, power is usually provided by a central government through state-owned-enterprises (SOE) for power generation, transmission, and distribution. However, limited public resources would lead the government not to be able to meet the growing demands of electricity alone, therefore a strong need to mobilize monetary resources from the private sector. This is especially so for the generation of renewable energy, which requires high capital costs and a high level of technological know-how during project development, construction, and operations. Furthermore, the mismatch between the up-front high capital cost requirements of renewable energy and revenue generation over a long-term period for the cost recovery needs to be bridged by innovative financing solutions with complex legal documents and proper risk allocations. However, these technical, operational, and financial skills required for renewable energy development are not usually of the government but the private sector.

## Typical PPP Structure of Renewable Energy Project

Renewable energy PPP project also follows a typical PPP structure, where a government grants a concession to private sector investors for a certain period. In turn, the investor, with required responsibilities, establishes a Special Purpose Company (SPC) and makes necessary arrangements to raise required funds to undertake the project through equity investments and debt instruments. The investor recovers its investment with a reasonable return and repays the debts from a series of revenues generated from the project over the long-term concession period. In the case of renewable energy PPP projects, like any other power PPP projects, investors' economic and financial risks are reduced or eliminated to a certain extent through a long-term Power Purchase Agreement (PPA). The PPA is usually signed between the SPC, which generates and sells electricity, and a utility company that purchases electricity from the SPC. The commercial terms for the sales of electricity, for example, the price and volume, conditions of payments, responsibilities of each party, contract period, and termination events, are defined in the PPA. Due to the low credibility of the utility SOE in developing countries, regular and termination payments and other key responsibilities in the PPA are often guaranteed by the government. The core of PPP arrangement lies in identifying and allocating the risks embedded in a project among various participating parties, which are considered to be best in handling the risks. A typical structure of renewable energy PPP project is illustrated in Figure 3.5.1.

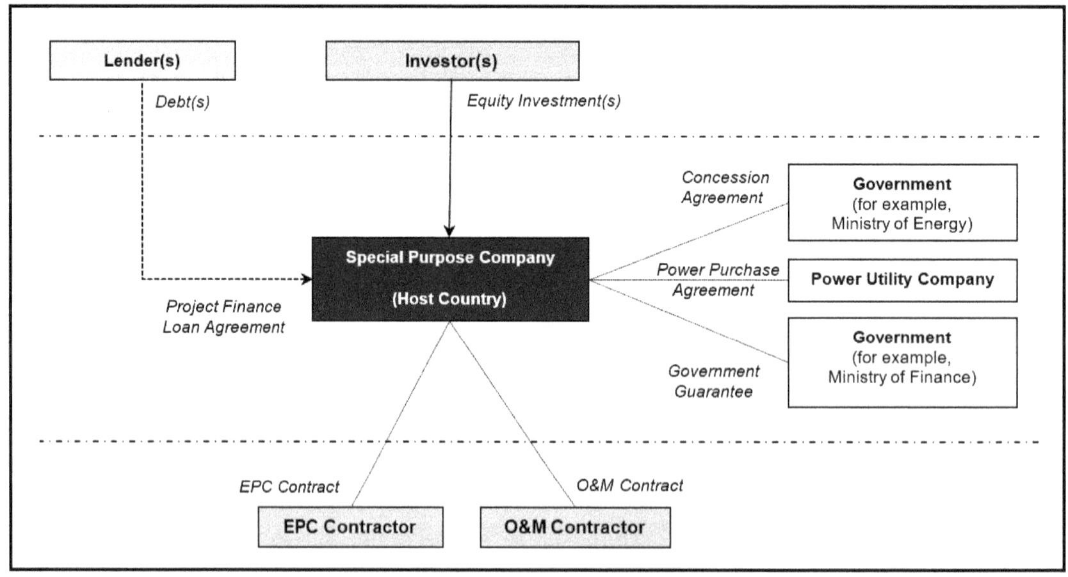


**Figure 3.5.1** A Typical Renewable Energy Public-Private Partnership Project in a Developing Country

## Inherent Risks in Renewable Energy Project

Unique risks that the government and investors usually face in the renewable energy PPP projects include, among others, resource quality, spatial planning, new technologies, administrative approval, local and environmental acceptance, and quality and price of maintenance services (Dinica, 2008). The distinctive characters of the renewable energy projects shape the unique features and risks of renewable energy PPP projects. Even though capital costs, that is, the up-front expense of building renewable energy projects during the construction stage, have dropped significantly since the early 2010s, renewable energy still poses a higher capital cost than other thermal energies. Despite low operation and maintenance costs, high capital costs usually make financial institutions perceive renewable energy projects as riskier, leading to a higher interest rate and requiring more stringent conditions to the investor. This fact is translated into the financial risks; therefore, the critical importance of robust financing mechanism needed in the renewable energy projects, where the financial gap should be innovatively bridged to foster the further development and wider diffusion of renewable energy technologies (Yue et al., 2001). High technical expertise and the management know-how required for project development and operations are associated with the construction and operation risks.

Additionally, the intermittent nature of renewable energy sources means that electricity is not continuously generated. It often cannot meet the peak energy demand if not combined with other energy storage solutions. Although the storing of energy may help ensure that power is available when needed most, it also entails higher capital costs, coupled with high operational and maintenance requirements, therefore posing additional financial risks and operational risks. Finally, economic incentives and policy support from the government, for example, agreed FITs, are often required to attract the renewable energy private sector developers by ensuring a stable revenue stream. They are stipulated in the PPA contract with a utility company, sometimes being guaranteed by the government. This leads to a risk of breach of contract by the government, a political risk in a project (Joskow & Tirole, 2005).

## Private Sector Participants

Participation of a private sector company in a renewable energy project as an investor is usually driven by the investment return of a project on its equity capital measured by Return on Investment. The same private investor sometimes participates in the project as Engineering, Procurement, and Construction (EPC) contractor and/or Operation and Management (O&M) contractor to generate additional profits from EPC and O&M work. In addition to financial motivations, albeit low investment returns as an investor or low profitability in EPC and O&M, the private sector participates in renewable energy projects for other reasons such as market expansion, deployment and market test of new technology, and accumulation of track records for future projects (Bennett et al., 2000).

Specific knowledge-based skills and experiences are strongly required for the private sector participants in renewable PPP projects, and they are usually screened during the bid evaluation process. The project investors are expected to have strong technical and operational know-hows in the energy sector with financial strength and stability. EPC and O&M contractors are often required to have proven records and technical expertise in renewable energy projects. Given the complexity of financing arrangement, financial institutions should be able to make correct assessments of various risks involved in the projects, reflect them in the pricing, and analyze their impacts on the loan repayment.

## The Public Sector

The public sector participants, either the government, SOE, or others, are also required to have specific skills and expertise, for example, a good understanding of the renewable energy technologies and trends, the ability to correctly assess and transfer certain risks to the private participants, evaluation of the price of the renewable energy project, negotiation with the power generators, effective and timely organization of community consultation, and monitoring capacity during the operation period. The lack of such required skills in the public sector, along with desperate needs for energy, may lead to poorly designed contracts that could, in turn, result in the unsuccessful implementation of renewable energy projects and/or ad-hoc unwanted renegotiations down the road (Martins et al., 2011). Furthermore, without knowledge of renewable energy technology and its market trends, the pricing may be determined at an arbitrary level, borne by the power users and eventually by taxpayers. Due to high visibility and its high level of environmental and social impacts on the community, the project may face difficulties in the future without proper consultation and community engagement processes.

The government's concerns are complex. It is required to be mindful of various dimensions of the project such as legislative and regulatory aspects, optimization of the proper energy mix, political opinions of the project, minimization of the retained risks and maximization of social benefits, and protection of taxpayers' interests. Nonetheless, the government has far more benefits to pursuing a PPP model in renewable energy generation in partnership with the private sector. The benefits include, among others, quick delivery of the project, learning up-to-date technological and managerial know-how, and harnessing financing capacities of the private sector (Jones, 1994). In return for these potential benefits, the public sector needs to show the private partners the stable revenue stream during the concession period to recoup their initial investments and make debt repayments.

Municipal and provincial governments are highly involved in most renewable energy projects, primarily due to environmental and social impacts on the local communities, such as noises and loss of visual landscape integrity. A local government's involvement includes identifying project sites, zoning plans, issuance of required licenses and permits, and local community consultation processes. Various forms of incentives, mostly tax incentives, are often provided from the central or upper-level to the local government to favor renewable energy development and accept a PPP renewable project in its province. Local governments generally support renewable energy projects because stable access to electricity is one of their key policy priorities to ensure residents' life quality and sustain a good business climate.

The following section introduces a PPP case for solar power generation in India and provides several lesson points for small-scale renewable PPP projects.

## Case Study: India Gujarat Rooftop Solar Power Project in Gandhinagar

### Case Overview

The State of Gujarat, located in western India with over 80 million residents, enjoys 300 sunny days per year. In recognizing the high solar energy potential, Gujarat province has embraced the idea of renewable energy to meet the state's growing energy demands. As Gujarat has been at the forefront of industrial development in India, the Gujarat government believed that renewable energy development would help sustain its significant national leadership in economic and social development while reducing the spread and depth of externalities and minimizing vulnerability to multiple spheres of economic growth. The push for renewable energy development was also motivated by the government's high recognition of the urgent need to diversify energy sources to preserve the state's endowed fossil fuels and to tackle climate change challenges simultaneously. The Gujarat government then adopted the Solar Power Policy of 2009 to install 500 MW solar power projects by 2014. The government also planned to make its capital, Gandhinagar, a pilot solar city, which can be instrumental in implementing the 2009 Solar Power Policy. To this end, the PPP-based rooftop solar photovoltaic (PV) technology was chosen as one of the strategic directions to achieve the policy goal, while effectively overcoming many technical, regulatory, and financial challenges regarding the solar rooftop projects (GEPD, 2009). With many other subsequent solar rooftop PPP projects, as of March 2020, the State of Gujarat was ranked the first in India for its domestic rooftop solar installation of 50,915 systems, which accounts for nearly 64% of the country's total of 79,950 systems. While this corresponds to about 177.67 MW power generation in the state each year, the installed rooftop solar systems' combined capacity is 322 MW, according to the Ministry of New and Renewable Energy.

Launched in 2010, the Gujarat rooftop solar power project in Gandhinagar is a landmark and pioneering small-scale project using solar PV technology under the 2009 Solar Power Policy framework. The project comprises the development, construction, and operation of two rooftop solar projects in the state capital city of Gandhinagar. The government sought private sector participation to finance and build two 2.5 MW pilot solar projects that could provide better access to power for an estimated 10,000 people (World Bank, 2012). For the project implementation, the Gujarat government granted private investors a concession to produce solar power of a total capacity of 5 MW. The generated power, in turn, has been purchased by Torrent Power, a private sector utility company under a 25-year PPA. The project went through a competitive bidding process based on a tariff that the bidders requested to quote. The world's 40 large energy technology firms had shown interest in solar projects. Four companies, Lanco Infratech, Azure Power, Sun Edison, and Mahindra Solar, were requested to submit the final bid. In 2011, the government selected Azure Power and Sun Edison, asking each company to install 2.5 MW solar generators. The project was commissioned in March 2012 (Rasika, 2012), and is now in full operation.

In this project, solar panels were installed on both public and private rooftops. The Gujarat government has provided the rooftops of about 25 state government buildings for around 4 MW power generation. The remaining 1 MW has been generated on 250 private properties, including apartment blocks, private houses, and commercial buildings. To ensure enough local communities' participation in the project, the government promised a "Green Incentive" of Rs. 3 (about $0.016 USD)/kWh to the participating city residents if they install solar panels on their rooftops. According to Rasika (2012), the monetary incentive was sufficient for inducing the residents' participation. It is projected that a rooftop owner would at best receive about Rs. 8,878 ($145) per month for a 1,000 sq. ft. of leased area, even with a very modest assumption of solar energy reception of about 200 KWh/sq. ft. per year and a conversion factor of 18%. This Green Incentive seemed to be innovative because the project, on the one hand, could be implemented without occupying and acquiring lands.

On the other hand, it also provides additional income sources to the participating residents for hosting the solar panels. The extra income was considered substantial, as the per capita income for 2009–2010 in Gujrat was Rs. 33,843 ($553) (GoG, 2013). Figure 3.5.2 shows the project structure of two Gujarat rooftop solar power projects of 2.5 MW capacity each.

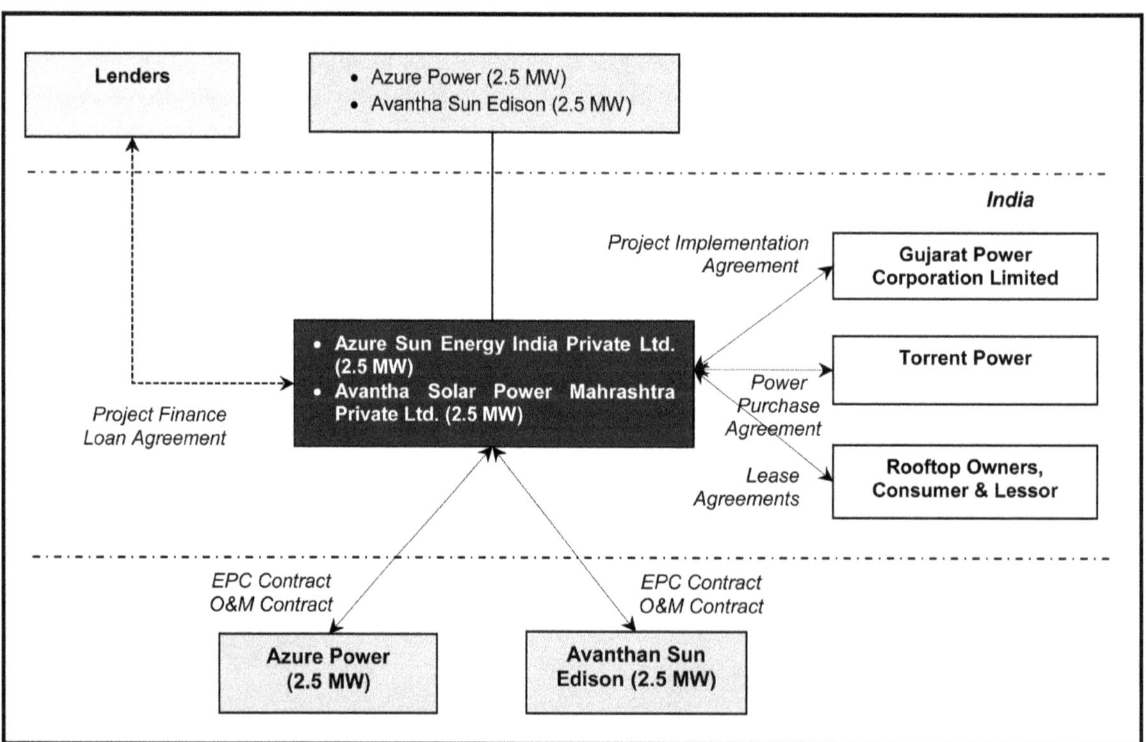


**Figure 3.5.2** Project Structure of Gujarat Rooftop Solar Power.

The Gujarat government intended the project to prove the concept of small-scale grid-connected rooftop solar power development, which exists in developed countries (in the United States and Germany in particular). The project was structured to address the risks and challenges that constrain the rooftop solar market in India and thus provide path-finding solutions for market development (World Bank, 2015). For instance, securing an adequate number of suitable roofs (institutional, commercial, and residential) is a significant challenge for any distributed and grid-connected solar rooftop project. The government committed to leasing public building rooftops to mitigate the risk, while a green incentive mechanism was devised for residential buildings that can help monetize otherwise idle assets. The leasing of residential rooftops was also possible when targeted marketing was executed to ensure prospective customers who might have lacked the understanding of solar power generation have become well aware of the rights and obligations as lessors and the concept of rental payments. Off-taker was also identified and invited to discuss all technical, commercial, and legal aspects from the initial stage of the project development, which had resulted in the viability of the project. Other main challenges in the pilot project include lack of clear regulatory guidelines for interconnection of sub-1 MW generation facilities in the state electricity distribution code as well as lack of approval of the process and documents (such as PPA, project implementation agreement) by the regulators (World Bank, 2015). These were addressed during the early stage of the project before its bid process.

Overall, as the first MW-scale solar PPP project in India, the Gujarat project was considered very successful. The state government could enhance energy access at affordable prices with virtually no state subsidies, mobilize the private sector's investment and technical expertise, benefit the participating residents with additional rental incomes, and reduce carbon emissions (World Bank, 2012). The replicability of the same model in different cities adds another merit to the project. Relying on lessons learned from this pilot PPP model, the Gujarat government implemented subsequent 25 MW rooftop solar power projects. Gujarat Power Corporation Limited arranged the new projects in its five large cities, all in small scales, that is, Vadodara (5.0 MW), Rajkot (6.5 MW), Mehsana (5.0 MW), Bhavnagar (3.5 MW), and Surat (5 MW).[1]

## Lessons Learned

There are important lessons drawn from the Gujarat Rooftop Solar Project for the renewable energy PPP projects in other developing countries. First, central and provincial governments' policy initiatives have been well coordinated to establish an enabling environment for renewable energy development, leading to the successful implementation of PPP projects in Gandhinagar. As part of India's National Action Plan for Climate Change, the Indian government launched Jawaharlal Nehru National Solar Mission (JNNSM) in 2010. The JNNSM has set its ambitious target of adding 1 GW of capacity between 2010 and 2013 and seeks to increase the combined solar power capacity from 9 MW in 2010 to 20 GW by 2022 (World Bank, 2010). One of the strategies to implement JNNSM was to bundle relatively expensive solar power with one from the unallocated quota of thermal power stations. The combined power generation approach was adopted to reduce the impact of a higher solar tariff on utilities. JNNSM also embraced a reverse bidding mechanism[2] that helped qualified bidders benefit from the declining global prices for solar components (World Bank, 2013). The Gujarat government's response to JNNSM was prompt and relied on the 2009 Solar Power Policy. The government implemented the state-specific regulations and guidelines for rooftop solar projects, adopting the "feed-in tariff" concept as a first-kind monetary incentive tool for India's renewable energy development (World Bank, 2015). It illustrates that PPP-based renewable projects would function well under the condition where a central government establishes a strategic direction for promoting renewable energy and implements its national strategy in harmony with state, provincial, or local governments' follow-up actions.

Second, the Gujarat rooftop pilot project indicates the significance of handling land constraints early in a project planning stage. Renewable energy projects usually face difficulties for site selection since it is mainly challenging to secure large parcels of lands where the right amount of natural resources, such as wind and sunlight, is continuously provided (Eliperin & Mufson, 2009). Besides, renewables have a low energy density compared to other conventional energy sources (Eliperin & Mufson, 2009). *Land acquisition* for solar PV or wind projects, regardless of its size, would be then translated into high up-front costs and greater environmental and social impacts about land conversion. In the Gujarat rooftop solar project case, private actors suggested the two rooftop-based solar power installments and the idea of utilizing existing local government buildings' rooftops. For the installment capacities fallen short of, residents were also invited for power generation. This way, being entirely accepted by the government led to the smooth implementation of the project while successfully lowering project costs and other resources that otherwise would be demanded land purchase negotiations.

Third, offering Green Incentive to project participants presents a win–win situation for both government and the local community. The Gujarat case is also called "Rent-a-Roof Project," as private companies lease rooftops from government and private residents who would receive Rs. 3 ($0.05) per unit produced. Solar panels are then installed and connected to the grid by project operators, and the operators, in turn, receive a FIT of Rs. 11.21 ($0.18) under a 25-year concession (World Bank, 2014). As such, this pilot project showcases a Green Incentive as a crucial design element for a compelling solar rooftop PPP business model. The incentive enables seamless collaborations among various stakeholders, including policymakers, regulators, individual rooftop owners (lease rentals), solar module suppliers, project developers, and utilities (meeting renewable purchase obligations by procuring solar power). Since the ability to pay for improved energy services is one of the major limitations in energy access problems in developing countries, Green Incentive, in sync with the preferred implementation model, would encourage clean energy usage after its installation. It would also prompt the scale up of renewable-based electrification projects. Green Incentives can also enhance the local community's active involvement during a project operation stage that has been typically ignored in most renewable energy projects, despite its critical role in achieving overall project performance (Chaurey et al., 2012).

Following up on this pilot project's success, the Gujarat government has attempted to increase the rooftop solar model to other cities in the state. For example, the government sought a 5 MW rooftop solar project in Vadodara, and WAA Solar Private Limited financed around $8 million of the total project costs. The business model's slight modification was made to allow plants' ownership to be transferred to rooftop owners, which raised potential rooftop owners' interests in the project. With a 25-year PPA made, the project was successfully implemented and provided increased energy services to around 9,000 residents (World Bank, 2014). Likewise, solar rooftop PPPs with Green Incentives are replicable. As long as policy and regulatory frameworks are clear, stable enough to attract investors, and flexibility in PPP contracts are granted to project developers.

## Conclusion

Energy security is one of the top policy priorities in a country, and climate change and its impacts have presented a twofold challenge of providing sustainable energy and divesting fossil fuel–oriented power generation. However, due to lack of financial means, limited technical expertise, and inadequate/insufficient regulatory mechanisms, developing countries would be more likely to supply sustainable energy with renewable projects. Those projects demand high up-front capital costs, establish regulatory guidelines and rules, and employ technical knowledge for project design and implementation.

PPP arrangements can be suggested as a procurement model to address such challenges. They can reduce risks from a capital-intensive cost structure, enable public actors to harness private sector's technical expertise, and encourage more effective project preparation (Martin et al., 2011). Key to the successful launch and undertaking of the project would be a careful consideration of design elements in PPP renewable projects' planning stage. The Gujarat Rooftop Solar Power project is a replicable PPP model for small-scale electrification projects in developing countries. The project's success would be attributed to multilevel governments' coordinated efforts for facilitating private investments by ways of incentive-based mechanisms such as lowered tariffs. Its uniqueness also includes avoiding unwanted negotiations over land acquisition for solar power generation, as the Gujarat project utilized the rooftops of public and private buildings. Green Incentive is a critical element that brings local residents' support for the project, inviting local residents to be part of power generators. Being replicated in other cities or states in India, the solar PPP model in Gandhinagar offers a promise for its replicability in other developing countries, insomuch as private companies make win–win operational arrangements with residents as well as a public sector create policy measures promoting renewable-based electricity generation.

While this chapter provides anecdotal evidence for crucial success factors in a solar PPP, a future scholarship can benefit from investigating PPP arrangements using different renewable sources such as wind. Also, it would be valuable to explore what inhibits or promotes the expansion of PPP-based renewable projects across other regions of the developing world, particularly in Africa suffering from the lowest electricity access rate in the world (IEA, 2016). In sum, this article suggests that well-designed renewable PPPs can be instrumental in improving energy access to meet rapidly growing domestic energy demands in developing countries. It would allow each country to participate in a global transition to a clean, low-carbon energy system to promote sustainable development.

## Endnotes

1. Developing Asia is defined by the IEA to include Afghanistan, Bangladesh, Brunei, Cambodia, China, Chinese Taipei, DPR Korea, East Timor, India, Indonesia, Malaysia, Mongolia, Myanmar, Nepal, Pakistan, PDR Laos, Philippines, Singapore, Sri Lanka, Thailand, Vietnam, and Other Asia.
2. http://ppi-re.worldbank.org/~/media/GIAWB/RE/Documents/RE-data-all.xls
3. Biomass-based electricity generation projects were numbered 51 among 1,690 total financed projects from the World Bank PPRE Database.
4. http://www.gpclindia.com/showpage.aspx?contentid=110
5. The reverse auction as a competitive bidding mechanism allocates projects to a set of successful bidders with the lowest tariffs adding up to the quantum of capacity earmarked for each batch. JNNSM Phase I allowed benchmark tariff fixed for each financial year by the Central Electricity Regulatory Commission (CERC) (World Bank, 2013).

## References


Abbott, K. (2012). Engaging the Public and the Private in Global Sustainability Governance. *International Affairs*, *88*, 3.

Bennett, E., James, S., & Grohmann, P. (2000). Joint venture public partnerships for urban environmental services: report on UNDP/PPPUE's project development facility 1995–1999. United Nations Development Programme and Yale University.

Bridle R., & Kitson, L. (2014). The Impact of Fossil-fuel subsidies on renewable electricity generation. Global Subsidies Initiative Report. Geneva: International Institute for Sustainable Development. https://www.iisd.org/system/files/publications/impact-fossil-fuel-subsidies-renewable-electricity-generation.pdf

Chaurey, A., Krithika, P. R., Palit, D., Rakesh, S., & Sovacool, B. (2012). New partnerships and business models for facilitating energy access. *Energy Policy*, *47*, 48–55.

Dinica, V. (2008). Initiating a sustained diffusion of wind power: the role of public–private partnerships in Spain. *Energy Policy*, *36*, 3562–3571.

Economist. (2014, January 5). Why is renewable energy so expensive? http://www.economist.com/node/21592685

Eilperin, J., & Mufson, S. (2009, April 16). Renewable energy's environmental paradox. *The Washington Post.*. http://www.washingtonpost.com/wpdyn/content/article/2009/04/15/AR2009041503622.html

Government of Gujarat (GoG). 2013. Socio-economic review. http://gujecostat.gujarat.gov.in/?page_id=12

Gujarat Energy and Petrochemicals Department (GEPD). (2009). Solar power policy. http://geda.gujarat.gov.in/policies_state.php

Gujarat Energy Development Agency (GEDA). (2015). Gujarat Electricity Regulatory Commission (GERC) order determination of tariff for solar energy projects. http://geda.gujarat.gov.in/policies_state.php

Grégor Q., Jarrousse, A., & Mouen, S. (2013). Developing renewable energies in Africa: A public-private partnership. *Private Sector and Development*, 25–27. http://www.proparco.fr/webdav/site/proparco/shared/PORTAILS/Secteur_prive_developpement/PDF/SPD18/SPD18_Gregor_Quiniou_Astrid_Jarrousse_Stephanie_Mouen_UK.pdf

Indian Ministry of New and Renewable Energy (IMNRE). (2016). Solar power capacity milestone of 5,000 MW in India. http://pib.nic.in/newsite/printrelease.aspx?relid=134497

IEA Renewable Energy Working Party. (2002). Renewable energy into the mainstream, 9. http://anetce.com/2002_iea_renewables54.pdf

IFC. (2014). India: Gujarat Solar. Public private partnership in series. http://www.ifc.org/wps/wcm/connect/d0a75c804b077348b4acfe888d4159f8/PPPStories_India_GujaratSolar.pdf?MOD=AJPERES

IFC. (2014). Harnessing energy from the sun: Empowering rooftop owners. https://www.ifc.org/wps/wcm/connect/topics_ext_content/ifc_external_corporate_site/sustainability-at-ifc/publications/p_report_harnessing_energy_from_the_sun

International Energy Agency (IEA). (2016). World energy outlook. http://www.worldenergyoutlook.org/resources/energydevelopment/energyaccessdatabase/

IPCC. (2014). Climate Change 2014: Synthesis report. https://www.ipcc.ch/report/ar5/https://www.ipcc.ch/report/ar5/

Jacob, A. (2005). Wind power market shows no signs of slowing. *Reinforced Plastics*, 49, 24–29.

Jones, B. D. (1994). *Reconceiving decision-making in democratic politics: Attention, choice, and public policy.* The University of Chicago Press.

Joskow, P. L., & Tirole, J. (2005). Merchant transmission investment. *Journal of Industrial Economics*, *53*(2), 233–264.

Koch, C., & Buser, M. (2006). Emerging meta-governance as an institutional framework for public private partnerships networks in Denmark. *International Journal of Project Management*, 24, 548–556.

Komendantova, N., Patt, A., Barras, L., & Battaglini, A. (2012). Perception of risks in renewable energy projects: The case of concentrated solar power in North Africa. *Energy Policy*, 40,103–109.

Komendantova, N., Patt, Anthony, & Williges, Keith. (2011). Solar power investment in North Africa: Reducing perceived risks. *Renewable and Sustainable Energy Reviews, 15*(9), 4829–4835.

Komor, P. (2004). *Renewable energy policy.* iUniverse Inc.

Kruckenberg, L. J. (2015). Renewable energy partnerships in development cooperation: Towards a relational understanding of technical assistance. *Energy Policy, 77,* 11–20.

Martins, A. C., Marques, R. C., Cruz, C. O. (2011). Public-private partnerships for wind power: The Portuguese case. *Energy Policy, 39,* 94–104.

Mittai, S. (2014). 750 MW solar power plant in India, likely to be largest solar power plant in world, gets World Bank financing commitment. *Clean Technica.* Retrieved May 1, 2017, from http://cleantechnica.com/2014/12/20/largest-solar-power-plant-world-750-mw-solar-power-plant-india-gets-world-bank-financing-commitment/

Pessoa, A. (2010). Reviewing public-private partnership performance in developing economies. In G. A. Hodge, G. Carsten, & A. E. Boardman (Eds.), *International handbook on public-private partnerships* (pp. 568–593). Edward Elgar Publishers.

Pattberg, P. H. (2010). Public-Private partnerships in global climate governance. *Climate Change, 1*(2), 279–287.

Pattberg, P. H., Biermann, F., Chan S., & Mert, A. (2012). Public-private partnerships for sustainable development: Emergence, influence, and legitimacy needs? *Review of African Political Economy, 40*(137), 485–495.

Rasika, G. A. (2012). India's PPP model for rooftop solar programme. www.energetica-india.net

Renewable Energy Policy Network for the 21st Century (REN 21). (2005). Renewables 2005: Global status report. http://www.ren21.net/wp-content/uploads/2016/06/GSR_2016_Full_Report.pdf

REN 21. (2016). Renewables 2016: Global status report. http://www.ren21.net/Resources/Publications/REN21Publications.aspx

Sovacool, B. K. (2011). *Developing public-private renewable energy partnerships to expand energy access.* Report for the United Nations Economic and Social Commission for the Asia Pacific, Bangkok, Thailand. Institute for Energy and the Environment, Vermont Law School.

Sovacool, B. K. (2013). Expanding renewable energy access with pro-poor public private partnerships in the developing world. *Energy Strategy Reviews, 1,* 181–192.

UNDP. (2011). Public private partnerships for service delivery (PPPSD), UNDP capacity development group, Johannesburg, South Africa.

UNEP. (2017). Global trends in renewable energy investment. http://fs-unep-centre.org/sites/default/files/publications/globaltrendsinrenewableenergyinvestment2017.pdf

UNFCCC. (2016). Paris Agreement: Report of the conference of the parties on its twenty-first session. http://unfccc.int/meetings/paris_nov_2015/items/9445.php

World Bank. (2010). Unleashing the potential of renewable energy in India. http://documents.worldbank.org/curated/en/504181468260121463/Unleashing-the-potential-of-renewable-energy-in-India

World Bank. (2012). *India: Gujarat solar. Public–private partnerships brief.* World Bank Group. http://documents.worldbank.org/curated/en/2015/06/24581474/india-gujarat-solar

World Bank. (2013). Paving the way for a transformational future: Lessons from Jawaharlal Nehru National Solar Mission Phase I. Energy Sector Management Assistance Program. https://openknowledge.worldbank.org/handle/10986/17480

World Bank. (2014). Replicating success in Vadodara: Rooftop solar PPPs in India. http://www.worldbank.org/en/news/feature/2014/09/25/replicating-success-in-vadodara-rooftop-solar-ppps-in-india

World Bank. (2015). Rooftop solar public-private partnerships: Lessons from Gujarat solar. https://library.pppknowledgelab.org/documents/2408

World Economic Forum. (2013). Scaling up energy access through cross-sector partnerships. http://www3.weforum.org/docs/IP/2014/EN/Communications/WEF_EN_Scaling_Up_Energy_Access.pdf

WHO. (2009). The energy access situation in developing countries. http:// www.who.int/indoorair/publications/energyaccesssituation/en/

Yue, C., Liu, C., & Liou, E. (2001). A transition toward a sustainable energy future: Feasibility assessment and development strategies of wind power in Taiwan. *Energy Policy*, *29*, 951–963.

## DISCUSSION QUESTIONS

1. What are the pros and cons of renewable energy PPPs from the government's, private investor's, and financier's perspectives?
2. What are the prominent uniqueness, benefits, and challenges of the rooftop solar PPP projects, compared to other solar PPP projects, as evidenced by the Gujarat case study?
3. What are the other noticeable trends of renewable energy projects in developing countries that you see from the database in https://ourworldindata.org/? Suppose penetration of a certain renewable technology in the electricity mix visibly increases in Sub-Saharan African countries during the last 5–7 years. What is that technology, and what do you think are the reasons?

Printed in the USA
CPSIA information can be obtained
at www.ICGtesting.com
LVHW081914260124
769864LV00009B/1384